taste

The secret meaning of things

First published in 1991
by Faber and Faber Limited

Revised and expanded edition
published in 2017 by Circa Press

©2017 Circa Press Limited
and Stephen Bayley

Circa Press
50 Great Portland Street
London W1W 7ND
www.circapress.net

ISBN 978-1-911422-06-8

Printed and bound in Latvia

Reproduction: Dexter Pre-Media
Design: Jean-Michel Dentand

taste

The secret meaning of things

Stephen Bayley

CIRCA

Our business here is the conscientious, continuous, resolute distinction of quality from mediocrity.

Alfred H Barr, on the principles of New York's Museum of Modern Art

Contents

Foreword It is very difficult

In her elegant autobiography *Images and Shadows* (1970), Iris Origo, who grew up in the cultivated Quattrocento atmosphere of the Villa Medici at Fiesole, near Florence, has an anecdote about her stepfather, Geoffrey Scott, author of *The Architecture of Humanism* (1924). This fashionable and influential book offered a refined defence of classicism after all the obloquy of the Gothic-inflected Ruskin years of the late nineteenth century.

Scott had worked with his friend, Cecil Pinsent, on the gardens of Bernard Berenson's famous I Tatti and later on other Tuscan gardens, including Origo's own La Foce. Thus he has some claim to have created a model of the Italian garden that has influenced generations of Anglo-Americans: a tastemaker in his own right. Indeed, the subtitle of *The Architecture of Humanism* is *A Study in the History of Taste*, although the actual book was more limited and partial than that.

But a larger idea had begun. So much so that Origo says Scott contemplated writing an ambitious synoptic history of taste, which the whole crowd at the villa agreed would have been a 'fascinating and entertaining book'. Apparently, there was a great deal of conversation about it in the garden, on the terraces and in the *saloni*. But despite the enthusiasm, there were problems. For weeks and weeks after the idea was mooted, a sheet of paper sat on Scott's writing table. It was bravely inscribed:

A History of Taste

Volume 1

Chapter 1

'It is very difficult ...'

'So far as I know,' his stepdaughter concluded, 'the work progressed no further.'

I have come a great deal further than Geoffrey Scott, perhaps without the elegance he might have achieved, but certainly with all the difficulties he so properly anticipated. Taste is an elusive subject, since it is both a mirror and a window. Scott was probably prudent to stick to his architectural theory and biographies and to leave the mirrored maze unexplored.

The difficulty in writing about taste is this: any reasonably objective survey of the histories of art, manners and literature shows that taste, at least as expressed in terms of our momentary preferences, *changes*. It is demonstrably – sometimes hilariously – the case that pictures, buildings, designs, books and behaviour that find favour in one generation are perversely despised in the next. Indeed, the cycle of taste – from modishness to disfavour and then to camp revival – is a familiar one upon which the spurious dynamics of the fashion industry depend.

Accept this volatility and you accept that there can be no such thing as objective 'good' taste, but only an evanescent, culturally and historically specific preference for certain things. How is the individual to determine the worth of his or her tastes in this world of continuously shifting values? Whether tastes are inherited or acquired, they will always be in question.

But are aesthetic convictions or beliefs, no matter how passionately held, as subject to the capricious depredations of time as platform soles and flared trousers, ripped jeans, footless tights, kipper ties, no ties, puffa jackets, mini-skirts, cargo pants and aviator shades? Surely some underlying aesthetic standards survive the brief seasons of fashion? Maybe. There is a tension in this book which some will find stimulating, others irritating. It arises from the conflict between my *observation* that taste changes, that values are fugitive, and my personal *conviction* that there *are* certain forms, shapes and ideas which transcend time and have a special, permanent value. Writing this book has tested my conviction against the evidence of observation.

Exactly why is it so repugnant to learn that the Duke and Duchess of Windsor had staff to hand-cut their lavatory paper and employed a footman to feed their pug dog meals in silver bowls? Why is it so laughable to learn that in the barrio of Villa Morra, a fashionable district of Asunción in Paraguay, the houses are tropical-Alpine-kitsch, a sort of Kitzbühel with date palms?

Why is Donald Trump's taste so disturbing? For his first television interview as President-elect, Trump appeared, imperiously, sitting on a golden throne in the style of the French Bourbon king Louis Quinze, with period-incorrect wall and ceiling paintings on classical, allegorical themes in the background. 'I like shiny new things', he once said. All of this faux-Versailles sits on cantilevered decks, behind mirrored glass about 200 metres above Fifth Avenue.

Was the President-elect aiming to enhance his prestige by accessing Bourbon values? The French invented the notion of *bon goût*, so they also invented the notion of *mauvais goût*. Good taste may be indefinitely debatable, but surely it has something to do with manners? And bad taste with inappropriateness?

Those avid for social promotion have often found a super-glossy suggestion of Versailles lends legitimacy to uglier nouveaux attributes. Besides, new money rarely chooses subtlety as its means of expression. The same clearly applies to this new President. Trump's taste is as revealing of the man as any of his Tweets.

Trump's Frenchified throne is in an apartment atop Trump Tower, the 1983 Manhattan landmark that announced his presence as a city-builder, and a tastemaker of sorts. Since, in his pre-intellectual system, highly reflective surfaces and precious materials have special value, it was perhaps significant that the site is next door to Tiffany, the up-with-the-Joneses jeweller. It was as if sympathetic magic might have its effect.

His chosen architect was Der Scutt (1934-2010), a middlebrow Modernist well used to pampering developers' egos. If nominative determinism means anything, you'd have to say that 'Der Scutt' spells trouble, sounding like a Death Knight in a low-budget swords-'n'-sorcery romp. However, his given name was also Donald, showing how in this quarter of the architectural world dissimulation in given names is more important than truth to materials.

At Trump Tower, rather as Augustus turned Rome from brick to marble, Scutt brought coruscating bronze glass to a part of Manhattan hitherto largely limestone, and thus dignified. The lobby is in pink marble whose extraction required a Carrara mountain peak to be removed. The *New York Times* critic Paul Goldberger, in a rare moment of aberration, passively cooed that it was 'warm, luxurious even exhilarating'. Others felt it vulgar.

Trump's throne-room was always the set piece. The first decorator was Angelo Donghia (1935-85) who had also worked for Liza Minnelli and Diana Ross. In this celebrity culture, Donghia was one of the first designers to get into brand extension, putting his name on bed linen even before Gloria Vanderbilt put her name on the butt of blue jeans. But Donghia's cool style (with grey flannel his signature) could not long accommodate the expressive needs of Trump's enlarging ego. So a nightclub singer turned decorator called Henry Conversano was hired. Conversano's design credentials include the Golden Nugget casino in Atlantic City;

for other clients he proposed revolving beds and 8-Pax jacuzzis, but his first job for Trump was a fourteen-seat onyx dining table.

Documentary details are sketchy, but let's assume Conversano, perhaps with artistic direction from his client, created the glitterball of rococo kitsch that is the often-photographed Trump Tower apartment today. As the *New York Times* said of Conversano's work, it is what 'heaven would look like if Liberace had been a decorator'.

In 1985, years before a singular political vision interfered with his pursuit of vulgarity, Trump had sent out to his friends gold-embossed dossiers on his latest pleasure palace, Mar-a-Lago, a 118-room villa on 20 acres in Florida, built in the 1920s of Dorian stone and shipped-in fifteenth-century Spanish tiles. This hacienda-burger is now the de facto Winter White House, as its original builder intended. Decisions of world-historical significance will be made in an environment of Conquistador Kitsch with a golf club attached.

At the time of Trump's Mar-a-Lago purchase, many people – particularly those, like me, schooled in the reductivist aesthetic of Modernism that until recently dominated contemporary thought – felt a revulsion so fundamental that it is tempting to call it instinctive. Mar-a-Lago was surely a warning signal of grossness to come. Incidentally, as if to suggest that vulgarity and illiberal politics are connected, in Paraguay they have, as well as tropical Alpine kitsch, neo-Trump architecture too. Trump may be the low-water mark of 1980s' taste, but he was not alone in his deference to excess and flash in that bilious decade. At the time, Australia experienced an economic boom that produced some splendid examples of nouveau vulgarity, rivals even to the future President. Alan Bond, a signwriter from Hammersmith, moved to Oz and, enriched through property development, financially engineered himself to being the status-rich sponsor of Australia's 1984 America's Cup team. But the family was interested in other sports. At the time, his wife used to cruise Perth in a pale blue Mercedes with leopard-skin upholstery. When a Bond daughter married, invitations were sent out in white leather wallets, which contained gold medallions embossed with the profiles of the bride and groom. Later, Bond went bankrupt with debts of Aus$1.8 billion and served four years in jail for financial malpractice.

Left: Donald Trump at Mar-a-Lago. The President's Palm Beach hacienda was built between 1924 and 1927 for Marjorie Merriweather Post, heir to the Postum Cereal Company.

Such trifles are what Thorstein Veblen once called the 'pecuniary canons of taste'. There may be a direct connection between vulgarity and bad business. Trump routinely exaggerates the height of his buildings, offering fake facts. During his Presidential campaign the *New York Times*, admittedly no friend of Trump, calculated that one third of his business ventures failed and one third were not nearly so successful as he made out. Indeed, his colossal corporate losses secured for the 2016 candidate a long holiday from income tax.

Post-perestroika Russia has made its own fabulous contributions to the wince-making archives of bling. Vladimir Putin has forty-three jets (one of which definitely has a gold lavatory, but perhaps they all do). He has fifteen helicopters. Beige dominates the interiors. A London designer called Celia Sawyer specialises in aircraft interiors crafted for the very rich: clients are notoriously sensitive about exposure, so facts are hard to come by, but one Sawyer interior has every surface, soft or hard, covered in gold. The only exceptions are the crystal luminaires.

Yet there is nothing inherently 'good' or 'bad' about the Windsors', Paraguayan, Trump's, Bond's, Putin's or Celia Sawyer's taste. Trump's dossier or Bond's invitation may be gaudy or vulgar, a Sawyer aeroplane may challenge aeronautical theory, but, given the crassness of the attempt to impress with an ostentatious display of wealth, these efforts would not have been more attractive had they been austerely set in Helvetica Light or Gill Sans and printed on the purest vellum, handmade by chaste Carmelite nuns, or crafted by adepts of Minimalism. Indeed, each was an example of very good and effective functional *design*, since they achieved with surpassing ease the intention of impressing.

In contrast, take the architectural design of a Bauhaus room, director Walter Gropius's own study, say, so admired by people like me and yet so distant from rich and successful people like Donald Trump. Here is the most rational design that the art and science of the 1920s could afford, a monument to the machine aesthetic that dominated early twentieth-century culture. Close observation of machines was meant to inspire a sense of 'functionalism' in the designer. But Walter Gropius's 'functionalism' is no more than the resolution of a circular argument that was very much of his own devising: functionalism is a good thing; geometric forms, industrial

Right: The Modern Movement in architecture attempted to get beyond taste and to define standards of design. Its scriptural home was the Bauhaus, where Walter Gropius's study was a shrine. There were many half-truths in Modern Movement theory, but no lies.

materials and primary colours are functional; therefore, geometric forms, industrial materials and primary colours are a good thing. You would have to say, 'Wait a minute, Walter. It can't be as simple as that.'

As the disappointing history of social housing in the Bauhaus tradition has shown, designs by Walter Gropius (1883-1969) are fine for those like Gustav Mahler and me who enjoy mind games, and share positivist beliefs in the benefits of heliotherapy and herbalism, but are less successful when foisted on blue-collar workers whose own aspirations are to live in a blaze of polychrome vulgarity like Donald Trump.

These two examples give away something of the game. Taste is not so much about what things *look* like, as about the ideas that gave rise to them. Intention is the key to understanding taste; we must judge the spirit that informs an object or a gesture, rather than the form of the object or the gesture itself, which is a matter of *design*. It was Sigmund Freud's personal feeling for form — what his biographer Peter Gay called an 'appreciation of beauty as a kind of perfection' — that made him so uncomfortable with the style of his masterpiece, *The Interpretation of Dreams* (1899).

This book, too, is about interpretation, but it concentrates on, or rather hints at, the *meaning of things*. My own idea of perfection — sometimes unstated, often explicit — lies behind all the phenomena I single out for comment, or for more complicated or subtle criticism or praise. I like simplicity and distrust complication. I prefer elegance to exuberance, silence to noise. This is my taste.

While writing I have become convinced that, discounting narrow philological or etymological studies, an academic history of taste is not so much difficult as impossible. So, this book is not a history, but a suggestive essay. Since a part of it was originally written in Italy, it seemed a good idea to divide it into two parts, somewhat like the *commedia dell'arte*. The first part is the *imbroglio*, the improvised story of an idea. The second is the *scenario*, which shows how taste has developed and changed in architecture, design, food and fashion. There is no getting away from the fact that the modern question of taste is utterly dependent on the ideas of consumption fostered in industrial and post-industrial cultures. As in the *commedia dell'arte*, *lazzi* (gags) interrupt the performance, but here they take the form of pictures and their captions, rather than histrionic asides.

Taste might evade absolute definition, but we are known by our momentary expressions of choice. There is an approach to studying patterns of preference and consumption that allows the meaning of things to be interpreted: every artefact and gesture is the disguise of a meaningful structure. Taste is about consumption and, in consuming, we reveal ourselves.

Unlike Freud's, my analysis and style may not be quite equal to the task. I may lapse too easily into facetious, image-seeking circumlocutions, squinting at ideas, all the while offending an inner ideal and perhaps sadly indicating an inadequate mastery of the material. Still, we are a little further on than Geoffrey Scott, with his empty sheet of foolscap and his poems.

Stephen Bayley

imbroglio

Taste The story of an idea

Look at Dr Freud's consulting rooms. The great man is sitting in a sombre Viennese interior, no doubt pleased with the popular reception of *The Interpretation of Dreams*. You can see the craquelure, smell the leather and the polish, sense the aspidistra, and sniff the dust. Even though it is a black and white photograph you can tell the dominant colour is brown. Tomes of grim, scholarly *Mitteilungen* suggest that psychoanalysis has the sanction of the past, that it is an ancient and respected academic medical practice.

Several things would be different if Dr Freud were practising in New York or London today rather than in the volatile Vienna of Loos, Schiele, Klimt and Werfel. One is that his consulting rooms would not look the same: nowadays leaders of the medical profession do not present their seriousness in terms of sombre bourgeois interior design. Instead, wealthy medical professionalism is today suggested by black leather and chrome furniture, middlebrow junk art, and glass tables piled high with photo monographs next to the water cooler.

Another is that the dark corners of patients' minds would on inspection be found to be corroded not by Freud's own anxieties about sex, death and mother (for nowadays these things are commonplace), but by … taste. This word, which formerly signified no more than 'discrimination', was hijacked and its meaning inflated by an influential elite who use the expression '*good* taste' simply to validate their personal aesthetic preferences while demonstrating their vulgar presumption of social and cultural superiority. The very idea of good taste is insidious. While I stop short of believing that all human affairs are no more than a jungle of ethical and cultural relativity, the suggestion that the infinite variety and vast sweep of the mind should be limited by some polite mechanism of 'good form' is absurd.

Everyone has taste, yet it is more of a taboo than sex or money. The reason for this is simple: claims about your attitudes to or achievements in the carnal and financial arenas can be disputed only by your lover and your financial

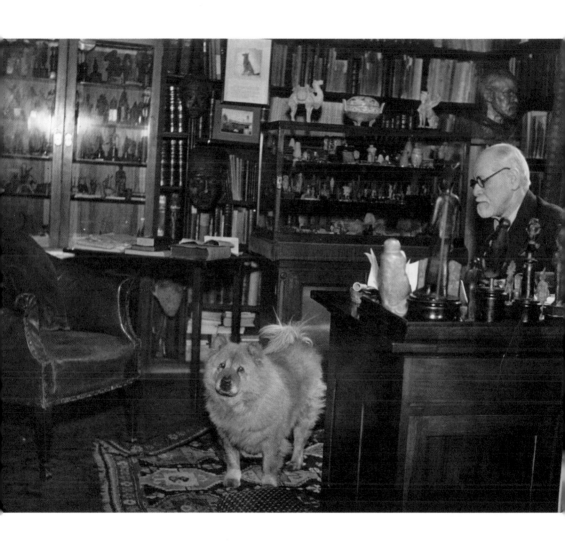

Above: Sigmund Freud in his study at Berggasse 19, Vienna. The professions have traditionally required imagery to buttress their status, especially in their offices. Freud chose sombre academicism.

advisers, whereas by making statements about your taste you expose body and soul to terrible public scrutiny. Taste is a merciless betrayer of social and cultural attitudes.[1] Thus, while anybody will tell you as much as (and perhaps more than) you want to know about their triumphs in bed and at the bank, it is taste that gets people's nerves tingling.

Nancy Mitford noted in her acute discussion of the term 'common' (as in 'He's a common little man') that it is common even to use the word 'common', which gives double-bluffers rich hunting grounds among the maladroit and insecure. Explicit social class, explicit material taste, social competition and cultural modelling are part of the post-industrial re-ordering of the world and as Nick Furbank wittily pointed out in his book about snobbery, *Unholy Pleasure* (1985), 'in classing someone socially, one is simultaneously classing oneself'. He might just as easily have said 'in criticising someone else's taste, one is simultaneously criticising oneself'.

The one certain thing about taste is that it changes. Taste began to be an issue when we lost the feeling for intelligible natural beauty possessed by the Neoplatonists and medieval artists and writers. Nature and art are, in a sense, opposites, and art has been the most reliable barometer of attitudes to beauty. As André Malraux noted at the end of the 1940s, in the modern world, art, even religious art of the past, is divorced from its religious purposes and has become a negotiable commodity for consumption by rich individuals or by museums.

Art was the first designer merchandise and there is no surer demonstration of fluctuating taste than the reputations of the great artists and the pictures they created. Averaged across centuries of first lionisation and then neglect, it is clear that these reputations have no permanent value: the estimation of the value of art depends as much on the social and cultural conditions of a particular viewer as on qualities embodied in the work itself.

We see in the past what we want to see. Economists call the effects of this survival bias. We call it taste. In the 1960s, Antoni Gaudí's architecture was rediscovered, although it had never really gone away, because it had hallucinatory qualities that the psychedelic generation recognised. In the 1970s, Art Deco became established as a respectable art-historical label, even though Alfred H Barr and Philip Johnson had banned it from the new Museum of Modern Art in New York on grounds of it being frivolous and merely decorative. Sometimes, of course, the merely decorative is exactly what's needed.

I am El Greco

The reputation of El Greco (1541-1614) is the paradigm of this cyclical phenomenon of survival-neglect-revival. Praised in his own lifetime, he painted in a style, exaggerated even by the standards of Mannerism, which Neoclassical critics found unsettling. The only way encyclopedists could interpret his attenuated forms and his spooky colours was to claim he was going blind and had gone mad. A century later, French Romantics travelling in Spain, including Théophile Gautier, recognised in El Greco's attenuated forms, nightmare colours and exaggerated mannerisms exactly those passions they wanted to versify, paint or articulate. Half a century on, Picasso singled El Greco out for major cultural rehabilitation.[2]

Once El Greco could only be understood in terms of medically recognisable disorders, but by the early twentieth century he was seen in a more positive, less pathological light and hailed as a source of *duende*, the romantic Spanish gloominess lovingly described by Lorca. This *duende* inspired Picasso: his *Les Demoiselles d'Avignon*, conventionally held to be the origin of Cubism, was as much influenced by El Greco as by Cézanne and, importantly, allowed Picasso to claim an earlier Spanish precedent for the movement he invented. As El Greco became a cult, other converts followed Picasso, including his friend Santiago Rusiñol, a rich aesthete responsible for the Catalan *Renaixença*.[3]

As arbiters of taste are inclined to, Rusiñol created a museum, Cau Ferrat, in Sitges in 1894 to vindicate his own preferences. In the opening ceremony, his two El Greco paintings were carried on a float to the accompaniment of a marching band while assistants scattered flowers. By 1898 Rusiñol had convinced his fellow townsmen to subscribe to a monument to the painter, which still stands in the Catalan port. At the same time, Picasso's studio was covered with photographs of El Greco, and in fact close parallels in both style and subject matter can be seen between Blue Period Picasso and late El Greco. The identification of one with the other went so far that in one sketchbook Picasso scribbled, *Yo El Greco* (I am El Greco).

El Greco is now established as an Old Master after centuries of alternating vilification and neglect. Or is he? The El Greco anecdote makes clear that what is fashionable in one generation often becomes preposterous in the next. When Kenneth Clark wrote his first book, *The Gothic Revival*

Right: El Greco, *The Vision of Saint John* (c.1609-14). Fine art is as subject to the depredations of time as high fashion. When El Greco painted like Titian he was accepted, but his later distortions gave him a reputation for madness.

Above: Sir George Gilbert Scott's Albert Memorial has been labelled a 'test for taste'. It was ridiculed even before it was finished. By the early twentieth century it was considered grotesque, but the revival of interest in Victoriana in the 1950s turned it into a much-loved monument.

(1928), it was almost as a *jeu d'esprit*: Victorian Gothic architecture had become a lost cause and it was a sophisticated and amusing literary rite of passage for a parvenu aesthete such as Clark – later assisted by John Betjeman, Osbert Lancaster and Evelyn Waugh – to talk it up, especially since Geoffrey Scott had recently made so influential a case for Renaissance classicism.

Crawling and verminous

The Albert Memorial is one of the Gothic Revival's masterpieces and was used by Clark as a frontispiece. During the First World War, on strolls through Kensington Gardens, the philosopher RG Collingwood (who coined the term 'Historicism') was shocked by its ugliness. He concluded in his *Autobiography* (1939) that the Albert Memorial was 'visibly misshapen, corrupt, crawling, verminous'. Despite this attack, he found the general effect of Sir George Gilbert Scott's design so powerful that he produced a study, 'Truth and Contradiction', which attempted to deal with the perplexing problems, perceptual and ideological, which the curious memorial caused him. A marvellous diversion in the history of taste, it was never published.

The Albert Memorial has often been described as a 'test for taste'. Despite Collingwood's critique, the memorial became absorbed into the repertoire of Englishness, while the memory of the sometimes cruel and squalid age that created it faded into comfortable nostalgia. The Gothic Revival itself, witness the successive editions of Clark's book, became more and more acceptable, until verminous became quaint and quaint became haunting. This process culminated in the founding of the Victorian Society in 1958, a club whose members can also be verminous, quaint and haunting.

Perhaps an even more dramatic demonstration of changing values in art occurs in literature. William Shakespeare's reputation as a genius of timeless relevance is a recent one, or, at least, recently renewed. To us he bestrides the narrow world like a colossus. And so he did to Samuel Sheppard, who in 1651 described him as 'sacred', but by 1662 Samuel Pepys thought *Romeo and Juliet* 'the worst [play] that I ever heard' and described *A Midsummer Night's Dream* as 'insipid' and 'ridiculous'. Half a century later Alexander Pope called Shakespeare 'divine', but there was also a moment in the eighteenth century when he was regarded as a talented barbarian of local interest and little more: Dr Johnson wrote in the 1765 Preface to his edition of Shakespeare that he 'has … faults, and faults sufficient to obscure and overwhelm any other merit'. Voltaire likened Shakespeare's complete works to a 'dunghill'. Thomas Bowdler found

Shakespeare so offensive that in 1807 and 1818 he edited the works for family consumption, so that 'Satan's cleverest bait' would no longer drag pure-minded youths towards a life of vice. Bernard Shaw despised him and Tolstoy wrote of 'an insuperable repulsion and tedium' on reading *King Lear, Romeo and Juliet* and *Hamlet*.

Civilisation has presumably not reached such a degree of global stagnation that the value of Shakespeare might not again be reassessed, and, in an age with different (although perhaps not superior) values, his literary art might be found wanting. Already there are moves to have Shakespeare removed from various school syllabuses because he is too white and too Anglo. Sublime artistry cannot, perhaps, survive the assault of dim ethnocentric political correctness. The ebbs and flows of history show us that the possibility of such a reversal exists. Our values are vulnerable. As Chaucer asked, 'if gold do rust, what then will iron do?'

More than mere historical anecdote, this spectre of continuous reassessment suggests an extraordinary dynamism, even uncertainty, perhaps even arbitrariness, in matters of aesthetic judgement, affecting everything from altarpieces to washing machines. Another example: the poet John Keats was fascinated by Hellenism, the fashionable love of all (or most) things Greek. In a library somewhere in Rome or London he focused on an engraving of the British Museum's Townley Vase (or some say the engravings of the Borghese Vase in the Louvre) and wrote of his 'still unravish'd bride of quietness' the 'Beauty is truth, truth beauty'.[4]

Beauty and truth bring together the formal and the moral, just as the acknowledgement of the existence of taste requires us to judge one in terms of the other: formality and morality might also be used to describe the purposes of modern industrial design. A Bauhaus teapot, for instance, is both a geometry lesson and a secular sermon.

The apparent universality and implied timelessness of Keats's judgement is made less clear and more poignant by the clutter of metaphor surrounding the poem. In trying to come to terms with the problem of beauty and decay (a concern of other poems, including *Ode on Melancholy* and *Ode to a Nightingale*), and, 'saddened by the mutability of natural beauty, he sought consolation in the more permanent beauty of art'.[5] But the perception of value in art changes.

A century and more nearer our own time, the pioneer American design consultant Norman Bel Geddes (1893-1958), addressing the spirit of the age, claimed that if Keats had been writing in 1940 he would have said the same about an aeroplane as he had about that old Grecian urn. We find

Above: Norman Bel Geddes, Airline No 4 (1929-32). Once upon a time, air travel was a spectacle of optimism and pleasurable excitement.

beauty in contexts we understand. In the Middle Ages the scholastic philosophers construed beauty to be an attribute of God, rather than of urns or aeroplanes; beauty and art were not necessarily related, indeed the idea of 'art' as a discrete activity was not acknowledged.[6] Keats's Neoclassicism, the prevailing taste of his day, required him to admire the Hellenic pot, while Norman Bel Geddes, suffused with the spirit of the mid-twentieth century, was as moved by the plane. In *Design This Day* (1940), Geddes's contemporary, Walter Dorwin Teague – apparently without irony – compared one of the Texaco filling stations he had designed to the temples of Greece.

Each age finds its own expression in material things and the faculty we use to identify those we find palatable or repellent we call taste. With the spread of materialism, consumerism and commodity fetishism, minute aesthetic criteria are being established as the basis for general social competition for the first time in civilisation. Everyday things we consume are – if perhaps only briefly – acquiring the sombre resonance of great art.

Because it involves everything we do in competition, taste can soon become a neurosis. Just as quality in design is most conveniently explained by the use of moralising terms such as honest, decent and sound, which have their origins in observations of human behaviour, taste is similarly rooted in performance, in that the exercise of it is somewhat akin to manners.[7] The architect Eugène Viollet-le-Duc (1814-79), an eloquent spokesman for structural rationalism in building design, applied the same principles to personal behaviour, believing that, '*Le goût consiste à paraître ce que l'on est, et non ce que l'on voudrait être.*' Or, taste is being what you actually are, not what you would like to be.

Semantically, taste is rich and confusing, its etymology as odd and interesting as that of 'style'. But while style – deriving from the stylus or pointed rod that Roman scribes used to make marks on wax tablets – suggests activity, taste is more passive. The old Latin tag '*De gustibus non est disputandum*' (there is no disputing about taste) is the oldest formulation of the idea 'One man's meat is another man's poison'. It is primary evidence that since Roman days the matter of taste has involved choice, whether individual or collective. Today, taste means both aesthetic and social discrimination, as well as gustatory sensation.

Etymologically, the word we use derives from the old French, meaning touch or feel, a sense that is preserved in the current Italian word for a keyboard, *tastiera*.

In English, the term 'good taste', meaning 'sound understanding', appears in the early fifteenth century, but it is not until the seventeenth century that the concept of aesthetic discrimination arrives in England: in the 1685 translation of Baltasar Gracián's *Oráculo manual y arte de prudencia* (1647) the term '*gusto relevante*' becomes 'quaint and critical judgement'. Interestingly, this book for the courtier has never been out of print since its first appearance, and more interestingly still for a book devoted to the professional cultivation of charm, it was made most famous in the German translation of Arthur Schopenhauer.

The metaphorical use of taste to mean judgement began in France, where Gracián's *gusto relevante* was rendered as *le goût fin*. A literal translation gave a new and troublesome word to English. The salons of France, where art, literature, antiquities and science were discussed in circumstances of considerable comfort and luxury, adopted the word and gave it a capital 'T'.

By the early eighteenth century the word taste was becoming familiar in essays on literature; the major transformation was complete and taste had become synonymous with judgement. A subtle and even elusive concept was born, elements of refinement and restraint attaching themselves to the definition only later.[8]

The Earl of Shaftesbury's *Letter Concerning the Art or Science of Design* (1712) is a typical marker of the phenomenon.[9] It was published just as critical discernment was about to become an intellectual sport. The *Letter* was written when art had been separated from its didactic and divine purposes and was well on the way to becoming a consumer product. At this moment taste did not have any particular values: it was only identified as a part of the human apparatus of discernment; you either had it or you didn't and there was no question of 'good' or 'bad'.

When man replaced God as the chief object of study, it was inevitable that the idea of beauty deriving from divine inspiration was replaced by a more secular, even materialistic, notion of aesthetic satisfaction. François de La Rochefoucauld remarked that 'Our pride is more offended by attacks on our tastes than on our opinions', an observation which puts into nice equilibrium the forces of cupidity and sophistication which dominate modern consumer behaviour.[10]

Taste has no rules

In a culture which had only one class with the economic capacity to make discriminating judgements, the matter of whether taste was good or bad was not so much irrelevant as inconceivable and its characteristics still wanted defining. Early pursuit of precision in this matter began by trying to locate where exactly in the body taste operated. To the Earl of Shaftesbury (1671-1713), having taste was like having an accessory for the soul. To Joseph Addison (1672-1719), as soon as taste was established, vice and ignorance would automatically be banished, presumably from loins *and* head – in that order.

David Hume (1711-76), who had said of Shakespeare 'a reasonable propriety of thought he cannot for any time uphold', defined taste as a 'sensibility' to every kind of beauty or deformity. Hume's view was that standards could be established, while Sir Joshua Reynolds (1723-92) upheld this view in the fine arts. Reynolds thought that genius and taste were very much the same thing, except that genius had the added ingredient of execution. To an academic painter like Reynolds, taste was to be found lurking in the same dominion as reason and was, therefore, in his view, equally exempt from any possibility of change.

The *Discourses* that Sir Joshua Reynolds delivered at the Royal Academy between 1769 and 1786 are a tour de force of aesthetic conviction; they are also the richest ground for sniffing out the English Enlightenment's attitude both to man-made rules and to God-given genius. Reynolds declared, 'Could we teach taste or genius by rules, they would no longer be taste or genius' (1770). But in grandly stating the case for rules, he made the most persuasive statement ever of the academic principle:

'Every opportunity therefore, should be taken to discountenance that false and vulgar opinion that rules are the fetters of genius. They are fetter only to men of no genius; as that armour, which upon the strong becomes an ornament and a defence, upon the weak and misshapen turns into a load and cripples the body which it was meant to protect … How much liberty may be taken to break through those rules … may be an after consideration when the pupils become masters themselves. It is then, when their Genius had received its utmost improvement that rules may possibly be dispensed with. But let us not destroy the scaffold until we have raised the building.'

Yet the worm of analysis kept burrowing in the foundation of Reynolds' classical certainties. 'How', you can imagine him always nagging himself, 'do we objectify our preferences?' Taste makers of the eighteenth century were concerned with whether judgements were based on mysterious, internal forces insusceptible to analysis, or whether there was a standard of taste which was rational and measurable, which could be scientifically determined and from which no reasonable man would withhold his approval. In this transition from the classical to the Romantic in art, David

Above: Sir Joshua Reynolds, self-portrait (c.1780). In every sense, a teacher of genius.

Hume suggested that beauty was not solely subjective to the viewer, but may be inherent in objects.

This suspicion was reinforced by Immanuel Kant (1724-1804), who reasoned that aesthetic judgements have universal validity. But Kant was wrong.

An explosion in production during the nineteenth century opened up consumption to social classes which did not include the president of the Royal Academy and distinguished philosophers; the idea of taste then came to represent not a commonly held view, but the antithesis of choices made in the marketplace, which, patronising experts always observed, expressed themselves in a debased and depraved form. In the fine arts this meant that painters were caught in the crossfire between Romanticism and popular culture.

The entire history of painting after, say, 1830 can be understood in terms of the dilemma faced by painters: whether to be society's picture-makers, or to be misunderstood private visionaries. Fyodor Dostoevsky (1821-81) described this as the choice between lofty suffering and cheap happiness. Similarly, manufacturers and designers did not know whether to satisfy existing popular taste, or to lead it by enhancing it. The question has not been resolved in the fine or the applied arts, but one thing is certain: by about 1850 it was very clear that aesthetic judgements – wheresoever applied and by whom – most certainly did not have universal validity. The age of consumerism has no time for Kant.

To account for this popular rejection of severe philosophy, the aspirational concept of 'good' taste began to emerge. Good taste was assumed to be a standard to which the masses would aspire, were they given the chance. The legacy of this underpins our behaviour in every activity from interior decorating to eating and table manners. Art historians have long struggled to understand what Birmingham manufacturers in the 1840s and shopkeepers of the twenty-first century understand intuitively: the mechanism by which civilisations and their preferences change and evolve.

Cultural historians, in pursuit of meaning in the chaos of history, take refuge in vague structural models such as Hegel's *Volksgeist*, an abstract entity embodying the national spirit, which imparts a common stamp to religion, politics, ethics, customs, arts and science. Marxism substituted economic conditions for the *Zeitgeist*, spirit of the age, but the frigid calculations of the political economists do not clarify the nebulous discussion. Mixed industrial economies substituted 'good' design for Marxist imperatives.

In an address to the Danish Society of Arts and Crafts and Industrial Design, in 1970, JK Galbraith (1908-2006), the economist who coined the term 'the affluent society', said: 'As living standards rise – as man multiplies the goods he consumes and the artefacts with which he surrounds himself – we are entitled to believe, or at least to hope, that quantitative measurements give way to qualitative ones.' A vain hope, since economists have no explanation for the mechanism of choice, even if its consequences are the very stuff of economics. How does change in taste affect supply and demand? How does a change in income distribution alter the ability of a market to satisfy certain tastes? But taste itself always lies out there … it is exogenous, unexamined. In their search for a value-free science, economists prefer to regard taste as a mystery, its nature only glimpsed through 'revealed preferences': choices registered in the marketplace. Economists rarely analyse, still less judge, the origins of taste, preferring to leave it to those of us who are less squeamish about the unquantifiable.

Whatever happened to 'good' design?

Good design was an inevitable consequence of the invention of taste. And soon after 'good' design got itself a bad name, the word 'designer' was mired in putrid froth. There is a very specific historical context. Circa 1979, the first signs of the 'designer' phenomenon were to appear on Gloria Vanderbilt's bottom. Indian jeans manufacturer Mohan – 'Mike' – Murjani knew there was no better way to tart up his product than having a famous name on them, so he pursued and failed to acquire the services of Jackie Onassis. Second choice was mature socialite Vanderbilt, who, in a contract that will form future case studies in business schools, agreed to model the product and have her signature embroidered on the rump. Thus, in one hideous, meretricious swagger of the marketing mechanism, 'designer' jeans were born.

The editors of the *Oxford English Dictionary* are tracing the descent of 'designer', a word that once signified an honourable vocation. As they toil, designer declines still further. Following the example set by Mrs Vanderbilt's arse, a lurid concoction of narcotics, hallucinogens and amphetamines was once witlessly described by the *Guardian* newspaper as a designer drug. Perrier became designer water. Now anything offered for sale that is irrelevant, matt black, white, gussied-up, expensive or just plain freaky weird is sold as a designer this or a designer that. So, a vocational term for a dignified profession, which includes Vitruvius, Sir Christopher Wren, Thomas

Above: Gloria Vanderbilt, the American socialite who begat the 'designer' phenomenon.

Sheraton, Henry Ford and Eric Gill, was debased to a slap-on epithet of no real meaning to join other dead or dying labels such as 'deluxe', 'executive' and 'turbo'.

Such epithets are dead or dying because they are stripped of real meaning. When language loses its basis in reality we are threatened by suffocation in a Babel of flashy values. Automobile manufacturers of the 1950s and 1960s, cynically refusing to improve the suspension, transmission or engines of their cars, added cute bits and big mark-ups to banal products and called them 'deluxe', as though a Vauxhall dealer could sell you a motorised Dunlop-borne pleasure dome instead of an under-engineered barge that droned, squeaked, smelt of plastic and made you feel sick. The ghost of meaning that once attached to the concept 'executive briefcase' is exorcised as soon as you articulate it. 'Turbo', a word once used exclusively by researchers into forced induction in heat engines, is now liberally applied to anything from chocolate to carpet shampoo, though the sweets and the soap are not fitted with an exhaust-driven compressor.

The absurd debasement of the designer was a fascinating episode in the history of taste, and all the more extraordinary when you consider that in the mid-twentieth century design had begun to usurp art in its power to delight and astonish the public. As soon as painters and sculptors ceased to communicate with people and chose instead to create commodities of debatable artistic interest exclusively for dealers and museums, it was inevitable that the public would take its aesthetic pleasures where it could find them: in the styling of cars, the cinema and in popular culture. Put another way, the century of consumerism has moved the entire man-made world into the province of aestheticism.

With the whole of material culture open to scrutiny and painting disappearing up its own art, it was necessary to make some claims for design. One of the first consisted of certain learned people declaring certain artefacts to be in possession of that mysterious and numinous attribute good design. Good design could mean something as long as there was some identifiable competition in the form of bad design. In Britain and the US in the 1950s and 1960s there was felt to be more of one than the other, and it perhaps meant something because then you found lots of manufacturers competing in the same field, some making good design and some bad. But good design was rarely defined precisely, because what was really being discussed was not so much design of any sort as taste. No survivors of the period are available to confirm this devastating observation, but you can still hear their ghosts, such as JK Galbraith, pointing to bleached ash Scandinavian furniture with webbed seats, products and typefaces in certain austere forms, colours of a certain restraint, and saying, with the fervour of the fundamentalist, 'that is good design'. Maybe, maybe not, but what they meant was, 'for someone of my age and educational background, that is to my taste'. But what the good design lobby really meant was: 'I know better than you.'

This sort of goodness began to discredit design in the eyes of the public, because it suggested the exclusivity of a remote clique. There is excellence in design, but it is altogether more scientific: you can measure it and weigh it. You know for certain when something is durable, affordable, useful, efficient, and – if you make it – profitable. What is less certain is whether you like it, whether bleached ash furniture tells other people things about you, which you would like them to know. Does it reveal the social and cultural influences operating on you? Is it sending the world secret messages about you? Does it betray your … taste?

Good design got itself a bad name because of this confusion, and the designer phenomenon was an inevitable consequence of it. Just as the qualifying adjective 'good' was plucked from universal vocabulary to give extra validity to certain products, so nowadays, in the deluxe, executive, turbo tradition, designer has become a tag of dubious cachet. It is, as Marxists will tell you, just one way that capitalists valorise surplus and make you think you want to consume something you don't really need. If, to paraphrase Dorothy Parker, you want to know what God thinks about 'designer' merchandise, just look at the people he gives it to.

But politics and religion aside, the designer fad only survived because of credulous consumers, uncertain of their taste, adrift in oceans of junk. The depravity of the design business is the implied suggestion that only jeans and mineral water and expensive things are designed – that it is rare and exclusive for something to be thus.

Both good design and the designer phenomenon were products of cynical ages, concepts that could only be validated by the continued existence of and demand for the bogus. According to JK Galbraith: 'It is said by the exponents of bureaucratic method that they serve the taste of the majority, and that taste is intrinsically bad. It will, indeed, be bad if there is no alternative, but given a choice, people have … a greater instinct for beauty than we often imagine.'

Above: Georg Jensen silverware (1929). Scandiwegian platters in naked metal were always said to be 'good design'.

Above: A Braun Station T1000 CD World Receiver (1965) designed by Dieter Rams, the German industrial designer whose landmark work for Braun made him the last survivor of the Modern Movement.

The cyborg shopper

Seventy years after Galbraith, markets are globalised and served by a faceless Internet. The shopping experience has been replaced by the luminescent glow of a screen, as consumers turn themselves into cyborgs every time they shop. Click-data reinforce assumptions made by algorithms based on earlier sets of click-data. The comfortably smug Eurocentric assumptions of mid-century modern economists, designers, opinion-formers and, let's say it, tastemakers seem absurd in the early twenty-first century.

Yet some things do not change. If we agree with Keats that beauty is itself variable, we are left with the perplexing conclusion that truth too is not eternally valid, but a function of specific social and cultural circumstances – as Donald Trump's 'fake news' suggests. Any dire ramifications arising from this are properly the province of philosophers and priests, but there are also implications for designers and consumers.

Clearly in any particular age there is a universe of choice in matters of colour, form, style and purpose, yet only certain options are generally considered worthwhile. Standards are always being established by outstanding minds in each generation. In the eighteenth century, an oligarchic control of wealth influenced all aesthetic judgements and these aristocratic requirements influenced society as a whole. Nowadays, different forces operate and our understanding of them is impaired by our confusion about the difference between taste and design.

Take any object. If you have access to data you can immediately tell whether it can be manufactured economically, whether it is durable, popular and profitable. These things can be measured in dollars and centimetres. Look at any building. Let's assume it has structural integrity so safety matters can be ignored, but how does it make you feel? It is these less tangible elements in any design that are the subject of this book. Why do certain designs seem to transcend fashion and achieve a timeless quality?

Is it true that the form of the most admired designs is such that you can immediately understand what the object does? Is it true that in all excellent design there is a harmony and coherence between the overall form and the individual details? Do all admired products, buildings and fashions have a certain equilibrium between the technique employed in the manufacture and the intention of the product?

The intention here is not to say that any taste is good or bad, but in the midst of arguments that suggest aesthetic judgements are liable to continuous review, can any claim be made for universality? Certainly, the Modern Movement can be interpreted as an attempt to restore rules to the theory and practice of architecture after a century and more of eclecticism: a 'return to order' was how Jean Cocteau put it. For perhaps fifty years of the twentieth century the modern aesthetic, disguised mostly under a veil of 'rationalism' blown stiff by the wind of social purpose, dominated European and American taste.

Quiet is better than loud

No one stated better the rules of that aesthetic than the German product designer Dieter Rams. A student of Ulm's minatory post-war Hochschule für Gestaltung, the designer whose work for Braun made first the white and then the black box a fetishistic commodity, Rams explained his philosophy of form: '*Einfach ist besser als kompliziert. Leise ist besser als laut. Naheliegendes ist besser als Gesuchtes.*' Perhaps Dieter Rams would not accept that his version of 'simplicity' (*einfach*), his version of 'quietness' (*leise*) and his interpretation of 'obvious' (*naheliegendes*) are themselves determined by aesthetic preference, and can make no claim to being undeviating absolutes. The preferences which Rams so artfully and eloquently expressed in his severely beautiful, but very restricted, designs for Braun appliances betray the social and cultural conditioning of the *Wirtschaftswunder*: they represent the *Zeitgeist*. Or did.

Dieter Rams used to enjoy driving his Porsche very fast on the autobahn. Different times demand different values. Nancy Mitford thought it was vulgar to display any sign of undue haste and therefore sent only business letters by airmail. How perturbed might Mitford have been by the speed of contemporary communications when 205 billion emails are sent every day?

With all the past immediately available for consumption and history deregulated by post-Postmodernism, with the world becoming smaller and smaller, taste more than ever is confused with fashion and with design. A vast number of those same 205 billion emails are sent on machines designed by Apple's Jonathan Ive whose personal inspiration was Dieter Rams himself. Rams brought a carpenter's eye to the Bauhaus aesthetic and changed the shape of radios and record players in the 1950s and '60s. Ive adapted that same aesthetic for machines that changed the shape of the world and revised human behaviour. Given the awful power of Apple's machines, they won public acceptance because they looked benign and sophisticated, not like Nikola Tesla's Teleforce, an early Death Ray.

As a metaphor for choice – if not for sensation in the mouth – taste is a peculiarly modern, Western faculty. The hieratic societies of the ancient past and of the Orient did not fret about the finer points of discernment,

Above: A Nagra IV-S tape recorder (1971), designed by Stefan Kudelski: the ultimate expression of analogue-era techno-romanticism.

THE LONDON AND BIRMINGHAM RAILWAY CARRIAGES.

Above: Marx introduced the word 'class' at a time when technical innovations deriving from industrialisation were partitioning society. Nowhere was this distinction more explicit than in the class system of the railways. Taste had been universal; now there was one for each class, if not for each individual.

at least not in so far as putting different objects and styles in competition with each other.

Even in the European Middles Ages the concept of taste did not exist. Medieval economies were based on survival and subsistence, while medieval art was didactic. The idea of art devoted to the excitement of pleasure is a recent one. Just as the idea of our having a unique 'personality' is recent too. Privacy also. Privacy is essentially a modern concept. Although medieval scholars had a great deal to say about proper social conduct, in a world that was not materialistic, their strictures were largely confined to canons of behaviour rather than consumerist choice.

But there are some interesting examples in the Middle Ages of things being acquired for edification and delight rather than for survival. Museums did not exist, but certain aristocrats acquired collections of curiosities as booty, as symbols of power and as hedges against economic disaster. Intended for private contemplation rather than public education, such collections are not to be understood as art; no great distinction was made between the beautiful and the merely odd. If the inventory is anything to go by, the Duc de Berry seems to have held in equal regard his collection of paintings and his embalmed elephant.

With art and life seen as one, medieval society did not distinguish between the moral and the aesthetic content of works of art. Hence disinterested aesthetic experience did not exist and therefore taste had no meaning before the beginning of the world of the consumer some four hundred years later. Beatrice Webb, aware of the modern citizen's preoccupation with being a consumer, described this role as perhaps 'the most pregnant and important piece of classification in the whole range of sociology'.[11]

Taste is in the soul of the consumer, a means of accommodating ideas about art and morality into lives that often provide for little of either. Whenever we find that art and morality are in conflict, it is because we are trying to reconcile a modern conception of the aesthetic with a medieval conception of the moral.[12] The structure of modern society – where consumption of artefacts has replaced the inheritance of them – required a concept of taste so that qualitative discussion, and social competition, could present established values – definite concepts by which performance could be judged and found impressive or wanting.

Taste may be an expression of personal values, but it also identifies an individual with a certain class. Since taste was invented by and for the middle classes, it is always the middle classes who suffer in discussion of it.

Bourgeois is French for middle class. Once meaning merely a town person, the word had acquired a pejorative sense as early as the seventeenth century: in Molière's *Le Bourgeois gentilhomme* (1670), being a town-dweller – when the court resided elsewhere – was clearly a social disadvantage. Although the term *bourgeois* fell into disuse during the French Revolution and was replaced by the less value-laden and more scientific *citoyen*, British writers preserved the concept for stigmatisation well into the nineteenth century.

In his *Book of Snobs* (1848), slyly subtitled *By One of Themselves*, William Thackeray calls snobbishness a 'diabolical invention of gentility', but puts gentility on the spot now and for evermore when he cautions that 'stinginess is snobbish, ostentation is snobbish, too great profusion is snobbish'. Thackeray immediately identified patterns and preferences of consumption with moral values. Matthew Arnold in *Culture and Anarchy* (1869) described the middle class as 'Philistines' prey to 'hideous and grotesque illusions' and inclined to seduction by 'worldly splendour, security, power and pleasure', an observation since validated by the glossy magazines and their advertisers.

In 1875, when the Midland Railway decided on a two-class system in its coaches, it was second class that went – first and third remained, the idea being to distance the one and suggest a level of aspiration for the other. Such tensions underpin the neatly constructed world of the consumer. Taste and class are almost inseparable. The greater part of economic activity in the West is devoted either to the pursuit of taste or to the disguise of class. It is the prosperous but unsure middle classes who are the most voracious consumers and therefore the ones most animated by considerations of taste.

Jewish Renaissance

To judge by the advertising, taste remains at the heart of personal motivation in matters of consumption. Ideas about group membership and group exclusion are either overt or esoteric in most consumer advertising and in the consumption that follows it. An account at Henri Bendel's New York store was once considered a requirement for Manhattan's contemporary aristocracy, which *New York* magazine defined more precisely, if less attractively, as 'small-boned women who lived for style'. When the downmarket fast-fashion chain store The Limited took over, that small-boned aristocracy was scandalised. The Jewish princess was once contemporary America's most accurate gauge of taste: deracinated, classless except for levels of consumption, proud by acquisition, a keen supporter of the 'arts and diseases', patron of designers, maker and breaker, arbiter of taste.

There are jokes about Jewish Taste. There is Jewish Renaissance as a style of interior design, much given by repute to gilt and velour. Cars were once painted Jewish Racing Gold. But as Jewish taste settled comfortably into the mainstream, new pretenders arrived to refresh the outrage of purists and snobs.

The word 'bling' entered *The Shorter Oxford Dictionary* in 2002, said to be onomatopoeia for light hitting a shiny object such as rapper Jay Z's diamond ring or his sequinned trousers or possibly even his bottle of Roederer Cristal. Here we are in the territory of Pimp Jewellery. It was Jay Z's *Money Ain't a Thang* that helped popularise the term, although the late Tupac (shot dead in Las Vegas in 1996) will also be known to history for his contribution to taste semantics. In a number called *Fuck Friendz*, Tupac invites listeners to: 'check out my diamonds bitch everyone gonna blink (bling bling bling)'. By 2008 *Time* magazine was describing French president Nicolas Sarkozy's term in government as the 'Bling-Bling Presidency'. Sarkozy is Jewish.

Taste and class feed off each other. Both words and concepts, each more impressionistic than scientific, came into being and use at about the same time. In Samuel Richardson's novel *Clarissa* (1748), class supersedes the earlier 'station' and by the later eighteenth century expressions such as 'of the lower class' were, so to speak, common. The same semantic shift took place in Germany where Karl Marx, for whom such considerations were a profession, began using *Klasse* to signify what had previously been known as *Stand* (estate). Marx said that class could only be understood in terms of an individual's relationship to the means of production (which is to say, as worker, consumer or owner). Taste can only be understood in terms of individuals' relationship to their need for consumption.

The creative people in advertising agencies are unconsciously aware that discrimination is a stimulus to consumption. The account planners are more alive to it. But their taste too is culturally determined, as an anthropologist with a global perspective can explain (or as any review of international campaigns for identical products will demonstrate). But colours, like ways of selling booze or cars, have different meanings in different territories. In Britain black is culturally associated with death and mourning, while in Venice or Spain it suggests grandeur and the grandee. Yellow is a sacred colour in China, but white is disagreeable for the same reasons that black used to be in Victorian Britain. European normality is merely a local preference. Martini, for example, never was a global product, and the technological criteria that obsess Audi engineers are no more universal a taste than *Wurst mit Rösti*. But German sausage and roast potatoes have not been so expertly marketed as the cars.

In his essay 'Reading Things' from *Faith in Fakes: Travels in Hyperreality* (1986), Umberto Eco asked, 'If Vienna had been on the equator and its bourgeoisie had gone around in Bermuda shorts, would Freud have described the same neurotic symptoms?' Probably not. Even in Europe, the history of evolving social taboos, whether bare knees or nose picking, demonstrates a susceptibility to change. To use Nick Furbank's illustration of the absurdities of discrimination which make the English upper classes such a rich source for critical observers: 'Lord Beauchamp thought it middle-class *not* to decant champagne.'[13] Lord Beauchamp clearly had it in for the town dwellers.

There are differences in tastes between different territories, as well as between social classes. The French have a more marked preference for offal than the Germans. In Chiavari, Italy, you can eat fish brains in the most expensive restaurants; try to serve them in Cleveland, Ohio, and you would be prosecuted by the Food and Drug Administration. There is also the element of time: taboos about food are in some cases recent. There is more than one nineteenth-century cookery book that gives instructions on how to carve calves' eyes. With the industrialisation of food-processing (and the distancing of the consumer which that process entails), a taboo about identifiable bits of edible animals evolved: generalised meat of no specific source was safe for middle-class consumption, but an all-too-obvious eyeball, ear, snout or trotter became unacceptable. By an interesting process of inversion, this particular taboo has been reversed, so that steak and chips is, at least in England, a proletarian dish and a lamb's pancreas an extremely sophisticated one.

European culture became refined through the practice of such arcane discrimination. Since the Middle Ages, when eating and drinking were even more social spectacles than they are today, conduct at table has been a ground for scholars to pontificate. In his magnificent book *The Civilizing Process* (1978), Norbert Elias describes medieval texts that feature discourses on socially acceptable behaviour.[14] The scholastics had a definite idea of proper conduct which passed into mainstream European culture as 'courtesy'. As with the word taste, courtesy's cognates in all European tongues have the same meaning: *courtoisie* in French, *cortesia* in Italian and *Höflichkeit* in German all signify exactly the same thing. Etymologically, this is 'how people behave at court'.

Manners became a means of objectifying certain taboos and giving expression to the self-image of an emerging bourgeoisie: middle-class, consuming town dwellers. In exactly the way that the concept of taste was to evolve into a code for accepted gentility, manners became more and more refined so that they no longer meant general conduct, but signified a certain caste's idea of acceptable etiquette. This interpretation of behaviour is not necessarily normal.

We respect cleanliness and order in the social consumption of food, but in his *Origin of Table Manners* (1978), Claude Lévi-Strauss observed that respect for eating quietly is a modern European phenomenon. He discovered that the table manners of 'primitive' people (he was thinking of the South American Indians) were not so much the crude fumblings of 'primitives' as an adjustable code that could be used as a language to communicate different moods and ideas. Eating habits are no innocent behaviour, but a method of broadcasting attitudes; some methods are vilified, others approved. As late as the nineteenth century, the French maintained the Spanish custom (alive still in Arabia) of belching after a satisfactory meal to demonstrate a favourable repleteness. Since the Renaissance, eating habits have been acknowledged as a form of non-verbal language.[15]

Table manners demonstrate what Lévi-Strauss called a 'compulsory message'. Cutlery is just one means of moderating our relationship with the external world. In medieval Europe it was customary to eat from a common dish. Crucially, for fastidious Westerners, cutlery achieves a distance between self and object. In non-Western cultures, eating implements are intended to preserve the food from the malign influence of the eater. In the West, the same implements are regarded as a means of maintaining internal purity and external grace. Health (so-called) is only the latest of an endless line of fads which have dominated European behaviour at table: wine was once denied to children not on grounds of well-being, but because their virulent young spirits might improperly acquire its potency. Health is itself a matter of taste: at least, we tend to have periodic foibles that are influenced by fashion more than medicine.

Since Baldassare Castiglione's *Il libro del cortegiano* (1528), the first modern book of manners, there has been an element in Western thought which places appearance above feeling. Castiglione's book was full of ideas that marked the beginning of the process, studied here, of

P. R. ladro napoletano

B. S. falsario astigiano

BOGGIA assassino falsario

CARTOUCHE

GIOCONDINA MARINI brigantessa

DESRUES avvelenatore falsario

interpreting artefacts in terms of behaviour. Castiglione's *sprezzatura* was the first expression of taste in everyday behaviour. A contrived, clever, courtly manner, its very artificiality put it at odds with nature. It was, by definition, artificial.

This form of self-awareness was a modern awakening. Establishing the standards for proper courtly behaviour was a way of structuring the world. From that moment behaviour was understood in terms of good and bad. But while courtiers, philosophers and anthropologists understand art and gestures, they are less certain about how objects and images communicate meaning. Cesare Lombroso, Professor of Psychiatry and Forensic Medicine at Turin (dedicatee of Max Nordau's notorious *Entartung* (1892), a book about 'degeneration' that was an inspiration to Hitler), took the eighteenth-century idea that beauty has a moral character to an extreme in his attempt to typify criminal types by their distinguishing features, but he was predicting a sort of pseudo-science that Hitler's approval of was eventually to discredit.

In post-war Paris there was a different mood of intellectual speculation. Roland Barthes (1915-80), Professor at the École Pratique des Hautes Études, knew his audience: it was a sophisticated one for whom reading was already a nearly sacred rite. French intellectuals of the 1950s were already familiar with Marx, Freud, their own native theatre of the absurd, their own new-wave films, the new novel, as well as pre-war Surrealism. With the ground prepared in this way, acceptance of Barthes's structural analysis was considerably easier than it would have been in England or the United States. Like the other 'new' critics, he was chiefly concerned with literature and language but, inevitably, his close reading of texts spilt over into close readings of objects. For so athletic an intellectual, it was but a short leap from, say, a stylistic analysis of Flaubert to a structural analysis of the Citroën, steak and chips, or detergent.

Paradoxically, despite his dedication to explication, Barthes's successive critical works get more and more obscure. In his early collection of essays, *Mythologies* (1957), he writes in an unscientific, lapidary and brilliantly terse and ironic manner. There is a witty revelation on each page. The later and far more detailed *Système de la mode* (1967) is perhaps his most powerful and most baffling work. Wit is replaced by algorithms and organograms. He looks at fashion as presented in magazines as a system, a structure in its own right. Fashion is an identifiable set of signs by which society communicates its concerns. Thus Barthes, in his search for interpreted meaning in everyday things, was to the catwalks of Paris 4ème what Lévi-Strauss was to the Polynesians.

Umberto Eco (1932-2016), late Professor of Philosophy at Bologna University, was more successful than Barthes in applying highfalutin literary theory to the everyday world. Eco has been accused of 'intellectual slumming', just as Barthes might have been accused of 'haute vulgarisation' in writing about Marilyn Monroe in the same sentence as the Académie française. Eco defended his assault on the modern world in this way:

'Today in Pompeii tourists are visiting murals depicting Romans with huge penises; originally meant as adverts for brothels, they are now considered great art. In the eighteenth century Telemann was thought a greater composer than Bach; in the nineteenth, Eugène Sue a greater writer than Balzac. In 200 years we may consider Picasso inferior to the man currently responsible for the Coca-Cola commercials … So we should never be afraid to analyse marginal or inferior manifestations of our culture'.[16]

Our views on the character of the world itself are equally vulnerable, and our respect for nature and individual countries has varied over the course of time. In pre-industrial, let alone pre-electronic, ages, nature was not necessarily benign. In medieval chronicles, nature is often presented as hostile and menacing. Mountains, quite properly, were once regarded as fearsome. The concept of the sublime landscape was, as life imitates art, largely influenced by the paintings of Salvator Rosa and developed by Mrs Radcliffe in her bravura accounts of the Apennines. Turner's better Italian pictures capture something of the vastness of the mood. It is significant that a love of nature was accommodated into culture at just the moment when industrial urban expansion threatened it. In this sense the entire Romantic movement was remedial. Sir Uvedale Price and Richard Payne Knight, neighbours in Herefordshire's Wye Valley as well as in spirit, and authors of, respectively, *Essays on the Picturesque* and *The Landscape* (both 1794), were among the most important influences on the English Picturesque movement – that sensibility which defined itself as art imitating nature and became refined into nature imitating art.

It was an astonishing episode in the history of taste. Price and Knight believed that material things have certain qualities that render them, say, beautiful, sublime or picturesque. Following Edmund Burke, who argued in his *A Philosophical Enquiry into the Origin of Our Ideas of the Sublime and*

Above: 'Nature', which is presently regarded as benign and beneficent, at least when it takes the form of 'unspoilt' landscape, was once, as in this mountain landscape by Salvator Rosa (1615-73), considered hostile and fearful.

Above: Italy-upon-Thames: Chiswick House, designed by Lord Burlington (with William Kent) and completed in 1729.

Beautiful (1757) that beautiful things have a capacity to relax the nerves, Price contented himself with enumerating the things that contained those relaxing qualities in the higher degree. Price clearly assumed that humankind had a particular sense attuned to perceive these qualities – an apprehension dismissed by William Thomson in his *An Enquiry into the Elementary Principles of Beauty* (1768): 'there are almost as many different opinions concerning taste, as there are persons who lay claim to it'. While most eighteenth-century debate on the subject was considered in these long, slow rallies, as if by accident, Price codified the rules which define and therefore limit our expectations of the English landscape, and which are still with us today.

Just as our relationship with nature is not fixed and determined, one country's attitude to another – now amused, now disinterested, now scornful – reflects changing taste as surely as the fluctuating reputations of great artists.

The Cornetto complex

The British reaction to Italy provides one of the most engaging and revealing examples. Few things seem more evocatively Victorian than the figure of Punch, but Mr Punch, whose features betray it, was originally Pulcinella of the Neapolitan *commedia dell'arte* of 1600. He only acquired his English wife Judy in 1818, at the end of a progressive – and unrequited – infatuation of one country for the other.

So complete was the English absorption of Italian architecture, marbles and paintings that when travelling through Italy in 1786-8, Goethe wished he had a 'cultured Englishman' as a companion. Italy was an idea as much as a country, so much so that, despite a generalised assumption among English travellers that Italians were popish, not to be trusted, idle and lascivious, their home country was held in very particular regard for centuries.

A transition occurred in the late eighteenth century, when milordly amateurism sickened into scholarship. Between William Roscoe's *The Life of Lorenzo de' Medici* (1796) and JA Symonds' *Renaissance in Italy* (1875), there was an explosion of popular books about Italian life, history and culture. Of these books, spontaneous, impressionistic, unscholarly, Charles Dickens' *Pictures from Italy* (1846) was perhaps the best written, if the least influential. FT Palgrave's edition of Murray's *Handbook for Travellers in Central Italy* (1843) was instrumental in changing British taste. Later, the guidebook was taken in two different directions: one by John Ruskin, the other by Augustus Hare. Born in Rome, Hare wrote several guidebooks to Italy and had a natural mother called Italima. These personal details are all witness to the cult of things Italian, which extended to religion and Romanticism. John Henry Newman, an Anglican clergyman, visited Rome in 1833; he left it well on the way to becoming a Catholic. Dismayed and enthralled by the Eternal City, he wrote: 'The first thought one has of the place is awful – that you see the great enemy of God … Next, when you enter the museums, galleries and libraries, a fresh world is opened to you – that of imagination and taste.'

Romanticism was the first democratic, mass-media movement in art, depending for its force on a combination of word and image, which in a sense provided the scriptural origins of pop culture. The Romantics popularised travel. Even the nomadic Byron got his first impressions of Italy second-hand. Of Venice he wrote:

Otway, Radcliffe, Schiller, Shakespeare's art,
Had stamped her image in me.

In poetry, Wordsworth, Keats, Shelley, Coleridge and Browning monopolised Italian subjects. In prose it was Edward Bulwer-Lytton and George Eliot. Roscoe's The Life of Lorenzo de' Medici was a source for Pre-Raphaelitism, but in a curious way the Pre-Raphaelite Brotherhood rejected Italian subject matter, just as their spiritual forebears, the Nazarenes, had begun to create in Rome from 1809 a style of painting that was entirely German. Thomas Stothard, who drew the figures for the engraved illustrations of Samuel Rogers' influential Italy (1830), had never actually been there; a synthetic stereotype was passed on to an entire generation. Although Holman Hunt, Millais and Rossetti had been inspired by engravings[17] of the Pisan Campo Santo when they founded the Brotherhood in 1848, they were all without direct experience of Italy and its art. Holman Hunt explained their reluctance to acquire it: 'In these days men of British blood … should not subject themselves to the influence of masters alien to the sentiments of the great English poets and thinkers.'

In 1849, Hunt exhibited a painting based on and accompanied by a long quotation from Edward Bulwer-Lytton's Rienzi (published in 1835 and dedicated to Alessandro Manzoni, author of I Promessi sposi). Rienzi is shown as the patriotic liberator of Rome. But contemporary Italian painting had no influence on mid-nineteenth-century British art. The Pre-Raphaelite Brotherhood was only one of a number of attempts to capture the purity of earlier Italian art, sometimes through the example of contemporary second-rate English literature. The rehabilitation of Botticelli, which preceded that of El Greco, was typical, as was Alfred Stevens' design for the proposed new bronze doors of the Geological Museum in Jermyn Street (1846-9), an exercise in higher pastiche.

Another example of a cultish vogue for things Italian was the brief fashion for the Garibaldi blouse, a version of Giuseppe Garibaldi's famous red shirts (which were in fact supplied to him by Thresher and Glenny of the Strand as part of London's contribution to the Sicilian expedition of 1860). The Italian liberator also became a popular model for Staffordshire figures. A biscuit created in 1861 by Peek Freans of Bermondsey, and still in production today, was named after him.

Inspired by the magnificent example of past Italian art, Sir Joseph Noel Paton – a painter whose *Dream of Michelangelo* (late 1840s) is in the William Morris Gallery, Walthamstow, London – wrote, in an era of copious mediocrity, an outstandingly bad poem:

No, Buonarroti, thou shalt not subdue
My mind with thy Thor-hammer! All that play
Of ponderous science with Titanic thew
And spastic tendon – marvellous, 'tis true –
Says nothing to my soul

The quality of Paton's verse is perhaps appropriate to a taste that went into decline almost as soon as it had finished its ascent. Two such unlikely bedfellows as Karl Marx and Queen Victoria both condemned the Garibaldi cult. The communist dubbed it 'a miserable spectacle of imbecility', while the monarch found herself 'half ashamed of being the head of a nation capable of such follies' (although she did have an Italianate villa called Osborne built for herself on the Isle of Wight). What Byron called Italy's 'fatal gift of beauty' could lead to dismay, and the taste for things Italian became less robust. Browning's lugubrious line, 'What was left, I wonder, when the kissing had to stop?' hints at a mood of disfavour.

Exposure to Italian music was an inescapable fact of life in Victorian Britain. Grand opera, maudlin songs for an accompanied pianoforte, and the itinerant organ grinder offered each of the British social classes vicarious contact with Italian culture. But as early as the 1840s the popularity of Rossini, Donizetti and Bellini was being challenged by the Germans Mendelssohn and Weber. By the time WB Scott paid his last visit to Italy in 1873, he found that Italy helped 'decrease my love of painting' and added,

50° ANNIVERSARIO DELLA MORTE DI GIUSEPPE GARIBALDI

MOSTRA GARIBALDINA

ROMA - 30 APRILE - 5 GIUGNO 1932 - X

Palazzo delle Esposizioni - Via Nazionale

4 GIUGNO: Inaugurazione del Monumento di Anita Garibaldi - 5 GIUGNO: Partenza del pellegrinaggio per Caprera

RIBASSI FERROVIARI DEL 50 %

ESENTE DA BOLLO   CORDANI - MILANO

'How does the traveller begin to loathe the Madonna.' In Britain, Italian music was kept alive not so much by composers as by singers and instrumentalists and impresarios (itself an Italian word). This change in status has contributed to the prejudice, still not entirely eradicated, that Italians are amiable buffoons. There is a hint of this in Mrs Beeton's *Household Management* (1861) which declares that 'With the exception of macaroni, [Italians] have no specially characteristic article of food.' *Cucina povera* was yet to be discovered by discerning sophisticates.

Improved communications were a fundamental influence in turning English taste away from Italy. Familiarity breeds contempt, so for as long as Italy was impossibly remote, artists were happy to provide imaginative confections of Italian scenery and the public was happy to be beguiled by them. Whereas in 1820 John Keats took four and a half weeks to sail from Gravesend to Naples, and in 1833 the painter Charles West Cope (whose picture *Italian Hostelry* – in fact painted in London in 1836 – hangs in Liverpool's Walker Art Gallery) took more than seven days and nights to travel by road from Paris to Milan, by the 1860s the railway had reduced the London-Milan journey to a mere fifty hours.

Mrs Beeton's amused dismay passes straight through to Norman Douglas, although in his case the subject is treated with more exuberance, charity and knowledge than Mrs Beeton could muster. In *Old Calabria* (1919), Douglas revels in curious details: Venosa displayed 'a reposeful dirtiness, not vulgar and chaotic, but testifying to time-honoured neglect, to a feudal contempt of cleanliness'; 'one old man ... was wont habitually to engulf twenty-two litres of wine a day'; 'mice ... are cooked into a paste and given to children'.

While there is some mockery in Douglas's account of pre-industrial Italy, there is also an element of *Et in Arcadia ego*, which was to be expressed in a new, romantic interpretation of Italy and the Mediterranean stimulated by the privations of the Second World War.

Norman Douglas's ghost stalks the pages of the marvellous cookery books written by Elizabeth David (1913-92). By the time Mrs David's *Italian Food* appeared in 1954, Italy, experiencing its own post-war *ricostruzione*, was overdue for a revival. In her introduction to successive editions, Mrs David repeatedly invokes authenticity. The subtext of her descriptions of

Left: A poster for an exhibition to commemorate the fiftieth anniversary of the death of Giuseppe Garibaldi (1932). Father of Italy and folk hero, the English named a biscuit after him.

England in the 1950s is a critique of English life and manners at least as important as that of the more loudly trumpeted contemporary Angry Young Men. Being concerned with sentiment as much as with recipes, the popularity of Mrs David's books proved the centrality of taste to the modern consumer.

Born to shop

Science estimates that more than fifty per cent of our brains is required to process visual data while only one per cent for taste. There are further peculiarities in the neurological aspects of this topic: a phenomenon known as the 'cross-modal effect' suggests that, for example, the experience of noise affects the taste of food and drink. This is a problem airline caterers have been aware of for some time: in-flight food is often designed with strong rather than subtle flavours. You are more likely to be served a big oaky Chardonnay than a delicate Grüner Veltliner, a voluptuous Oregon pinot noir and not a light Beaujolais.

The meaning of taste in history has swooped and veered between physical sensation and aesthetic predilection. Wordsworth was worried that a taste for poetry might be confused with something so indifferent as a taste for rope dancing or for sherry.[18] The same can be said of the Italian word *gusto* or of the French *goût* and the German *Geschmack*. It is a concept at once substantial and suggestive, the metaphorical transfer from passive sensations to intellectual acts of discrimination. Taste with a capital 'T' developed from an abstraction to an attribute. As Raymond Williams noted in *Keywords* (1976), 'We have only to think of related sense words, such as touch or feel in their extended and metaphorical usages, which have not been abstracted, capitalised and in such ways regulated, to realise the essential distinction.'

In 1755, Johann Joachim Winckelmann, a gay librarian from Dresden, went to live in the Roman palace of Cardinal Albani, taking with him a bag full of German Rationalist philosophy. He was appointed Prefect of Roman Antiquities in 1763, and his early distinction between Greek and Roman marbles laid the basis for modern archaeology. He also laid the scholarly basis for Neoclassicism, a taste in art, architecture and design that became – in an age on the verge of mass production – perhaps the first consumer cult.

Winckelmann found in Greek art a confirmation of his personal theory of beauty. He considered that simplicity, harmony, functionalism (in both structure and adaptation to the local environment) and respect for materials were all prerequisites for the achievement of beauty in architectural design. He did not see that either colour or ornament had any part to play in it. Beauty resulted from a certain arrangement of shapes and forms that were in some way expressive of the ideal. This was what he meant by his demand for 'noble simplicity'.

In providing a theoretical basis for the Neoclassical aesthetic, Winckelmann was a profound, if esoteric, influence on the history of European and American taste. A contemporary of his, Jeanne Antoinette Poisson (1721-64), had a more immediate contribution to make to the newly developing European material culture. Known to history as Madame de Pompadour, Mademoiselle Poisson's astonishing career demonstrated the close relationship between social aspiration and contemporary taste – a relationship that has been more or less inseparable ever since.

Pompadour made tangible the elevated idea of 'taste'. It ceased to be metaphorical, and became instead a particular vision of haut-bourgeois style. She turned *arriviste* middle-class snobbery into a minor movement in the history of art, creating 'positional' goods two centuries before the term was invented. Hers was the *objet du goût*, her legacy the discretionary part of the marketplace, where all modern consumers are adrift between the Scylla of conformity and the Charybdis of error. Madame de Pompadour, it could be claimed, was the inventor of the consumer product.

Ever the one for the grand gesture, the ambitious young Poisson was pleased to drive, as circumstances demanded, either a pink or a blue phaeton across the path of Louis XV as he hunted or pursued his botanical interests in the forests around Paris. With style, she wore pink in the blue phaeton and blue in the pink one. The gesture did not go unnoticed by the monarch, who, bored with the queen, had also recently lost his mistress. He picked her up at a fancy-dress ball held at Versailles in 1744. Apparently without irony, Poisson went as Diana the Hunter. She easily captivated the King with her wit and coruscating conversation, her singing, dancing and musicianship. Reports say nothing of her prowess as a huntress, but dissimulation was not a concern at Versailles.

The King gave her an estate at Pompadour and the title of marquise. She gave him everything except her body, an exercise in restraint that in the era before Freud was not properly understood, but which throws into dizzying confusion her willingness to pose enticingly and fleshily in the nude for François Boucher's voluptuous *Toilet of Venus* (1751), once in the collection of the Comte de La Béraudière. Her nude portrait, while not without a strong erotic *frisson*, was intended for her own apartments at

Versailles, not for the titillation of the King. It is an image designed to confer status, in this case divine, on the sitter. The once humble Poisson had a high regard for her own worth. At court she became notorious because, with true middle-class snobbery, she conducted herself with chilling hauteur.

Jules Beaujoint published this ditty in his *Secret Memoirs of Madame la Marquise de Pompadour* (1885):

The Birth of Jesus made
At Court a stir indeed,
And Louis in a coach drove off
To Pompadour with speed,
Said he, 'The Child we'll go and see',
Said she, 'No, not at all;
They'd better bring the Child to me,
I never made a call.'

Madame de Pompadour's exercise of taste was facilitated by ready access to money and is thus a prototype for modern consumerism: it is often said that her collection was the most remarkable assemblage of possessions ever acquired by a French citizen. While Louis XV had the greatest difficulty in getting between her legs, she slid easily in and out of his bank account. Nancy Mitford's *Madame de Pompadour* (1954), based on sources that include du Hausset, Croy, Bernis, Luynes and Maurette, has her saying, 'He doesn't mind signing for a million, but hates to part with little sums out of his purse.'

She bought house after house to decorate for the King: Crécy near Dreux; Montretout at Saint-Cloud and La Celle nearby; others at Compiègne and Fontainebleau. She filled the Hermitage at Versailles with fresh flowers every day. She had the architect Lassurance design a house called Bellevue near Sèvres (which had scented china flowers from Vincennes), and Les Reservoirs at Versailles. Her Parisian house, the Hôtel d'Évreux, is now known as the Élysée Palace, a legacy that has had incalculable esoteric influence on the taste of French presidents.

Madame de Pompadour was the *ancien régime* version of the 'born to shop' phenomenon. Her pursuit of material acquisitions was on the sinister

Left: A Roman marble statue of Laocoön, discovered in 1506.

side of neurotic. They included Dresden, Meissen, potpourris from Chantilly, sculptures, carvings and ornaments by Pigalle, Verbeckt and Falconet, pictures by Chardin, Van Loo and, of course, François Boucher.

There were also storehouses filled with other pictures, porcelain (2,000 pieces of Sèvres), tapestries, linen, tools, carriages, wine and autograph furniture (including an escritoire by J-F Oeben, now in the Jack and Belle Linsky Collection of the Metropolitan Museum of Art. At the Rothschilds' Waddesdon Manor in Buckinghamshire, a Disneyworld of French taste, there is a gold and porcelain snuffbox with portraits of her dogs, Inès and Mimi, painted on the lid – another example of how the Pompadour *arriviste* taste crosses generations. A nice footnote: in 2008, burglars broke into Waddesdon and ransacked this collection in a most discriminating fashion.

Although, according to Jules Beaujoint, 'the Marquise was not a blue-stocking', she left a library of 3,826 books covering such subjects as commerce, finance, industry, philosophy, theology and history. Pompadour – whom Beaujoint describes as a woman of 'severe taste' – was artistic dictator of France in the years before the Revolution: she had Ange-Jacques Gabriel design the Petit Trianon, the perfect proportions of which were later to inspire Le Corbusier in his belief that all fine architecture is the product of an invisible grid, *tracés régulateurs*. She also created the Cabinet du Roi at Versailles, and, with her intuitive flair for dealing with craftsmen and designers, arranged the Gobelins tapestries, the damasks, the secretaries, the bibelots and the pictures. Perhaps as a consequence of her preferred diet of vanilla, truffles and celery, Pompadour, France's first arbiter of *goût*, died at the age of forty-two.

The story of Madame de Pompadour, with its engaging details, is not of mere anecdotal interest. Her extraordinary position as artist of the state gave her huge power and influence to indulge her aesthetic preferences. Her canvas was not stapled to a stretcher, but covered all of modern material France. Her achievements created the role of tastemaker, whose ghost exists today, but her understanding of marginal utility and the role of desire in design led to the *objet du goût,* which has passed by a route described elsewhere in this book, from mistresses of kings to owners of chain stores.

In Britain, less elevated bourgeois taste at the time of Pompadour was represented by furniture, ceramics and the idea of the *souvenir*. Popular

Right: Madame de Pompadour posed for François Boucher's *The Toilet of Venus* (1751). That the measure of exquisite good taste, wherever *arrivistes* gather, is even today expressed in terms of eighteenth-century French art, architecture and design says much about the influence of Madame de Pompadour.

design was already in the marketplace in the late eighteenth century. Neoclassicism expressed this taste sometimes uncertainly. Josiah Wedgwood (1730-95) and his artist John Flaxman extended trade far beyond Sir Joshua Reynolds' conception of the world, converting a peasant craft into an industrial business supported by the ancestor of the modern skill of marketing. He gave class to the primitive kilns of Staffordshire and became a major influence on the development of taste.

Wedgwood's creamware service was inspired by the chaste simplicity, noted also by Winckelmann, of antique art (although in fact antecedents of Wedgwood were doing much the same thing in Rome). However, this was not just an aesthetic preference; from the mass producer's point of view there were practical and economic imperatives for this desired simplicity in that simple designs were easier to make than the more elaborate Rococo ones.

Good and proper

In furniture there was a desire to achieve certain standards of dignity and order. The Preface to George Hepplewhite's *The Cabinet Maker and Upholsterer's Guide* (1794), a compilation of designs for jobbing craftsmen to copy and for the gentleman pleasurably to survey, declares, 'To unite elegance and utility, and blend the useful with the agreeable, has ever been considered a difficult, but an honourable task.'

Hepplewhite's designs were described as 'good and proper', an interesting phrase that hints at the relevance of manners and appropriateness to English taste. The *Guide*, besides being a hymn to gentility, reveals itself as a confident arbiter of taste: 'Mahogany chairs have seats of horsehair, plain, striped, chequered &c. at pleasure … Japanned chairs should always have linen or cotton cushions.' Hepplewhite's designs were so adaptable and so durable and successful that they have been continuously reproduced but it was not until the mid-nineteenth century that a technical revolution in furniture manufacture radicalised taste.

Innovations in ceramics came sooner. Interestingly, improvements in the processes of making ceramics, in the brave Wedgwood tradition, coincided with an emerging Neoclassical taste – the artificial stone produced at Coade's factory in Lambeth helped to make the Neoclassical version of the antique popularly accessible at low cost. Since the collection of classical statues at Fontainebleau had become famous, they had served as marks of modernity, as Montesquieu explained: 'These statues cannot be sufficiently looked at, for it is from them that the Moderns have built up their system of proportions.' There was an element of elitism, even snobbery of the intellectual sort, in possessing such a canon. But Montesquieu knew this: his *Essai sur le goût* was published in 1757.

By about 1700, foreign craftsmen in Rome were preparing lead reproductions of ancient statues for commercial manufacture, for those who could afford neither original antiques nor the more costly bronze copies. While Wedgwood was not above making heads of ancient worthies as souvenirs, the real popularisation of antique imagery and ideals came from Mrs Coade and from John Cheere's sculpture yards at Hyde Park Corner, illustrated as the frontispiece of William Hogarth's *Analysis of Beauty* (1756), itself an exemplar of modern taste in the arts. With Josiah Wedgwood, John Cheere (1709-87) was the first Englishman to realise the potential market for tokens of taste. By collecting Cheere's mass-produced souvenirs, anyone could have a collection of marbles as ennobling as the French King's.

By the mid-nineteenth century, such reproductive didacticism was institutionalised. In Paris a Musée des Copies was established by Adolphe Thiers and in London in 1864 Domenico Brucciani opened a gallery of plaster casts in Russell Street, Covent Garden, portentously called a 'Galleria delle Belle Arti'. Brucciani's statues were not only educative (in that they prepared visitors for their trips to Florence, Naples and Rome); they also found their way into all the provincial art schools of Britain, as required since 1859 by the Lords of the Committee of Education of the Privy Council. In a prototype gesture of suburban disdain for Italy, *The Art Journal* reasoned that the success of Brucciani's collection lay in the fact that Covent Garden provided an environment 'much purer' and therefore more conducive to contemplation than Italy itself. At the same time, when certain casts found their way into private hands, status was conferred on the owner. This form of intellectual property was highly valued. Contemporary garden statuary is a mongrel descendant of this fad for copies.

The development of taste as an idea and as an aesthetic prescription parallels the rise in popular expectations, which grew with the increase in spending power. Taste and money are inseparable in nineteenth-century culture. Honoré de Balzac was obsessive about money (even while he romantically despised the monied classes); his descriptions of interiors created by financiers and industrialists betray the dependence this generation of consumers had on the antique in forming and projecting their taste.

Overleaf: The Hôtel d'Évreux, Paris (1722), purchased by Louis XV for Madame de Pompadour.
It is now the Palais de l'Élysée, official residence of the President of France.

Hortus & Palatium Ebroicense   16.e V^{üe}

The term 'consumer' had come into use as a description of bourgeois economic activity in the eighteenth century. In the new markets of the rapidly industrialising nations, making and using became known as making and consuming. It is interesting to chart the relative decline of the old-fashioned, more genteel word 'customer' against the rise of the more abstract, aggressive 'consumer'. Semantically, customer suggests familiarity and regularity and a one-to-one relationship with a retailer or a manufacturer, while the remote consumer is a more relevant, impersonal tag in global markets giddy with excess. 'Consume' almost always has an unfavourable, even hostile, connotation, as in 'consumed by fire'. Tuberculosis was known as consumption during the whole period when it was a killer disease, and Vance Packard's *The Hidden Persuaders* (1957) makes great play with the derogatory term 'consumer society'.

The history of the word consumer reveals the development of the Western economy. Mass production and all that it entails – investment, long lead times, low unit costs and ready availability – replaced a system where simple makers could articulate and satisfy needs; the new distant customers alienated from the production process became consumers. Deconstructing meanings in this way helps explain how taste operates in the contemporary world. Just as the modern idea of money involves faith or credit (from the Latin *credo*, I believe, or I trust), the concept of taste came to fill the vacuum created by the possibility of limitless consumption brought about by the possibility of limitless credit. The etymology of credit makes it clear that money, like taste, is very much an act of faith.

The Frankfurt School social scientists Walter Benjamin and Theodor Adorno noted the extraordinary paradox that under capitalism taste is not autonomous – as one might expect in a system that promotes competitive individualism – but tends to be collective. Thus, academic Marxists taught market researchers what are the most effective contemporary symbols of privilege and instruments of status.

The status symbol is as significant today as it was in Madame de Pompadour's time, but it takes different forms and serves different purposes. It is not surprising that in the eighteenth century tokens of taste were classical statuary and in the nineteenth moral values. In the twentieth – a century in thrall to the machine – consumer durables became touchstones of value, and none so numinous as the wristwatch. Its very familiarity and availability has, by a Darwinian process, forced special and intricate patterns of discrimination on consumers. What Antinous was to Cardinal Albani, the expensive wristwatch was to the tastemakers of the late twentieth century. The late Giovanni Agnelli of Fiat had a fine personal foible: he wore his on the outside of his cuff.

Although not the most expensive, the most exceptional watch-as-status-symbol is the Swiss Rolex, since its reputation is based on technical merit (a patent for its remarkable watertight system was granted in 1926). This gave rise to an aura of professionalism and expertise that has since proved especially attractive. Ever since Mercedes Gleitze wore a Rolex Oyster for a heavily publicised cross-Channel swim in 1927, Rolex has been more than merely a watch.

Before the First World War wristwatches, as compared to fob watches, were considered effeminate, but when artillerymen needed the convenience of a wristwatch (as bicyclists had just before them), they became important symbols. Ever since, the basic architecture of the wristwatch has depended on innovations made for the trenches. The number of press advertisements for new bracelets coming on to the market between 1914 and 1918 attests to its growing popularity, even though conservative spokesmen for the watch industry thought it was an idiotic fashion to expose so sensitive a mechanism on the most restless part of the body.

Rolex: Apollo edition
Because of the stigma of effeminacy, the wristwatch has always been marketed in a pointedly masculine way. Cartier's most famous wristwatches are the 'Tank' (made for the US Army Tank Corps, another innovation of the First World War), while all Rolex models make some sort of persuasive appeal to professionalism – that of the diver, the aviator, the racing-car driver or the opera singer. Today, the names of individual Rolex models all suggest impressive expertise: we have the Rolex Explorer and Submariner and may one day even have the Rolex War Lord, the Rolex Drug Smuggler and the Rolex Exterminator.

Ever since the 1920s the Swiss company has concerned itself with developing its customers as much as its watches, and for nearly forty years the simple theme has been 'famous people wear Rolexes'. They call it relationship marketing and in this case the relations are a distinguished crew including Yehudi Menuhin, Kiri Te Kanawa, Reinhold Messner and Norman Foster. However, Dave Trott, a voluble socialist Buddhist adman known for his views, once commented:

'I wouldn't be seen dead in one. What it says is that you have no originality and you need to wear an accepted badge to say you have made money. It's like people used to wear clothes and shoes with the YSL label

Above: Josiah Wedgwood (1730-95) was inspired by what he imagined was the chaste simplicity of antique art. Eighty years later archaeology proved that classical buildings had been garishly decorated. The eighteenth-century conception of 'antique' was a projection on to the past of contemporary taste.

on the outside or buy a Porsche 911 and never drive outside Soho. It's a cliché.'

But rival ad agency boss John Hegarty more shrewdly retorted: 'Rolex says, "I've made it. I've achieved that, done it, sorted that area out". It is about two things: awareness and achievement. It is also obvious with a Rolex that you have money because they cost so much.' Hegarty also said, 'It's all about taste'.

The same was once said of the Apollo Belvedere. But unlike Apollo, Montres Rolex SA knows that sales go up when it increases the price. A Rolex chief executive explained: 'We are in the luxury business. We are selling taste, selling fashion, selling status. If you have a Rolex you are a member of a select international club.' The director Franco Zeffirelli considers a Rolex 'above fashion. It is standard … in my own work I never try to be fashionable. Never. And the same could be said for the watch I have chosen to wear'.

It is significant that Rolex users are so self-conscious about their choice of wristwatch and that to many of them its value lies either in its overt expression of professionalism or in its reticent expression of neutrality. The proper maintenance of the middle class's self-regard depends on their values being necessarily good, superior to those of the upper as well as the lower classes. This is why snobbery is essentially a distinction of the middle classes and why the Rolex is an essentially middle-class watch.

As Dave Trott averred, famous products acquire tribal followers. Indeed, each requires the other in a bear hug of symbiotic consumerism. Because of the admiration Gulf women had for the French couturier, he became known as Yves Saint Laurent of Arabia. Porsches may appeal to disciplined German-accented technophiles who see value in tradition and admire the *Forschung* and *Entwicklung* that goes into the cars, but they are admired by other people as well: a banker socially promoting himself into an expensive Cotswold Village was told by snitty locals that no one would speak to him if he ever drove his bright red *Neunelfer* between Sandford St Martin and Great Tew.

But now tribal behaviour of one kind is being replaced by another. The Internet has allowed retailers to analyse huge data sets in pursuit of better understanding consumer preferences. Experts in large-scale pattern recognition scrutinise Amazon and Spotify. They know what we think. And they think they can predict what we think. Algorithms now tell us our taste, they tell us. In *You May Also Like* (2016), Tom Vanderbilt says: 'Taste is like traffic, actually, a large complex system with basic parameters and rules, a noisy feedback chamber where one does what others do and vice versa, in a way that is almost impossible to predict beyond that at the end of the day a certain number of cars will travel down a stretch of road, just as a certain number of new songs will be in The Hot 100.'

It is both more and less simple than that.

Brixton and Vienna

Between 1850 and 1910 the population of Britain grew from 27 million to 45 million. The growth was in the urban classes. When this huge, new and (by some standards) ignorant class emerged, supply and demand was no longer controlled by the *cognoscenti*, but by the principles of market economics. This produced such a fundamental revolution in behaviour that it soon became clear that Sir Joshua Reynolds was wrong: there was more than one taste and a great many decent people apparently did not share his.

The new middle classes neither knew nor cared about Reynolds' polite strictures, but preferred to clutter themselves with meretricious junk, mass produced by cynical manipulators of the means of production in Birmingham, Sheffield and Glasgow. A bookcase got up to look like the west front of Lincoln Cathedral was typical. For the nineteenth-century consumer, the rules of taste were replaced by market forces; philosophical musings gave way to homely tracts admonishing avaricious and fashion-crazed housewives for their want of judgement and their excess of competitive acquisitiveness.

Charles Eastlake in his *Hints on Household Taste* (1868) described with the unfluctuating certainty of someone comfortable with his prejudices the proper application of the principle of taste to all the minutiae of domestic life. He argued that the artistic chaos of most homes resulted from no one being trained to make aesthetic judgements (and in saying this he echoed the rationalism of the eighteenth century). He believed that guidance in the matter of what he called 'right taste' should form a necessary part of every genteel woman's education. His use of the absolute 'right', as opposed to the somewhat less certain 'good', reveals most clearly his conviction that one taste alone is correct. Nor is he innocent of the charge of puritanism, revealed in his abhorrence of consumerism and its appetite for novelty:

'When did people first adopt the monstrous notion that the "last pattern out" must be the best? Is good taste so rapidly progressive that every mug which leaves the potter's hands surpasses in shape the last which he moulded? But it is feared that, instead of progressing, we have, for some ages at least, gone hopelessly backward in the arts of manufacture.'

Above: The wristwatch provides even men of conservative tastes with an opportunity to express personality. The classic man's watch is the Rolex. The Cartier 'Tank' watch was created during the First World War, its military nomenclature helping to create a new market.

This charge of shoddy workmanship levelled at the workshop of the world was a powerful weapon in the aesthetician's armoury. It is true that applied ornament was often used to camouflage manufacturing faults, but in his criticism of popular decoration Eastlake became confused about taste and design:

'This commonplace taste … compels us to rest on chairs and to sit at tables which are designed in accordance with the worst principles of construction and invested with shapes confessedly unpicturesque. It sends us metal-work from Birmingham which is as vulgar in form as it is flimsy in execution. It decorates the finest modern porcelain with the most objectionable character of ornament.'

In his strictures Eastlake may have been influenced by Augustus Pugin (1812-52), visionary architect of the Gothic Revival, who made the same point, more forcibly, in his *An Apology for the Revival of Christian Architecture in England* (1843):

'It is impossible to enumerate half the absurdities of modern metal-workers; but all these proceed from the false notion of disguising instead of beautifying articles of utility. How many objects of ordinary use are rendered monstrous and ridiculous, simply because the artist, instead of seeking the most convenient form and then decorating it, has embodied some extravagance to conceal the real purpose for which the article has been made!'

The rich brew of art and morality, the roseate view of history, caught the mood of the time, and – setting a disastrous precedent for British culture – suggested that the solution to the immediate artistic, moral and social problems of England existed at the end of a long journey back to the Middle Ages. Here Pugin imagined a world of God-driven beauty and harmony, of innocent men, of organs booming basso profundo solid, spiritual goodness. There was no smog and no proletariat, only placid, satisfied peasants. Viewed from one of Gustave Doré's infernal and sooty railway arches, it was a persuasive vision.

But beneath the apparent certainties of Victorian England lay paradoxes that are still unresolved today. There is more snobbery in one copy of the nineteenth-century middle-class journal *Punch* than in an entire run of the patrician eighteenth-century *Gentleman's Magazine*. Pride in Britain's industrial eminence was moderated by disquiet at the quality, purpose and appearance of most of what was produced. While paternalism suggests a positivist belief in progress and improvement, the aesthetic zealots sought their inspiration in distant history. The concern for the moral welfare of the

Above: John Edward Soden, *Man Smoking in a Parlour* (1862): a Victorian domestic interior full of *horror vacui*.

Above: Prince Albert invented the idea of a Great Exhibition to improve public taste. The 1851 exhibition in Joseph Paxton's Crystal Palace, in London, was immensely popular. A primal media event, it suggested that the entire world was available for consumption.

working classes, though real, was also pragmatic, in that the country was more troubled by fears of public disorder and urban insurrection than popular views of the Victorian age allow. Above all, the interests of a ruling minority were contrived to appear to coincide with the good of the many.

The idea of taste has a peculiar force which nineteenth-century philanthropists were quick to exploit. Visions of depraved and enlightened taste were the invisible illustrations in self-help tracts, designed to help demoralised consumers. The paternalistic cultures of the nineteenth century set up museums to guide popular taste to more elevated (which was to say formal, antique) levels by exhibiting objects held to be of the highest artistic perfection. A necessary extension of this idea of presenting exemplars for imitation was, at least to the paternalist, the provision of equal and opposite exemplars for avoidance.

Nowhere were such philanthropy and opportunism, public purpose and self-interest, combined with more genuine enthusiasm for popularising art than in the person and career of Sir Henry Cole (1808-82). From an unpromising training as a civil servant in the Public Record Office, Cole created a curriculum vitae to rival any; he was chillingly described as 'over active' by one of Queen Victoria's aides, and at mid-career he played the leading role in the conception and execution of one of the century's most significant cultural events: the Great Exhibition of the Works of Industry of All Nations held in London's Hyde Park in 1851.

Cole's most influential accomplice was Prince Albert, whose interest in manufacturing ranged from export performance to the viciousness of superfluous decoration (although he did himself specify a racy-sounding tartan linoleum for Balmoral). While the aims of the exhibition organisers had been didactic, the mood of the public was celebratory. Promoted as an exercise in national pride, the underlying purpose of the Great Exhibition was to educate through exposure to the best and the worst, allowing visitors to draw their own conclusions. The intended lesson in taste may have been lost on many of the revellers, but the popular success of the enterprise encouraged Cole and his supporters to renew their educational efforts yet more energetically by other means. The profits from the Great Exhibition were used to buy some of the exhibits so as to form a permanent study collection of contemporary industrial art for public edification.

The Chamber of Horrors

Cole bought 2,075 items of foreign manufacture, 1,500 goods from the East India Company and 890 from British manufacturers. In descending proportion these comprise metalwork, fabrics, enamels, furniture and ceramics. According to the *Catalogue of the Great Exhibition*, 'Each specimen has been selected for its merits in exemplifying some right principle of construction or of ornament … to which it appeared desirable that the attention of our Students and Manufacturers should be directed.'

There were some crucial distinctions, betraying many a prejudice. Eastern products were generally illustrative of 'correct principles of ornament', but suffered from 'rude' workmanship. European specimens show 'superior skill' but are 'defective' in the principles of their design. When European products attempt direct imitation of nature, the results are 'very inferior … to the ruder scarfs of Tunis'. This bizarre study collection – 'illustrating the correct principles of ornament' – was opened to the public at the Department of Practical Art's Marlborough House premises.

The gallery displaying 'The False Principles of Design' soon became known as Cole's Chamber of Horrors, a sort of industrial freak show. With true paternalistic zeal Cole produced a catalogue that listed the false principles, so visitors could be forewarned against later forays in the marketplace. These false principles included: lack of symmetry, disregard of structure, formless confusion and superficial decoration. Alas, Cole's skill with public relations did not match his flair for didactic entertainment and the Chamber of Horrors was short-lived; complaints and withdrawals by the pilloried and vilified manufacturers best versed in false principles soon made the business of organising loans impossible rather than merely difficult.

During its short career the Chamber of Horrors attracted both public ridicule and healthy scepticism; officials found it risible, yet unsettling, but Cole had touched a nerve. His museum had to revert to the traditional idea of solemn, unquestioning contemplation of works of applied art. An astonishing experiment in setting up a public clinic where the maladies of manufacturing industry could be inspected by consumers failed, but provided a model for imitation.

Similar objections from the trades curtailed another experiment in creating a museum of bad taste in Prague. Here Gustav Pazaurek (1865-1935) had considered showing visitors to the Northern Bohemian Museum gross and horrible things for the home, an ambition he had to forgo until he reached the more liberal province of Württemberg, where, as Director of the Industrial Museum in Stuttgart, he created his Museum of Art Indiscretions. In this he included a modern suit of armour, intended for a parvenu castle; tin boxes coloured to imitate faience; wood looking like granite; iron faked to look like Wedgwood; and 'presumptuous' metals: tin looking like silver,

Above: The 'Chamber of Horrors' at Marlborough House, London: watercolour by William Linnaeus Casey (1856).
Bad examples make a good impression.

zinc looking like bronze. He also did not like chocolate busts of the Kaiser, at the time proving a popular line in certain tasteless *Konditoreien*.

Like Henry Cole, Pazaurek's aesthetic outrage was sustained by moral force. Cole damned the false, while Pazaurek condemned anything intended to deceive the ignorant. Although one might detect the germ of Modern Movement ideology in the insistence of truth to materials, Pazaurek was as quick to damn the errors of undue simplicity as of undue excess. But faults of construction were as repugnant to the Museum of Art Indiscretions as preciosities of materials. Here we find an element of functionalism creeping in: unstable vases, thermally inappropriate materials for containers, eccentric ornaments (empty shell cases and imitation helmets), thermometers fashioned like riding whips and uncomfortable chairs made from stags' antlers were presented for criticism. Souvenir trash, patriotic trash, religious trash and advertising trash were also included.

Pazaurek's complete list makes enchanting reading, its contents as bizarre as Tradescant's Ark. He cites:

Inferior materials, knotty wood, poor alloys, toxic substances, cheap processes, concealed flaws, distorted moulds, spotted glaze. Objects made of human or animal parts including bone, skin, fingernails, rhino horns, ostrich eggs, antlers, teeth, vertebrae, feathers, fish scales, lizards, lobster claws, butterflies and beetles, egg membrane, nuts, spices, ferns, fungus, coloured sand, ice and bread. Painstaking hobbies that overtax materials. Handicrafts that ignore the inherent properties of a material. Anything made of an inappropriately costly material. One material crafted to ape the character of another. Shallow material puns. Surrogate materials pretending to be more valuable ones, or vice versa. Flat patterns made into 3-D objects, or vice versa. Anything made either too heavy or too light. Anything with sharp edges; a vessel that does not pour; a handle uncomfortable to hold; anything which cannot be cleaned with ease. Combination objects, not optimally suitable for either purpose. Functional lies, including architectural ornament. Functional objects in forms that have no intelligent relationship to their purpose. Machine production that apes the effects of handicraft. Frivolous inventions. Forgeries. Obtrusive or odd proportions. Manic ornamentation. Decoration used to disguise flaws. Unskilled or unintelligent use of decoration, such as ignoring the natural logic of a botanical motif. Surface invasions: marbling wood or paper, gilding porcelain or glass. Any decoration created by accident: ink blots, poured glaze, melted wax, pictures drawn in a trance. Originality. Mockery or misuse of national emblems. Anachronisms and exotica. Exaggerated finishes including iridescence, fluorescence.

Primitivism and folk art. Jingoism, souvenirs, folklorica, sportsmen's artefacts, religiosity. Brutalising objects that encourage aggression Anything made for children. Wasted resources, especially single-use or disposable objects. Pollution. Animal trophies. Sexism and racism. Exaggerated claims of exclusiveness.

This is a warning list that, a century later, can scarcely be improved upon.

Household words

The righteous gale force of Henry Cole and, later, Gustav Pazaurek was based in lighter breezes of aesthetic anxiety that ventilated the stuffy complacency of the mid-nineteenth century. Henry Morley (1822-94) became a close associate of Charles Dickens, who had become acquainted with his work on reading a series called 'How to Make Home Unhealthy' in the *Journal of Public Health*. Morley soon followed the *Zeitgeist* and switched from public health to popular taste, from the inner to the outer man.

His clever parody, 'A House Full of Horrors', was published in 1852 in *Household Words*, a journal established by Dickens to monitor the growing cult of the middle-class home in the middle of the century. It was the social equivalent of the self-improving, democratic pamphlets that circulated at the same time among the new industrial workers. Morley describes the nightmares suffered by one innocent visitor to the Department of Practical Art, a certain Mr Crumpet, as he finds himself surrounded on his return home to the new suburb of Brixton by the very objects he has been didactified into abhorring:

'The matter is this: I have acquired some Correct Principles of Taste. Five weeks ago I went to the Department of Practical Art in Marlborough House to look over the museum of ornamental art. I had heard of a Chamber of Horrors there established, and I found it, and went through it with my catalogue. It was a gloomy chamber, hung round with frightful objects in curtains, carpets, clothes, lamps and what not. In each case the catalogue told me why such-and-such a thing wasn't endurable.'

In particular:

'That tray with a bit of Landseer's pictures on it, you will find to correspond with the seventy-ninth item in the Catalogue of Horrors, at which you will find these following observations. It is "An example of popular but vulgar taste, of a low character, presenting numerous features which the student should carefully avoid: First, the centre is the piracy of the picture; Second, the picture on which most labour has been bestowed is thrown away … It is wrong to hide a picture by putting a teapot on it".'

Mr Crumpet becomes dismayed to discover that he is actually wearing some of the unendurable clothing on show. From then on his newly acquired sensitivity in matters of taste has alarming consequences:

'After hanging up my hat in the hall, I had great trouble in straightening my hair as I went into the ladies, it would stand upright at the horror of my friend's hall-paper. I had seen it in the Chamber of Horrors – perspective representations of a railway station frequently repeated. Why is it that people do not understand what I have understood quite well for the last five weeks; that pictures of any kind, and above all, perspectives, are unusually out of place repeated around a wall … When a picture is repeated up and down and round about the place, the result is a nightmare.'

Morley gently concludes that while Cole's medicine was worth taking, a smaller dose might have been advisable. Mildly ridiculous even in its own day, Cole's prescriptions would be unthinkable now. With the passing of extrovert paternalism went behaviour so lacking in irony or in the supposed objectivity of intellectual reasoning. It was an exercise only possible in an age whose executives were backed by mighty moral certainties.

Henry Cole has provided prototypes for many things, from the professional civil servant to the Victoria and Albert Museum, but perhaps the most significant of all is his role model for the embattled middle-class aesthete, outraged by the impropriety and pretension of lesser folk, dismayed by the obdurate philistinism of those of higher rank. Good taste was what made Henry Cole feel good and less threatened. Bad taste was the other thing.

Cole's use of the museum as an active medium (rather than a passive collection) was not unique. In the United States, Mellon, Frick and other nouveaux riches were establishing, at the last historical moment when such a thing was possible, their own private collections rivalling in splendour and swagger the national collections of Europe. Their presence, both physical and spiritual, gave the public certain expectations of art – and still does. What animus drove the collectors? The answer is this: an art collection validates the status and confirms the arrival of the parvenu.[19] The Firestone heiress said her compulsion to collect eighteenth-century furniture was similar to the effect peanuts had on her: have one and you want the whole lot.

Museums buttressed self-made egos and gave to emergent nations the sanction of the past. They stabilised art, but art needs to be volatile, so to redress the stability of the marble halls, the concept of the avant-garde emerged. The avant-garde (which, at least semantically, has military

Above: Kitsch is not just a matter of taste; it can be defined. It occurs only in civilisations where choices are offered to the consumer.

AKADEMISCHER VERBAND FÜR LITERATUR U. MUSIK

MOTTO: "EIN SCHEUSAL VON EINEM HAUS"
(AUS EINER WIENER GEMEINDERATSSITZUNG)

IM SOPHIENSAAL

MONTAG, DEN 11. DEZEMBER 1911 UM HALB 8 UHR
ABENDS VORTRAG DES ARCHITEKTEN ADOLF LOOS

MEIN · HAUS · AM
MICHAELERPLATZ

MIT SKIOPTIKONBILDERN

Karten bei Kehlendorfer I, Krugerstr. 3 zu K 4, 3, 2, 1, —.50

Mitglieder des „Akademischen Verbandes für Literatur und Musik in Wien" und des „Vereines
für Kunst und Kultur" zahlen halben Preis · Die Mitgliederaufnahme erfolgt tägl. von 10—12 Uhr
vormittags im Hause I. Bezirk, Reichsratsstrasse 7

and then political origins) is fundamental to an understanding of modern taste. Somewhere out there is a huge graveyard of French expressions, memorials to past conceits and fancies that died when France ceased to dominate global culture. Avant-garde belongs alongside other antique expressions including *thé dansant* and *noblesse oblige*; it comes from a period when culture was a battlefield, when creativity could be quantified by capitalising the offence, hence the appropriateness of a *nom de guerre*.

Pugin and Eastlake could not be said to be avant-garde. With the middle classes entrenched in their comfortable philistinism and their false principles, artists since, say, 1880 have operated on the fringes. With the concept of the avant-garde the idea of novelty became, at least for the time being, inseparable from progress in art. The idea that art has leaders and followers has imposed a structure on our imaginations that has been difficult to shift. Baudelaire presented a paradox that captures the contradiction inherent in the ceaseless quest for novelty: 'The chief task of genius is precisely to invent a stereotype.'

The avant-garde brings up the rear

The avant-garde was a reflection of society's image of itself, but seen in a distorting mirror; decadent poets, wacky artistic types throwing paint in the public's face, slaves to the senses and brutes to their lovers, were convenient inventions which in fact emasculated art by stringing a cordon sanitaire around artists, defining their territory as out of bounds. The dangerous Bohemian in hat and cloak with a fevered imagination behind a smouldering brow made glossy by absinthe and pale by late nights and later mornings had a trembling lower lip. Only the eyes were fixed with the singular purpose: *épater les bourgeois!* This was exactly what Alfred Jarry did when he shocked the audience at the first performance of his play, *Ubu Roi* (1896), with the opening line: 'Merde'. It is a measure of the durability of the avant-garde that nowadays this is almost all that is remembered of Jarry's script.

And later, when familiarity had dulled the shock value of the sleaze, the avant-garde found expression in another strange bird, but one of a rather different feather – the technocrat. Here again, in a rapidly industrialising world, there was an image both to lionise and to demonise. From just after

Left: The poster for a lecture, 'Mein Haus am Michaelerplatz', by Adolf Loos, 11 December 1911.

85

the First World War, avant-garde artists abandoned their fedoras, cheroots and dirty habits and became missionaries from another territory equally alien to the stay-at-home bourgeois: the laboratory and the factory. Whereas if you had been researching a television programme on the avant-garde in 1880 you would have had to go to Paris and sip wormwood liquor with oddball painters and poets while dancing girls demonstrated the contemporary deficiencies of laundering, by 1920 your producer would have had to send you to Germany to meet Hungarian émigrés in boilersuits teaching metalwork, photography and calisthenics to wide-eyed, flaxen-haired, firm-thighed delegates of the master race. Nowadays to discover the avant-garde, you have to look in history books.

In the nineteenth century, art became a commodity, and the avant-garde was a reaction to this. Restless neophilia, supported by Baudelaire's Romantic interpretation of the artist's purpose, is as much a product of consumer culture as kitsch, its mirror image. The two extremes help define the middle ground of consumer values. The feverish quest of the artist is to capture the beauty that Ezra Pound characterised as that evanescent gasp 'between one cliché and another'. The avant-garde rejects convention and taste is not so much disregarded as deliberately confronted. A certain sort of thin-lipped, joyless, overstuffed, polished taste existed in every Victorian parlour, even Freud's, and especially in those redolent with morality. The existence of the avant-garde had a curiously stabilising effect on already conservative middle-class taste: if taste is a matter of choice and discrimination, what choice can there be when only the radically new is acceptable?

Henry Cole's century was as obsessed with the past as ours is with the new. Eclecticism in architectural style had put all of history into the marketplace – to Mr Crumpet's distress. Henry Cole's false principles are one example of a search for meaning in a clutter of senselessly reproduced stylistic motifs. Adolf Loos (1870-1933), Viennese architect, polemicist and *fin-de-siècle* man-about-the-Ringstrasse, was one of those keen to reject the eclectic delusions of the nineteenth century, which had so dismayed Crumpet. Loos wrote: 'Ever since humanity discerned the stature of classical antiquity, one single thought has united all great architects. They think: I am building the way the ancient Romans would have done. We know that they are wrong. Time, place, purpose, climate and setting all make this impossible.'[20]

Loos saw the history of civilisation in terms of mankind's progressive emancipation from ornament (a conceit more workable, perhaps, in Brixton

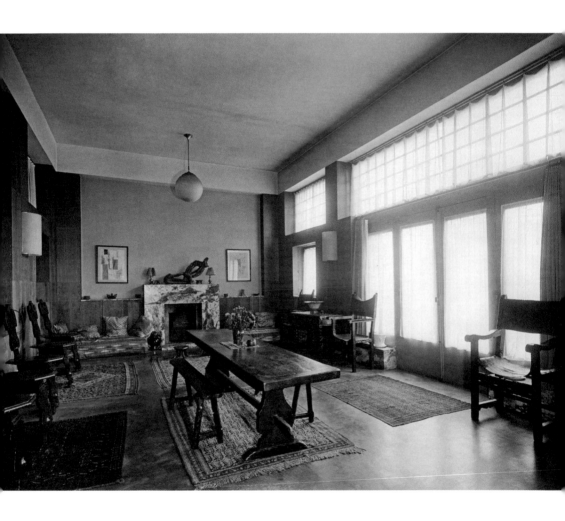

Above: The dining room of the Tristan Tzara House, Paris (1925-26), by Adolf Loos.

than Vienna). He equated decoration with degeneration, pointing out criminals' liking for tattoos. It is not too fanciful to suggest a similarity between Loos's rejection of artifice and ornament and Freud's exposure of the devices and delusions that disguise the essential primitivism of the psyche. The extraordinary climate of Vienna about 1900 was, for a nation largely unaffected by the Industrial Revolution that brought us Mr Crumpet, the product of a crisis in classical reason.

This crisis, which we can see in what Freud thought, what Klimt and Schiele painted, what Schoenberg composed and what Loos built, produced extraordinary fertility in art and social science. It is perhaps worth cautioning that this splendid flowering coincided precisely with Austria's political and economic decline, and may indeed have contributed to it. No longer able, or even much inclined, to influence external events, artists became introspective and somewhat desperate. Freud excavated the soul, Klimt and Schiele made a sensuous and lascivious sort of eroticism into fashionable high art, and Loos tried to make architecture systematic. Arthur Schnitzler, the most successful playwright of the day, whom Freud described as his alter ego, filled the theatres with his plays on sex, death and the soul. His best-known novel was called, characteristically, *Sterben (To Die)*.

Meanwhile, adrift from any particular social group or class, avant-garde artists justified their elected alienation as a necessary tension-builder in the process of creation. As a consequence, alienation became a test for high art, rather as drowning in witch rituals was proof of purity. Simultaneously, a fashionable lack of content in abstract art (c.1906-66), forced artists to develop exquisitely high standards of self-consciousness, self-reference and self-veneration. In painting, the generalised quest was for reduced form, a goal pursued at the expense of meaning and communication and in the teeth of public censure. Some painters, including Brice Marden, achieved total meaninglessness. Soon, public censure gave way to public apathy and indifference – and, for instance, to the founding of the Saatchi Gallery, where avant-garde art was apotheosised in the service of social mountaineering.

Avant-garde was an extreme perversion of taste. One is reminded of Gustav Pazaurek's disdain for 'Originality'. Sometimes it is in dramatic confrontation with nostrums of good taste; at others, to take an absurd example in the work of a sculptor such as Richard Serra, it is a triple distillation of refined good taste and therefore comes very near to being something else entirely. Under the despotism of the avant-garde, art was reduced to serial fads. During the fidgety age of Postmodernism, copying and a restless neophilia were elevated, while both the avant-garde and kitsch have become emasculated – or become the same thing, depending on your point of view.

Although a diligent researcher would quickly find an early-nineteenth-century reference to the radical avant-garde,[21] the concept makes most sense when politics and art bifurcated, and that happened most convincingly in Vienna. The Viennese avant-garde, perhaps more so than any since, was both the product and the scourge of the bourgeois society that gave rise to it.

There have been many Whig interpretations of art history that draw facile connections between the artistic revolution of Vienna in 1900 and the social engineering which the Modern Movement attempted after 1920. The two are very different, but they share avant-garde characteristics in their pointed rejection of safe bourgeois taste. Heath Robinson in *How to Live in a Flat* (1936) satirised the fashion for Modernism:

'Whereas formerly the best furniture was made by carpenters … the trade is almost entirely in the hands of plumbers, riveters, blow-pipers, and metal-workers of all sorts. As a result, the ultra-modern living room resembles a cross between an operating theatre, a dipsomaniac's nightmare, and a new kind of knitting. The advantages of steel furniture, of course, are that it does not harbour worms, requires only an occasional touch of metal-polish, and can be bent into all manner of laughable designs … It is quite possible … to construct a chromium-steel dining-room suite in one continuous piece – that is, without lifting the pen from the paper. This can be moved bodily from room to room – and even set up on the roof, in the event of anybody wishing to dine there – in about one third of the time needed to shift an old-fashioned mahogany suite. Moreover, when the conversation at the dinner table flags and all present are wondering what the dickens to say next, the host can create a diversion by inviting his guests to guess where the suite begins and ends, and awarding a small prize, such as a book of stamps or an unopened tin of peaches to the winner.'

Modernismus, Schmodernismus

The Modern Movement was an attempt to make the avant-garde popular, its leaders – unwittingly – imposing their own exclusive tastes upon reluctant populations. The vegetarian lady novelist sitting in a tubular-steel chair reading Schnitzler, her feet on a rug with an abstract pattern, was an easy target for conservative architect and novelist Sir Reginald Blomfield (1856-

Above: Osbert Lancaster satirises the Modernist interior, in *Homes Sweet Homes* (1939).

1942). In *Modernismus* (1934) he, like Pazaurek, attacked the idea of novelty: 'What impresses us most in these struggles for something new, is not their originality, but their immodesty, the folly of thinking that it is worthwhile to abandon the beaten track and stand on one's head in the ditch in order to attract attention.' Blomfield deplored the fact that 'The Modernists blandly ask us to exterminate any aesthetic preferences and instincts we now possess, and offer ourselves as passive victims.'

Blomfield himself designed the Menin Gate at Ypres and the Regent Street Quadrant, each a muscular re-edition of Neoclassicism and imposing too. But every page of Blomfield's coarsely argued text proves that he did not know of, say, Le Corbusier's romantic early work at La Chaux-de-Fonds (which the architect himself in fact suppressed). Those who did, knew that Le Corbusier was engaged on a mission of continuous refinement, development and discovery. *Modernismus* is too simplistic a book to accommodate a more sophisticated analysis of the flawed ambitions of Modernism, but Blomfield was right in questioning the exact standards by which the Modernists declared their taste to be perfection: 'What we complain of in the propaganda of Modernism is its confusion of thought, its persistent habit of begging the question, and of laying down as accepted principles what are, in fact, merely dogmatic assertions.'

What the Modern Movement got wrong, in all its special pleading, was its confusion of idealism with purpose, its mistaking paternalism for the commonwealth, and, as MH Baillie Scott remarked, its impudent claim to having a monopoly of practical efficiency. If you were that vegetarian lady novelist in Cambridge c.1930, you might well enjoy your tubular steel, your Schnitzler, and your non-representational rug, but that would be a matter of taste, not of scientific certainty. The assumption that the technical solutions to furniture and building design of 1929 were permanent was, as Blomfield said, based on mistaken sociology and arbitrary psychology. The icons of the Modern Movement were as historically specific as the nineteenth-century obsession with modesty, which led the Victorians to dress table legs in little pantaloons. Just as they felt it necessary to disguise household apparatus and buildings, so the Modern Movement demanded the clear articulation of an internal mechanism through external form.

But then Blomfield's objections to the Modern Movement were also a matter of taste – and his particular taste was influenced by snobbery: as a patrician grandee, he disliked the foreignness of Modernism (hence the sly title of his book which he puts into German form), and he disliked its Jewishness even more: 'I detest and despise cosmopolitanism.' Blomfield warned that the Modernists' taste for order would not win friends and in its place he offered evolutionary traditionalism. Today it is axiomatic that the Modern Movement's absolute belief in the idea of progress was a weakness: sadly, new forms have not stimulated a revolution in the human spirit. Osbert Lancaster spoke for the majority when he wrote in *Here, of all Places* (1958):

'This apparent failure of the reformers in the realm of domestic architecture is, one fancies, one of psychology. The open-plan, the mass-produced steel and plywood furniture, the uncompromising display of structural elements, are all in theory perfectly logical, but in the home logic has always been at a discount. Le Corbusier thought a house should be a machine-for-living-in, but Frank Lloyd Wright countered only if you see the human heart as a mere pump.'

The Modern Movement was the most extraordinary international exercise of the avant-garde will. The fabled unwillingness of architects and designers to accommodate the tastes of the public was hardly calculated to ingratiate themselves with the toiling masses on whose behalf they made such extravagant claims. This version of the avant-garde failed, despite some powerful rhetoric and some magnificent monuments to provide a widely acceptable unifying symbolic order. If the Modernists had known Mr Crumpet better, they would have been aware that the explosion of mass consumption meant the eternal loss of even the idea of a homogeneous society, and hence of a single value system.

The avant-garde only ever captivated the high culture of an intellectual elite (which has been aped by a self-conscious elite from Peggy Guggenheim to Doris Saatchi to Tracey Emin). But, as the art critic Clement Greenberg (1909-94) pointed out in an influential essay, 'Avant-Garde and Kitsch' (1939), 'Where there is an avant-garde, generally, we also find a rearguard.'

Greenberg popularised the term, which until then had been almost exclusively the province of obscure German philosophers and aestheticians, such as Fritz Karpfen, whose book *Der Kitsch* (1925) was among the first on the subject. Kitsch – which comes from the German word meaning to cheapen – and the avant-garde look very different, but are correlative in substance: they are the equal and opposite manifestations of that unique historical awareness (Blomfield called it 'hysteria') which produced the concept of modernity. They are the fruits of bourgeois capitalist society in what Marxists call its decline and the rest are glad to see as its evolution. Just as the avant-garde places novelty and originality above all else, so banality and vulgarity are lionised in kitsch. Both violate everyday conceptions of good taste.

Kitsch is unthinkable without industrialisation and feeds off it. Something kitsch almost invariably involves an adaptation from one medium to another, from appropriate to inappropriate, transformations made possible by advances in technology. It is all very well to have tongue-and-groove wood panelling, if that is what you fancy, because that is a matter of taste. Wallpaper looking like tongue-and-groove is, however, kitsch. Similarly, kitsch almost always diminishes size and scale. On sale in Japan, for instance, is a lavatory paper dispenser in the shape of Mount Fuji. Witless adaptation, diminution and relentless cheapening characterise kitsch.

In a funny way, the achievement of nearly universal literacy in industrialised countries turned cultures that were once homogeneous into segregated classes. The virtuosi were a privileged elite with easy access to art, music and literature, and among this minority it was not difficult to settle on standards and expectations for art. By about 1900, reading and writing had become everyday skills. Literacy, according to Clement Greenberg, 'no longer served to distinguish an individual's cultural inclinations, since it was no longer the exclusive concomitant of refined tastes'.

Unable or unwilling to transfer peasant culture to the city, the new urban proletariat and petty bourgeoisie were equally ill-equipped to participate in the traditional high culture of one of Sir Joshua Reynolds' salons. Kitsch was, to use another German word of uncertain provenance but perpetual value, an *ersatz* version of high culture called into existence by a new form of demand. Greenberg, a left-wing champion of Modernism, scathingly describes the trash sold to those he considers insensible to 'genuine' culture: 'Kitsch, using for raw materials the debased and academicised simulacra of genuine culture, welcomes and cultivates this insensibility. Kitsch is mechanical and operates by formulas. Kitsch is vicarious experience and faked sensations. Kitsch is the epitome of all that is spurious in the life of our times.'

Kitsch has the external characteristics of art, but is actually a falsification of it. The Modernist view was that kitsch was unreflective enjoyment. At worst, kitsch was seen as a pernicious influence against which 'genuine' culture must be constantly vigilant. Not only is kitsch an inevitable consequence of industrialised society; it is dependent on mechanical and electrical reproduction for its existence and transmission. Kitsch is made

Overleaf: Frank Lloyd Wright discusses a model of the Guggenheim Museum with students at Taliesin, Spring Green, Wisconsin. His famous helical temple of art was inspired by a Manhattan parking garage.

in factories and consumed in bulk, growing the while; it blurs the distinction between art and life and supplies information in place of meaning.
The hunting-scene Formica placemat is one example. A gilt chandelier is another. A presidential throne yet another.

A leap of bad faith

There are different types of kitsch, but they all share an element of *inappropriateness*. A carpet woven in the pattern of an ornamented ceiling complete with beams and mouldings (shown at the V&A's Department of Practical Art, London, 1852), an ashtray made of postage stamps (Museum of Art Indiscretions, Stuttgart, 1909), 1960s 'colonial' kitchen (Gillo Dorfles, *Kitsch*, 1969), Ronald Reagan's bedroom (1983), or Trump Tower (1983): each strives for an effect which is at odds with its true and proper purpose. Each is a demonstration of bad faith. But never forget that in Britain legislators work in a building designed by a syphilitic madman prone to medievalist fantasies. We call it Parliament.

An instantly recognisable form of kitsch, as common today in Japanese restaurants serving sushi on wood-effect, plastic platters as it was a hundred years ago when a bar of chocolate was made to look like the Kaiser, is the transfer of a work of art to an inappropriate medium. Before Postmodern architecture, this sort of nonsense was the definitive kitsch object, because it so manifestly undermined one of the highest forms of genuine culture – the original work of art. Mass reproduction of unique works is in itself a violation of one the most precious tenets of Western art, and reproductions applied to mundane merchandise heighten the violation of traditional values. The destruction of what aesthetes call 'the privileged moment' when a viewer communes with a unique work of art is caused by a debasing familiarity with reproductions. This applies to music as well as to painting (and to a lesser extent to architecture and literature: someone once complained that *Hamlet* was made up of old quotes).

The regular abuse of fragments of classical music in advertising sets up banal associations when the piece is played in full: for a while, Bach's *Air on a G String* was inescapably associated with cheap cigars when such things were advertised on television, the chorus from the last act of *Turandot* with an Italian airline. The leading Postmodern architect Michael Graves (1934-2015), who once sat in a warm glow of scholarly propriety at Princeton, took the abuse of classical values further by endorsing cheap shoes in US press advertisements. His career never really recovered, but he had already damaged his credibility by designing for Alessi a silly stove-top kettle with a tweety-bird whistle and a handle that became untouchable when the water boiled. Martin Pawley's mischievous theory that Postmodernism leads to ruin is borne out everywhere.

If the avant-garde is consciously individualistic and self-referential, then the expression of communal values is, by definition, anti-art, which is to say, kitsch. This is just one of the ways in which the avant-garde expresses its modernity when compared with the art of the past (whose highest aim was to articulate contemporary spiritual, philosophical or political ideals). It also explains why the political art of the twentieth century – one thinks of Nazi athletes, Soviet tractor drivers – is of necessity kitsch. Milan Kundera develops this idea in his novel *The Unbearable Lightness of Being* (trans. 1984): 'The feeling induced by kitsch must be a kind the multitude can share. Kitsch may not, therefore, depend on an unusual situation; it must derive from the basic images people have engraved in their memories: the ungrateful daughter, the neglected father, children running on the grass, the motherland betrayed, first love.'

To the Victorians, as well as to the Modernists, who in some curious ways resemble them, kitsch was irredeemable, but our less-certain age is not so dogmatic. Kitsch can be rehabilitated by context, or at least by intention. In his book *Kitsch* (1969), Gillo Dorfles discusses the Manhattan skyline, which comprises many individual monstrosities, yet the overall effect is stupendous. But the extent to which a sophisticated environment can transform the meaning of the objects it contains prompts Dorfles to caution, 'This is why we will never be altogether sure that fake marble columns, *papier-mâché* statues, wood imitation wallpapers, glass animals from Murano and even mother-of-pearl shells and Brazilian hardstone in the shape of ashtrays, although themselves undoubtedly kitsch, are beyond recovery.'

The deliberate cultivation of outrageous bad taste has long been a favourite device of the avant-garde. A sly, knowing sophistication at odds with safe bourgeois values suggests that an excess of good taste is just as lamentable as evidence of bad. Taste that is too good is a telltale of conformity and insecurity, what George Bernard Shaw called moral cowardice. In this exquisitely balanced equation the amount of admissible bad taste is subject to fine measurement by social scrutineers. Artistic, aristocratic and wealthy elites set their own rules, but ordinary citizens have to be more cautious. There is a parallel in the well-rehearsed cycles of fashion: a suitable amount of time must have passed for a revival to be acceptable, but there is a fine line between being at the forefront of a revival and simply being out of date.

As soon as it loses its original offensive impact, avant-garde hyper-kitsch is soon subsumed into the mainstream as another 'school' for art historians to ponder and catalogue. In the early 1980s the most radical Milanese designers, including Alessandro Mendini and Ettore Sottsass (1917-2007), were producing furniture for Studio Alchimia and for Memphis, whose designs were calculated to offend. Through slavish treatment in global glossy magazines, this wry mischief fed the brackish stream of Postmodernism. Andrea Branzi used patterns derived from Mondrian and Kandinsky paintings on his *poltrona falsa* because they were 'good and cheap'; Mendini spoke boastfully of his *Galleria del Copismo*. By the time these gaudy, banal bastardisations of 1950s suburbanism artfully contrived to oppose every assumption of the Modern Movement had been included in more than 200 international glossies and appeared in Karl Lagerfeld's Paris apartment, they had become just another style of rich man's chic. Now used everywhere, from Victoria Coach Station to department stores and food packaging, the Milanese movement, which started as an ironic gesture by Sottsass, soon became, quite appropriately, the most derisively celebrated visual cliché of the late twentieth century.

Quoting from suburbia

Memphis was a reminder that contemporary eclecticism differs from nineteenth-century historicism in this regard: today everything quickly becomes a cliché and therefore potentially kitsch. Like Postmodern architecture, of which it is a poor relation, Memphis refuted positivist faith in progress, and, defined negatively in opposition to Modernism, signalled only an ironic awareness of the end of all movements. Its media success was fuelled by the notion that popular culture is at odds with the high or genuine stuff. Before the assumptions of Modernism were regularly called into question, the self-appointed guardians of the avant-garde derided popular taste. Thus Virginia Woolf snobbishly stigmatises the hapless middle classes: 'The true battle in my opinion lies not between highbrow and lowbrow, but between highbrows and lowbrows joined together in blood brotherhood against the bloodless and pernicious pest who comes between ... highbrows and lowbrows must band together to exterminate a pest which is the bane of all thinking and living ... middlebrow seems to me to be everywhere.'

Right: Poltrona di Proust (1978), by Alessandro Mendini.

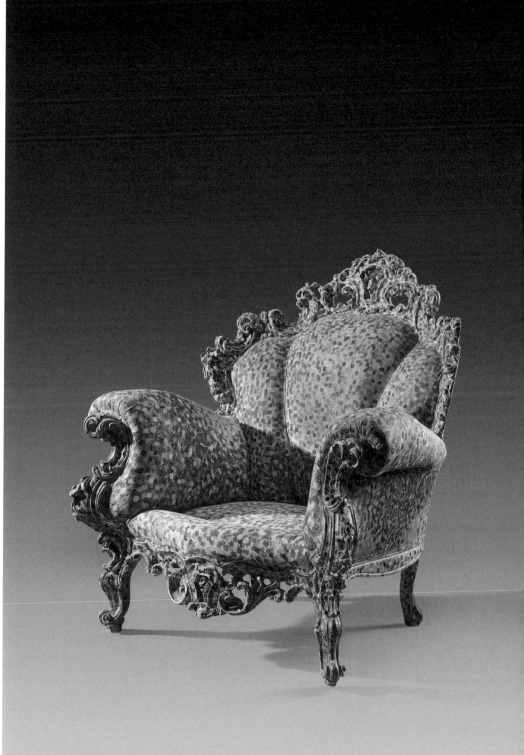

Highbrows believe that they alone can appreciate culture. Good taste in their interpretation is constantly under insidious attack from the philistine lowbrows with their coarse pretensions (which continuously threaten the exclusivity of highbrow culture). Clement Greenberg was a highbrow. Until very recently highbrows could write without irony this sort of condescending gobbledygook in the pages of *Partisan Review*: 'Middlebrow culture attacks distinctions as such and insinuates itself everywhere ... Insidiousness is of its essence, and in recent years its avenues of penetration have become infinitely more difficult to detect and block.'[22]

Meanwhile, the highbrows (defined by AP Herbert as the sort of people who look at a sausage and think of Picasso) are happy to patronise the lowbrows, listening to their jazz and taking an interest in their 'vernacular' art or their cooking. The lowbrows do not threaten because they are uninterested in highbrow values.

What is most interesting in this discussion of the self-evident is the precise mechanism by which the dominant classes impose their own distinctions between high and low, or 'good' and 'bad'. To Baudelaire, bad taste was 'intoxicating' because it offered the aristocratic pleasure of not pleasing, thus confirming that whenever taste is discussed, notions of class cannot be too far away. Snobbery is one of the most effective mechanisms by which this dominance is maintained. The manifestations of snobbery, or turning class into performance art, are also often taken to be 'good' taste. Listen to Harold Nicolson in *Some People* (1927): 'Sir Sidney Poole had asked me to dinner; Mrs Lintot had called me by my Christian name; and the Grand Duke Boris had said, quite distinctly, '*Monsieur, j'ai connu votre père* . . . Lady Dury had bought a Tang horse.'

Had Lady Dury just bought a Thermos flask, Nicolson would not have thought it worth mentioning. Snobbery is a remarkable and profound invention, an institution at least as formidable as the prison system and certainly as characteristic as the age that created it. It can be attributed to Thackeray and dated quite precisely to the years when the laws of consumer culture were being established; *The Book of Snobs* was published in 1848. Snob was undergraduate slang for low bred and – in a device later adopted by Nancy Mitford – Thackeray made it plain that it is snobbish to worry about snobbery.

Critics transferred this social game to the world of material things, where it became known as 'good' taste. Deadly competition burst out about what objects mean. It is remarkable how very charmless things regarded highly in 1850 appear today. Here is further proof that taste changes. When Owen Jones dreamt about interior design in *The Grammar of Ornament* (1856), 'There are no carpets worked with flowers whereon the feet would fear to tread, no furniture the hand would fear to grasp, no superfluous and useless ornament which a caprice has added and which an accident might remove,' his ideas sound astonishingly prescient, but the quickest glance at what Owen Jones himself designed shows that the words themselves flatter modern ears only to deceive contemporary eyes – his designs look as hideous as much of the stuff he reviled. While he praised those things in which 'nothing could be removed and leave the design equally good or better', the passage of time demonstrates that a good deal remained to be removed from designs of his own making.

The terms 'good taste' and 'bad taste' do not represent absolutes, but their usage is distinctive and telling, since it reveals the preferences and prejudices of particular social groups. They are crude ways of assigning value to things, but their validity derives only from the power and prestige of the social group that uses them. Most often, the value is not inherent in the object itself, but in the intention of its consumer. If good taste means anything, it is pleasing your peers; bad taste is offending them. But cultivated bad taste, or kitsch, can achieve either result.

Taste is more to do with manners than *appearances*. Taste is both myth and reality; it is not a style.

scenario

Architecture Painting the lily

'Taste, taste, taste,' the architect Frank Lloyd Wright once remarked; 'cows have taste!' His idea is clear: in the proper practice of architecture taste plays no part. Successful building arises out of something other than socially or culturally conditioned aesthetic preference, most probably from fundamental principles of design and laws of construction. Andrea Palladio could mend a smoking chimney and design a facade with the orders artistically orchestrated into major and subsidiary divisions, creating a beautiful, functional whole the while.

Ever since refinements in engineering separated the practical from the artistic in building and made anything that was imaginable possible, architectural design has been virtually reduced to a matter of taste. Given recent advances in construction technology, buildings will stand up with or without architects. Fast-track building has, quite literally, left design behind. Modern buildings, with their computer floors and voids, their vast provision for data cabling, are not stand-alone monuments like the Duomo in Florence, or Grand Central Station in New York, but merely evanescent architectonic hardware with a finite life. In big new corporate developments, where the building itself is not intended as an advertisement – the big corporation puts its marker down on Fifth Avenue or in the City of London's Square Mile – it is, with its spaghetti of fibre optic cables and its line-of-sight microwave dishes for nanosecond trades, merely an adjunct to the company's telecommunications budget.

In fast-track building, construction begins before the design process is complete, so that, in inflationary times, the expensive bits get under way first. First there is the piling, then the structural steel, then metal floor decks, then pouring concrete for floor slabs. When the frame is complete, windows, curtain walls and insulation are fitted at the same time as the mechanical and electrical services. If there's a moment left over, someone designs a snazzy shape so the clients think they've got some 'architecture' for their money. This is what the great Australian critic Robin Boyd derided as 'featurism'.

In the United States it became accepted practice for a developer to hand over only the decorated shell, core and public spaces to the tenant, who then had to hire an 'interior architect' to finish the job. While Brunelleschi laboured to make the details and the proportions of the Pazzi Chapel in Florence evocative of something like divine peace, the First Republic Bank of Chattanooga, or Get Rich Quick plc, needs a structure with a life of fifteen years, which can be appreciated at 55 mph from the freeway or while stationary in the congealed traffic of the City of London. If at all possible, the insides betray the thrusting ambition of the chairman of the board. With such an ugly disjunction between form and technique it is scarcely surprising that the greater part of contemporary architecture is pure kitsch.

At about the moment of the City of London's deregulation and the consequential explosion of liberated money-grubbing known as the 'Big Bang', aesthetic considerations were secondary to the imperatives of finance and its pilot fish PR, and the Prince of Wales became an outspoken and controversial commentator on architecture. The Prince's discovery that architecture is more than mere building and his consequent intervention in the public debate were generally welcomed, even if his credibility was compromised by his sole exercise in patronage being the creation of the lifeless retro-kitsch fantasia that is Poundbury in Dorset, a suburban dystopia designed at the royal behest by a choleric Luxembourgeois called Leon Krier.

Not since Prince Albert – of whom Arnold Bennett observed, 'He had a lot of taste ... all of it bad' – has a member of the Royal Family been so concerned with architecture and design. Although his views were often (to put it no lower) contradictory, by virtue of his special prestige the Prince of Wales began an extraordinary adventure: to become an arbiter of taste.

Incensed by the apparently thoughtless brutality of much 'modern' architecture, Prince Charles called for a 'revival' of classical architecture. In a curiously contemporary version of the pathetic fallacy, the Prince suggested that aping the architecture of Hawksmoor would take us, balance-of-payments deficit and all, back to the graceful world of the salons, with the plinkety-plonkety elegance of a Scarlatti sonata to accompany our reveries. It was a pleasing idea, but a misleading one.

Right: The Moritzkirche, Augsburg, Germany (2008-13), by John Pawson.

All insolence is fortified by rags and ruins

The paradox was that the Prince's taste for classical architecture was itself a modern one and had no sanction from the past; as Viollet-le-Duc said of restoration, '*Le mot et la chose sont modernes*.' What exactly is the royal understanding of classical architecture? Whatever they may now think of it in Kensington Palace and Highgrove, classicism is not a style that has always enjoyed universal approval. In *The Stones of Venice* (1851-3) John Ruskin excoriated the genre:

'Let us cast out utterly whatever is connected with the Greek, Roman or Renaissance … It is base, unnatural, unfruitful, unenjoyable, and impious. Pagan in its origin, proud and unholy in its revival, paralysed in its old age … an architecture invented … to make plagiarists of architects, slaves of its workmen and sybarites of its inhabitants; an architecture in which intellect is idle, invention impossible, but in which all luxury is gratified, and all insolence fortified.'

Ruskin's loathing of the classical genre is nowhere better illustrated than in his quite fantastic invective against the *sotto in su* (foreshortened and *trompe l'œil*) ceiling painting by Giovanni Antonio Fumiani in Venice's church of San Pantalon. A bravura exercise to our eyes, in it Ruskin saw 'the afflatus of vile ambition … the roof puffed up and broken through … with breath of the fiend below … the rags and ruins of Venetian skill, honour and worship, exploded all together sky high'. Here he found 'miracles of frantic mistake … flaunting and thunderous hypocrisy … [a] universal lie'.

Certainly, Ruskin did not like classical painting in this genre, although Fumiani was a contemporary of the great Filippo Juvarra whose work is an epitome of the classical. Thunderous hypocrisy? A universal lie? Prince Charles's call for a revival of this colourful phenomenon came at a moment of transition, not to say uncertainty, in British life. The royal polemic, aimed chiefly at planners and developers, assumed that there are certain aesthetic absolutes (the Prince calls them guidelines) which the powers that be, or at least that were, have ignored in their pursuit of profit. Of the planners he said: 'As things stand, they are only justified in rejecting a proposal if it is absolutely hideous; anything merely ugly must be allowed to get through.'[1]

What the Prince of Wales said was remarkable not only for its outspokenness, but also for the questions it begged (some listeners claim to have detected more than a hundred). Significantly, no mention was made of the question of taste. The Prince's aesthetic guidelines were presented as universally attractive – a high-handed (if not high-minded) version of the popular theory that, but for the cravenness of the public and the wickedness of the planners and developers, the cityscape of London in the late twentieth century would have been as attractive as people imagine it to have been three hundred years before (when the streets were sewers of horse shit and corpses). It was not the first time that revolutionaries and royal families shared a desire to turn back the clock.

It does not take long to deconstruct the Prince's historic message. The subtext presented an imaginary city built when aesthetic principles were better understood by palace and pauper alike. He argued for a limitation on the height of buildings, a proscription of certain materials, advocated the proportion of windows, and even the requirement to build in a certain style; such rules gave us Georgian London and would allow St Paul's to dominate the skyline of the capital. All very well, provided you *like* Georgian London and accept the dominance of Christian classical architecture in our cities as sempiternal.

Of one particular development, Paternoster Square, close to St Paul's, Prince Charles said:

'Let there be an information exhibition showing the area as it *was* [my italics], the plans of Wren, Hawksmoor and Lutyens ... It should be a beautiful area on a human scale, built at ground level not on top of a car park square. I'd like to see sheltered arcades, courtyards, a public square, with small shops and businesses at ground level – above all to cater for the needs of, and to create something special for, the three million tourists who already visit St Paul's each year ... I would like to see the medieval street plan of pre-war Paternoster reconstructed, not out of mere nostalgia, but to give meaning to surviving fragments like Amen Court and the Chapter House, now left like dispossessed refugees in an arid desert of godforsaken buildings. I would like to see a roofscape that gives the impression that St Paul's is floating above it like a great ship on the sea. I would also like to see the kind of materials Wren might have used – soft red brick and stone dressings perhaps, and the ornament and detail of classical architecture.'

Prince Charles may have had an internal vision and purpose, but this muddle-headed argument for a tourist trap of quaint, cute architecture must be attributed to a confusion of advisers and is perhaps best

Overleaf: Giovanni Antonio Fumiani's *San Pantalon* (1684-1704) in Venice is the largest oil-on-canvas painting ever made. Its Baroque busyness excited the critic John Ruskin into a fuming rage.

undermined by reference to one assertion alone. How appealing and charming 'soft red brick' sounds, how humane and desirable. Yet structurally efficient brick is not significantly softer than concrete, and Victorian board schools and workhouses tell a different tale about the seductive qualities of this material. The Prince of Wales may have become a remarkable popular champion; he may, like Cocteau, have lied to tell the truth; but his criticisms of architecture revealed as much of the tastes of his caste as they do of his flawed insights into modern building technology.

The concern to recapture 'character and charm' is peculiarly located in a specific time capsule: London, according to the Prince of Wales, was fine in the seventeenth and eighteenth centuries. Contemporary Manhattan, it is suggested by omission, not so. Paris during unspecified periods, fine. No mention of Germany or Italy (save one eighteenth-century reference to London being at least as noble a city as Canaletto's or Fumiani's native Venice). Buildings lower than the entablature of St Paul's are fine; ancient monuments should necessarily be preserved; technological culture is bad.

To some this was a backward-looking, sentimental farrago of special pleading, but in it lies the germ of the idea that the observance of rules will produce better architecture. Architecture has almost always been subject to rules, but in the past they have arisen not from idealistic princes looking for a responsible role, but from the influence of a religion whose values were universally accepted; the dominance of a ruling caste whose authority was complete and total; the overwhelming force of technological innovation; or from a combination of all three.

The rules of the Greek architects at the height of classical civilisation were technical and mathematical, part of a tradition that can be traced back to the period of Homeric myth. They adopted a repertoire of form and detail to masonry instead of timber. In the early Middle Ages Carolingian architects developed the stern engineering principles of Roman buildings, creating memorable symbolism in the *Westwerk* of their churches, which led to the great Gothic cathedrals. The architects used every available innovation in technology to express in their buildings a universal aspiration towards God. And, as Rudolf Wittkower has shown in his *Architectural Principles in the Age of Humanism* (1949), Renaissance architects depended on cosmology and geometry for the formal and spatial perfection of their buildings.

Georgian on my mind
Palladio refined the rules of all preceding versions of classicism into what for many people are the most pleasing buildings ever made. In the eighteenth

century – a godless age with man in charge – architects were particularly interested in achieving aesthetic perfection through the study of proportion. Georgian taste derived from the Renaissance and from the early seventeenth century, when house-trained classicism, imported from Italy, began to attain a generalised respect. The 'Georgian' period in English history produced buildings so universally admired because client, architect and builder tended to share a point of view; they were intent on making the most of *contemporaneous* possibilities, and were fortunate to find a language of design that was honest to the available building techniques and expressed their intentions. To copy the soft red brick and the classical detail is to mistake effect for cause.

The Modern Movement of the twentieth century can be seen, at least from the perspective afforded by a receding millennium, as an attempt to re-establish classical rules forgotten during the wild party of Victorian architectural excess. As Sir John Summerson put it, the Modernists 'had an authentic sense of reaction. They had seen that the environment was detestable and that they could change it'.[2]

Prince Charles and Le Corbusier have this in common: they both believe that better architecture depends on rules and principles. Neither is available for interview, but each would probably deny that his preferred rules are merely culturally and socially conditioned preferences. In fact, each has eloquently expressed his own version of taste in architecture.

If there ever were any such reliable rules, they have been blown apart by revolutions in building techniques and new materials. When prefabricated window units are brought over in a truck from Germany and slotted into position by crane, the authority of the architect as an *arbiter elegantiarum* is diminished. And while stone may indeed be a material with a 'truth' to express, the same cannot be said of synthetic spider thread (where a gene from a golden orb-weaving spider is secreted into a goat egg) or self-healing concrete. What are the urgent 'truths' waiting to be expressed here?

The contemporary debate in architecture begun by the Prince of Wales in 1984 hints at a complex underworld of ideas that support the English perception of self and culture. In the rhythms and textures of English life you can detect the idea that elsewhere there is a dream world that can somehow become accessible. A shortcut to it involves putting classical doodads on otherwise unremarkable buildings, as in Royal Poundbury.

The landscape of this dream world is picturesque: nature is benign and the only man-made interruptions are comely country houses. Of all the great things the English have invented, according to Henry James,

the well-appointed, well-filled country house is pre-eminent. Perhaps he would have said the same about motorway queues of well-appointed Range Rovers loaded with kit for the country weekend.

Besides leaving the country with an unforgettable sense of loss, the First World War nurtured the irony that underpins and undermines so much of English culture. A generation brought up on certain expectations of landscape, on certain attitudes to nature, and to abroad, found poppies and heard lark song in the foul mud of Flanders. As self-defence in the trenches they read Greek poets and eighteenth-century writers: pastoral literature provided escapism from the most hellish of circumstances. When the survivors returned, their sharp appetite for the eighteenth century was gratified by country houses, sometimes inherited, sometimes newly built. It is not fully appreciated that the cult of the 'Georgian' country house is in fact an architectural invention – some would say whimsy – of the twentieth century.

All prospects of social or material progress in England are bedevilled by this taste for historical retreat. Hence the Range Rovers (whose original advertising literature made a very self-conscious appeal to the hunting and fishing set). Most Englishmen of a certain class would prefer to live in a shoddily built, thermally inefficient, insecure travesty of classical architecture than commission a new house in a city.

Modern architecture was frustrated in England because the country has a vast stock of fine, authentic old buildings, and those who don't already possess them seem determined to acquire or replicate them. To the existing inertia provided by an inventory of architectural treasures has been added the dead weight of backward-looking convention: new old houses are also being built. The fact that the English largely disdain any form of innovation in architecture is sure evidence of an imaginary national Arcadia, which the true believers maintain might be imperilled if rational building were ever to be taken seriously.

Quinlan Terry is the most articulate spokesman of the new country house movement, the architect in the vanguard of the long march back into history. His eloquence is explainable, since he claims direct inspiration from God, but – just to be sure of his credentials – has established for himself a fake Palladian style, as inappropriate in twenty-first-century building as a periwig and the locutions of Alexander Pope would be in broadcast journalism.

Left: Zweifalten Abbey, near Reutlingen, Germany (1739-47), constructed in the German Baroque style under the direction of Johann Michael Fischer (1692-1766).

Nonetheless, the ham quality of Terry's designs pleases his philistine clients, who cannot see that his architecture fails to match the efforts of the humblest jobbing Georgian builder. It is perhaps just as well that Terry says, without apparent embarrassment, 'I do not design for the masses.' Indeed, that would be too difficult a task. Terry's every remark betrays the assumption that architecture is the province of the moneyed, landowning classes (as sex was once said to be): in a recent debate he demonised 'borrowed money' in his assault on modern architecture.

There is a whole literature to validate, quantify, record and give credibility to the English obsession with country houses. A decade after the First World War, Christopher Hussey, architectural editor of *Country Life*, published his elegant book *The Picturesque* (1927), a learned study of an earlier episode in the history of taste, which the English could not forget. A parallel development was the skilful hijacking of the National Trust by James Lees-Milne and others: a body created by Fabian socialists to preserve the landscape of England was converted by rhetoric and social prejudice into a club determined to preserve the architectural memorials of a certain age and a certain class. This magnificent act of preservation retarded English architecture for the good of no one save those people already living in country houses and weekend tourists in Volvos who buy jam and kitsch tea towels with printed illustrations of Blenheim and Chatsworth.

The privations of the Second World War also produced an intense nostalgia for the mythic country house, described so flavoursomely in Evelyn Waugh's *Brideshead Revisited* (1945). But in his preface to the second edition of 1960, Waugh registered his dismay at the way in which the country house idea had become exploited and debased:

'It was impossible to foresee ... the present cult of the English country house. It seemed that the ancestral seats, which were our chief national artistic achievement, were doomed to decay and spoliation like the monasteries in the sixteenth century. So I piled it on rather, with passionate sincerity. Brideshead today would be open to trippers, its treasures rearranged by expert hands and the fabric better maintained than it was by Lord Marchmain.'

Waugh is saying that the country house idea has become phoney: if we consider an old country house that has been restored, then what we are looking at is a sly and artful confection; if new, it is a pretentious one. Yet the magazine *Country Life* has grown and grown and in so doing has created a secondary market for fantasy architecture publications – one, a short-lived title called *Landscape* (revealingly, despite its title, almost entirely about country houses). Their constituency has grown too, and now extends far beyond the original hedging and ditching territory; these magazines are popular guides to a culture that is more *arriviste* than its zealous champions would want you to believe.

Not only is the 'Georgian' country house a recent innovation in the history of architecture (Victorians preferred massive, gutsy, castellated piles, stinking of the strength, wealth and power of the brewery and soap fortunes that so often built them), but its interior design, while appealing persuasively to a sense of the past, bears little relationship to true historical precedents. Indeed, Robert Adam, a leading 'contemporary classicist', explains that when his clients have parked their Range Rover in the porte-cochère, they, generally, like to enter an interior that is 'minimalist'.

It is worth relating here that John Fowler, who joined Sibyl, Lady Colefax to form Colefax and Fowler in 1938, the firm of interior decorators which is the benchmark of the style, was not an architect, landowner or scholar, but a furniture salesman from Peter Jones department store in Chelsea. The basic assumption of interior decoration, as someone remarked of the trade's doyenne, Elsie de Wolfe, is to introduce new money to old furniture. It is England's loss that the relationship does not work the other way.

Since the end of the Second World War there has been plenty of old and new money spent on country houses. The roll call of leaders of English life capable of seeing quality in building only when it evokes a past that never existed is as impressive as it is depressing. Robin Leigh-Pemberton, Governor of the Bank of England between 1983 and 1993, built himself a breathtakingly accurate and bogus William and Mary house at Torry Hill, near Maidstone, just before 1960. While he would discourage the forging of banknotes, Leigh-Pemberton felt it proper for a man in his position to live in a sly reproduction.

Conservative politicians seem specially to enjoy dissimulation. Michael Heseltine, when Minister of Defence, hired Quinlan Terry to build a garden pavilion in Northamptonshire. The style was amateur-dramatic-society Palladian pastiche – the architectural equivalent of the minister having troops descend from assault helicopters carrying halberds and flintlocks. When the Duke of Westminster hired the architect John Dennys to design the Modernist Eaton Hall near Chester, another duke – the Duke of Bedford – excoriated him. In a telling line perhaps inspired by his own propinquity to the M1 motorway, the Duke of Bedford exclaimed that such a style might be appropriate for a bypass in suburbia, but it certainly was not for a gentleman's seat in Cheshire. Then, as if in a *tableau vivant* about changing taste, another Duke of Westminster, the late Gerald Grosvenor, de-modernised Eaton Hall and began work on a new 'old' country house in the Cheshire landscape. The new old Eaton Hall was designed by the Percy Thomas Partnership to look a little more like a French chateau than a photocopier parts distribution warehouse. It was anomalously finished in 1991. In the context of this debate it is clear that 'appropriate' is rich shorthand for the symbols and aspirations of a certain class and their imitators.

Rus in suburbe

Revulsion against the modern world was given another form with the creation of suburbia. The English had to invent suburbia because after the First World War there were too many people who couldn't face modern life in the city, but who couldn't afford a time capsule in the country. Since 1964, British prime ministers have, with the exception of David Cameron, generally been suburban socialists or suburban meritocrats. Thus it is significant that John Fowler, who used to sell furniture in Peter Jones, designed the interiors of Chequers, in Buckinghamshire, the official country house of the prime minister. His infamous shabby chic suited their parvenu taste – what the French call *petit goût* (to distinguish it from the opposite and equally laudable *bon goût* and *mauvais goût*).

One theory of cultural history suggests that ideas originating near the top of the social-political-intellectual pyramid trickle down to the bottom and influence the populace. This model is perhaps too simplistic (as society, politics and the intelligentsia tend to be completely distinct pyramids), but in any case it has been upended. At a time when the Prince of Wales and his advisers aimed to arbitrate about taste, his mother, the Queen, gave her second son Andrew, Duke of York, a perfect small monument to suburban *petit goût*.

There is nowhere more suburban in England than Bracknell, in Berkshire. It is the home of those *lares* and *penates,* 3M, BMW, Waitrose, Avis and British Aerospace. Once upon a time, a few miles beyond the ring road in the walled garden of Sunninghill Park, on land owned by the Crown Estate Commissioners, the Duke and Duchess of York built their marital home. As the first new royal house since Balmoral and Sandringham it was a noteworthy event, but at a transitional moment in the development of English domestic architecture, Sunninghill was especially interesting. Consciously so or not, it was a manifesto of contemporary aesthetic and social values.

Above: New houses in Poundbury, Prince Charles's model community in Dorset, designed by Robert Adam.

Above: 'Le goût Rothschild' – once described as 'plutophilia' – illustrates the absurdities of *arriviste* taste.
In France the Rothschilds built a vaguely 'English country house' at Ferrières (1855-9), designed by Joseph Paxton.

The architect, Sir James Dunbar-Nasmith, one time professor at Edinburgh's Heriot-Watt University and a man with an appetite for 'conservation' although no eye for design, chose a style that was not exactly Georgian, but, if anything at all, Texas Tudorbethan, reminiscent of certain suburban prototypes, familiar in Ilford and Wembley and, indeed, Fort Worth and Dallas. Gables and ridges dominated the skyline and some decorative timberwork compounded what the Duke of Bedford would have called the bypass effect. From a long low building, chimneys rose picturesquely above the line of the ridge. From the south a smaller gabled pavilion gave on to a patio and conservatory. The fixed point in this joke oak architectural blur was the Duke of York's helipad. Like government ministers, he does not disdain those modern innovations he finds most convenient.

After an episode of poolside toe sucking, caught by a fearless paparazzo, the Yorks divorced in 1996. In 2014, the local council gave permission for Sunninghill to be demolished. In October 2015, bulldozers moved in. Many will see symbolism here.

The regression at Sunninghill from the eighteenth century to an earlier, albeit imprecise, age is significant. It tells us as much about contemporary taste as did the Duchess of York's wedding list, which, according to the *Daily Mail*, included 'nothing modern or freaky'. Harold Brooks-Baker, editor of *Burke's Peerage*, writing in that newspaper, said of their choice of fake Georgian furniture, hunting-scene placemats and pheasant ornaments in silver with gold inlay, 'This is the wedding list of an eighteenth-century Prince who never intends to get up and an old-fashioned bride who never expects to cook.'

The Royal Family's architectural taste helps to sustain an image of an England not so much gone for ever as having never existed – until now. 'Comfortable, timeworn, eccentric and elegant … that's English country style … the beauty, romance, nostalgia and originality of these houses … have evolved over many years. From their lovely examples … you will be inspired to bring the distinctive look of the English country home into your own.' The words are those of an advertisement for a new picture book, perhaps noticed by the Duchess of York, which appeared in a Sunday edition of the *New York Times* in 1987, the year after the Yorks' marriage.

The suggestion is that we are concerned neither with technology, function, rules and principles, nor with the search for democratic excellence so movingly and persuasively described by Walter Gropius in his own apologia, *Scope of Total Architecture* (1956). Rather we are to engage in a nugatory quest for a mythic Arcadia and in a round of competitive social display where you score triple points for philistinism.

It is usually forgotten – or perhaps not realised – that beauty often arises out of the proper husbandry of the design principles our culture eschews. The artificial and easy creation of cosy, styled time capsules, whether by Colefax and Fowler, Quinlan Terry or the Duchess of York and her advisers, is as futile an occupation as the search for a new colour, or the purblind quest for historical recovery. MH Baillie Scott (1865-1945), the Arts and Crafts architect who contributed a catalogue of forms and details to the repertory of suburban building, wrote in *Houses and Gardens* in 1906:

'To consciously aim at achieving "style" in design, either old or new, is to follow a Will o' the Wisp. For the pursuit of style, like the pursuit of happiness, must necessarily lead to disappointment and failure. Both alike are essentially by-products, and the quality of the by-products is in direct ratio to the worthiness of the ideal pursued. One may liken style to the jewel in the hilt of a sword, which flashes brightly when the blade is drawn in a worthy cause and to which the warrior absorbed with the matter in hand will give but slight attention … he who aims at style is he who would paint the lily rather than watering it.'

Yet country house enthusiasts – inspired, according to one, by 'artistic appreciation and nostalgia, combined with social curiosity and a strong dose of snobbery' – will speak of the charm of the elevation and the comfort of reading about a house like your own in a glossy book once advertised in a New York newspaper.

This is not perhaps sufficient reason, justification or excuse for derivative details, unexciting forms, complacent and unimaginative plans and a witless reliance on safe, familiar materials and details. Every pronouncement about country houses and classical revivals – whether from conservationists, the Prince of Wales, or, via Quinlan Terry, from God himself – speaks volumes about taste. The English care not about the art and science of building, but about offering up a certain set of social values and principles; country houses and the version of life they sustain say more about Britain than modern architecture ever can.

Dishonesty entered the world of architecture in the nineteenth century when, for the first time, the whole of history became available to ambitious nouveaux riches whose capacity to get anything done far outstripped their powers of judgement. In every case they chose a historicist style in order to give credentials to their very recent achievements. Perhaps the outstanding example of this was the castle style. Nineteenth-century authors were well

Above: In England, the Rothschilds built an absurdly ugly Renaissance-style chateau, Waddesdon Manor (1874-89), designed by the French architect Gabriel-Hippolyte Destailleur. It is now one of the National Trust's most visited properties.

aware that Walter Scott was trying to gain a 'pedigree' by having Edward Blore build a pseudo-baronial castle for him at Abbotsford, Roxburghshire, in 1816. The architect, CR Cockerell, while an admirer of Scott's novels, wrote that 'I cannot help attaching an idea of ridicule to these mock castles which can never fulfil the notions one has of the times in which they were built.'

Yet you could fill a book with examples of gentlemen's houses in the castle style … and of literary allusions to them, from John Bunyan's Doubting Castle to Robert Browning's castle, 'precipice encurled/In a gash of the wind-grieved Apennine'. But as the Church of England hymn is perhaps the most powerful literary form created by the Victorians, Cecil Frances Alexander provides a telling example. In *All Things Bright and Beautiful* (1848), which offers sure evidence of current typology, the significance of the lines 'The rich man in his castle/The poor man at his gate' is painfully clear.

Bodelwyddan in Wales is typical of the bogus castle style. An Elizabethan house, it was classicised about 1800, according to the taste of the times, and then castellated about 1830. Samuel Beazley (1786-1851), an obscure architect, could claim three castles in the same decade: between 1833 and 1838 he built Leys Castle, Inverness; Studley Castle, Warwickshire; and made alterations to Cahir Castle in Ireland.

The taste was not, of course, restricted to England, although in France and Germany the reasons for building or rebuilding *châteaux disparus* or *verfallene Schlösser* were usually more directly romantic: Gustave Doré's illustrations to the 1873 edition of Balzac's *Contes drolatiques* give the example in one case, while the Schloss Lichtenstein, just off the Karlsruhe-Mannheim autobahn, inspired by Wilhelm Hauff's 1826 novel of the same name, gives the other. What could better suggest the inheritance of history, of bloodlines going back to Charlemagne, than a house dressed in fake medieval military architecture?

In his memoirs, *The Whims of Fortune* (1985), Guy de Rothschild describes the building of his family seat at Ferrières, just outside Paris, which was transformed from a modest country seat to an architectural manifesto of the nouveau riche sensibility. Nouveaux riches had been scorned since Molière, but in the France of the Directoire and the Empire a new class of speculators and adventurers came into being. With money to spend, they overshadowed the traditionally penurious aristocracy yet wished to be viewed in exactly the same light.

James de Rothschild, Guy de Rothschild's great-grandfather, 'decided to build a residence on this domain worthy of his success and social ambitions – no doubt also a subconscious symbol of revenge by a former ghetto child'. An émigré in France, he built in pseudo-English style. And when Ferdinand de Rothschild, an émigré in England, bought Waddesdon Manor, near Aylesbury, from the Duke of Marlborough in 1874, he built a pseudo-French Renaissance chateau. Exotic validation has ever since been a nouveau riche technique of acquiring a form of status that cannot properly be tested. 'If room could be found for an endless collection of objects whose sole justification was sentimental, then there was ample accommodation available for concrete reminders, not of happy moments of the householder's past, but of the satisfactory state of his financial present' was how Osbert Lancaster put it in *Homes Sweet Homes* (1939).

Whether Guy de Rothschild was aware that his analysis of his grandfather's motivations anticipated Charles Revson's coldly impressive remark, 'Living well is the best revenge', is not clear from the context, but it is a significant contribution to the anthology of remarks which further an understanding of the nouveaux riches; William H Vanderbilt's 1883 remark to a reporter – 'The public be damned' – is also typical of the genre.

Ferrières and its thousand acres of grounds was designed by Joseph Paxton (1803-65) and completed in 1859. The house has its own place in architectural history and the gardens theirs in the history of landscape. In a discussion of taste, it is the interior contents and arrangements that are most revealing of how wealth distorts the meaning of things. In 1893 the *Pall Mall Magazine* observed: 'The houses of the great, the decoration of their tables, their dinners, their dresses, their carriages, all are followed by every class, with a fidelity only limited by their pecuniary ability.' Much the same thing, although less well and thoroughly done, might today be found in Beverly Hills, Rose Bay, Wilmslow or Virginia Water.

The interiors of Ferrières were decorated by a minor painter, Eugène Lami (1800-90), in a manner we might call Napoleon III mishmash: a bold assemblage of earlier styles and motifs. The 'white drawing room' was in the style of Louis XVI; tapestries were hung against a white background, white marble statues framed the windows and *trompe-l'oeil* angels floated on the cloud-scudded ceiling. In the next room, the *salon des cuirs*, a Govaert Flinck hanging of *The Triumph of David* was translated on to individual Cordoba leather panels, creating what Guy de Rothschild described as a seventeenth-century effect, modified somewhat by Italianate Renaissance marble columns. The main drawing room had a huge wooden Bavarian fireplace. Pure kitsch.

The main hall, top lit by a device of Paxton's, housed most of the pictures. James de Rothschild's attitude to art may be understood from the fact that he commissioned Ingres to paint five copies of his wife's portrait, a vulgarising gesture cut short by the revolution of 1848. There were also van Dycks, Gainsboroughs, works by Frans Hals, Roman portrait busts, armour, a billiard table, Italian cabinets inlaid with ebony, ivory, marble, onyx and semi-precious stones, a piano, an eclectic assortment of furniture, and tables groaning under the weight of artfully arranged precious objects. Quite without irony, Guy de Rothschild says the effect was one of 'harmonious disorder':

'Perhaps this is what the decorators and antique dealers describe as the "Rothschild Style", alluding to an atmosphere that is found in most of the homes inhabited by members of my family: a Napoleon III décor, personalised not only by all sorts of *objets d'art*, but above all by a sense of comfort and intimacy which intermingles furs, flowers, plants, family photographs, precious miniatures and rare books.'[3]

Just as the Rothschilds' establishment at Mentmore had modern amenities including hot water, central heating and artificial forced ventilation, the guest rooms at Ferrières were exceptionally well appointed, with private bathrooms and canopied beds. Each room was upholstered with 'pheasant', 'bird' or 'bouquet' fabrics. When the King of Prussia came to stay he exclaimed: 'What an incredible place! A king would not have dared to build it. It took a Rothschild!'[4]

Upstaging royalty and getting praised for it has been the aim of all nouveau riche taste ever since. When Napoleon III himself visited Ferrières in 1862 (dressed incongruously in the national costume of Brittany), Baron Rothschild arranged for the chorus of the Paris Opera, with Rossini conducting, to perform *The Death of the Pheasant* at a shooting dinner.

Parallel with the creation of new country houses for the new rich, made prosperous by banking, beer or patent medicines, was the development in cities of new ways of living – in apartment blocks and in hotels not intended for the rich but for the merely prosperous: their architectural styles and their internal arrangements speak volumes about contemporary taste, about the expectations we have from architecture and from building services.

The most impressive hotels of the early nineteenth century were American. Charles Dickens described Boston's Tremont as only a 'trifle smaller than Bedford Square'. Bourgeois expectations were expressed not only in terms of style and architectural arrangements, but also in terms of manners: at the Grand Hotel in Northumberland Avenue of 1881, the management unusually allowed – even encouraged – non-residents to eat at the table d'hôte. London's Grosvenor Hotel of 1860 was built, 'appropriately' for the continental rail terminus, in a French Second Empire style, with pavilions designed to impress at the ends of the massive roof structure.

In New York, Edward S Clark, head of the Singer Sewing Machine Company, built the 'Dakota' apartment block on Central Park West before the park was finished. A sort of proto-urban country house it was so named because of its remoteness. Soon, however, the Upper West Side was full of apartment blocks, which in the terminology of the time were known as hotels. The Hotel Lucerne of 1904 on West 79th Street is typical. The Charlesgate Hotel of 1891 on Beacon Street in Boston benefited from the introduction of elevators.

The hotels and apartment hotels anticipated some of the developments codified by that extraordinary phenomenon known as the Modern Movement in architecture and design. Like the fashion for country houses, the Modern Movement was inspired by the First World War. Its history has been exhaustively choreographed by an international troupe including Nikolaus Pevsner, Bruno Zevi and Kenneth Frampton. In the context of taste in architecture, Modernism is significant as a return to rules, an attempt to redefine classical order, after nearly a century of fumbling experimentation.

The shock of the ordinary
Simplicity was a novel addition to the choices available to a new consuming urban public. Since the 1830s, Michael Thonet had been mass producing bentwood furniture which matched technique with purpose to achieve a timeless harmony which seemed to elude other manufacturers, and which provided a model for architects and theorists, including Le Corbusier. It was in Austria, where the German Thonet established his factory, that Adolf Loos adapted Arts and Crafts views about simple materials, blended them with his own slick and idiosyncratic version of the manners and fashions of the English gentleman and turned them into a philosophy that was to be profoundly influential on the taste of the Modern Movement.

When Loos asked in *Ins Leere gesprochen 1897-1900* (published 1921), 'Which is worth more, a kilogram of stone or a kilogram of gold?' he was addressing himself not to the nouveaux riches, who had their own answer, but to architects, whom, he believed, should view all materials as equally valuable. This conceit anticipated by a decade Loos's best-known remark, usually misquoted, in which his taste for simplicity reached its exquisite extreme: 'Not only is ornament produced by criminals, but also a crime is committed through the fact that ornament inflicts serious injury on people's health, on the national budget and hence on cultural evolution.'[5]

The taste for simplicity in design (and, indeed, in life itself) led architects throughout Europe and America to see the machine both as a means of achieving the longed-for rational modern design, and as a metaphor for that achievement. This romantic attitude to the machine is itself an expression of taste, not the unalterably correct approach to design which its proponents believed it to be. The first half of the twentieth century was alive with mechanistic imagery: to Stalin artists were engineers of the soul; to William Carlos Williams a poem was a machine made of words. The machines that inspired architects then were the elemental ones employing beautifully clear and uncomplicated Pythagorean geometry and Newtonian mechanics; the Modernist philosophy could not sustain the change from applied maths to non-linear equations which came with electronics.

Like Functionalism (with which machine romanticism is sometimes confused), it is a point of view that is being expressed, an aesthetic preference that is being proclaimed, rather than a universally valid set of laws being revealed. Berthold Lubetkin (1901-90) wrote in *Building Design*, 'Such a mistake to call it Functionalism … it is the wrong word, people think it means a mechanistic approach when there is so much more to architecture – love and beauty.' The romance of the machine is a distinctively twentieth-century phenomenon – in the nineteenth century, buildings (and machines) were often disguised. At the turn of the twentieth century in Germany the Deutscher Werkbund began promoting the concept of *Typisierung* – a process of standardisation – and in response to it the architect Bruno Paul designed *Typenmöbel* (furniture which sounds far more aesthetically advanced than it looked). However, the most rigorous innovations came about during the First World War, or as a direct result of it. In 1917 the *Deutscher Normenausschuss* (later developing into DIN-type approval) came into being. Perhaps the most remarkable, if least obvious, innovation of the DNA was the introduction around 1921 of A-standard sizes for stationery used by the Reichskuratorium für Wirtschaftlichkeit in its efforts to impose standardised bookkeeping for all German industries. The architectural equivalent, in terms of function and utility, was the social architecture of Erich Mendelsohn and Ernst May, and the polemics of Bruno Taut. Reminiscing at the end of 1987, Sir John Summerson, who was influential in bringing Modernism to Britain, said that seeing Bruno Taut's work in *Der Sieg des neuen Baustils* (1927) was 'what crystallised modern architecture for the first time into a unified movement for me'.

Above: Ice skaters in Central Park, New York, with The Dakota apartment building (1884) seen in the background.

Crystallised or not, a great deal of serious nonsense was spoken about Functionalist architecture, although it did produce some heroic buildings. The first European housing estates, the *Siedlungen* of Bruno Taut himself, for instance, were, according to Philip Johnson and Henry-Russell Hitchcock, too often built 'for some proletarian superman of the future' (*The International Style*, 1931). Between 1921 and 1922 Rudolf M Schindler (1887-1953), a Viennese émigré in the United States, built himself a house on Kings Road in West Hollywood, which was the sort of building that TH Robsjohn-Gibbings later satirised in his sly book *Homes of the Brave* (1954).

Schindler, tired of a weary and corrupted Europe, saw Southern California as a new frontier where a perfect life would be possible. Here he built a utopian dwelling, a collection of independent studios opening on to private gardens. The architectural design was intended to radicalise all conventions: two families shared one dwelling and did a time-share in the kitchen. Schindler designed striking but ergonomically hostile furniture. There were no conventional bedrooms, but 'sleeping baskets' on the roof. These baskets were in fact simple frames, covered with canvas in the event of rain. The Schindler house was quite mad.

The symbolism of efficiency reached its extreme in the middle-period architecture of Le Corbusier (1887-1965). (That he was on a campaign is indicated by his pseudonym: Le Corbusier was the *nom de guerre* of Charles-Édouard Jeanneret.) Heavily influenced by his contact with Germany (where he had worked in Peter Behrens' studio), Le Corbusier was responsible for the century's most romantic and poetical expression of contact with the machine. The austere German *Typisierung* was translated into the more chic *objet-type* – the Thonet No 14 chair, and the standard wine goblet, which Le Corbusier used in his paintings and in his interiors. 'Mass production demands a search for standards. Standards lead to perfection,' he wrote in *Vers une architecture* (1923). He believed that engineers were 'healthy and virile, active and useful, balanced and happy in their work' and he coined the ultimate expression of the taste for things mechanical in calling houses 'machines for living in', just as the aeroplanes he so admired were machines for flying in.

Despite misquotations, despite being plagiarised by talentless hacks, Le Corbusier's influence was so powerful that the story of architecture for most of the twentieth century was the story of whether you accepted or rejected his view of the world, which is to say his taste. No single building truly by the hand of Le Corbusier exists in either England or the United States (although Harvard's Carpenter Center and New York's United Nations building have some claim), but for sixty years his was the dominating vision – until a recent change of taste has tested his assumptions and found them wanting by some contemporary standards.

Vers une architecture appeared in England in 1927 as *Towards a New Architecture*, published by John Rodker, whose distinguished avant-garde list included the first editions of TS Eliot's *Ara Vos Prec*, Ezra Pound's *Hugh Selwyn Mauberley*, the first translation of Lautréamont's *Les Chants de Maldoror*, and a proposal for James Joyce's *Ulysses*.[6] The translator of *Towards a New Architecture* was Frederick Etchells (1886-1973), a Francophile aesthete who made ends meet during the translation by doing makeweight designs of fake Georgian houses for the Grosvenor Estate. In his introduction to the English edition, Etchells wrote:

'A man of today, reading this book, may have the impression of something akin to a nightmare. Many of our most cherished ideas in regard to the "Englishman's castle" – the lichened tiled roof, the gabled house and patina – are treated as toys to be discarded, and we are offered instead human warrens of sixty storeys, the concrete house hard and clean, fittings as coldly efficient as those of a ship's cabin or of a motor car, and the standardised products of mass production throughout.'

It was a brave statement from someone who was to publish a somewhat different book, *The Architectural Setting of Anglican Worship*, in 1948, but a number of disclaimers (and some subtle cuts) were sufficient to encourage even the doyen of English country-house architects, Sir Edwin Lutyens, to review the book favourably. Lutyens could see that Le Corbusier was not an austere Trotskyist intent on eradicating the past: both the cadences of his prose as well as its content recall Viollet-le-Duc, the greatest of French architectural thinkers. Similarly, while Le Corbusier was demonised as an inhumane Brutalist, no close reading of his writings, nor a close examination of his buildings, could support this analysis.

Right: The Rockefeller Guest House, New York (1949-50), by Philip Johnson.

Simplicity is not poverty

If during Le Corbusier's heroic period – from, say, 1917, when he settled in Paris, to the mid-1930s – purification of architecture was his ambition, the resulting purity was sensuous and beautiful, not arid. In *Précisions sur un état présent de l'architecture et de l'urbanisme* (1930) he declared: 'Simplicity is not equivalent to poverty; it is a choice, a discrimination, a crystallisation.'

According to Le Corbusier, modern decorative art is not in fact decorated, and, like Sir Henry Cole or Gustav Pazaurek, he made his choices clear: Thonet chairs, filing cabinets, aeroplanes – good; Lalique, Galle, Sue et Mare – bad. But Le Corbusier did believe, at least for a while, that the laws of architecture that he was revealing would eradicate questions of taste. There was, he might have said, no alternative. Although his career changed and developed continuously, Le Corbusier's reputation has been a victim of his own rhetoric.

The Postmodern revisionists require him to be seen as an austere 'functionalist' intent on reducing life to hydrocarbons and Bolshevism, yet even his villas of the 1920s, when his designs were at their most austere, were inspired by a symbolic vision similar to that which inspired Wren and later Prince Charles. The difference is that the source of Le Corbusier's vision was the modern world (which is why he illustrated cutaway drawings of racing car stub-axles in his artistic journal *L'Esprit Nouveau*). His buildings actually looked like the Farman biplanes and ocean liners he so admired.

The mistake has been to treat Le Corbusier as if he were a monolith, but this can at least be interpreted as respect for his overwhelming stature. His various and articulate detractors have preferred to regard him as such because a monolith is simpler to tackle, if not to destroy, than rambling settlements. Vision is more easily neglected. The extent of Le Corbusier's ambition and the dimensions of his artistic achievement can best be judged by the significance attached to the demonstrable failure of his vision in recent years, even though he was not actually responsible for those international urban blights: town planning, urban motorways, skyscrapers, overscaled city centres, regimented apartment blocks and built monotony. Alas, as Ada Louise Huxtable remarked, 'Eventually, the acceptance of modern architecture came about through a combination of technology and economics that was able to achieve what lessons in taste and morality could not.'[7] Towards the end of his life Le Corbusier himself remarked, 'Life is right and the architect is wrong.'

Le Corbusier was convinced that form was a manifestation of tangible concepts and laws. From this it was but a short step to conclude that perfection was attainable, which would eliminate the embarrassment of choice forever. But late in life he began to understand that what he once believed was unalterably good, perfect and true – the law of machines – was in fact no more than a particular, even if very persuasive, aesthetic preference. Postmodernism has done more for journalism and publishing than it has for the history of architecture, but it has at least made frank discussion of wilful (and frequently illiterate) aesthetic preferences commonplace.

The prelude to Postmodernism was the celebrated failure of Modernism. In Britain, if a little less so in the United States, Le Corbusier and modern are virtually synonymous. St Louis's infamous Pruitt-Igoe development, dynamited by despairing city officials in the 1970s, is a realisation of Le Corbusier's 1930 Radiant City proposal. And how very hostile and dull it seemed when transferred from paper to an urban lot. Then, on 11 September 2001, the New York World Trade Center towers were destroyed in the Al Qaeda atrocity. The architect of The World Trade Center was Minoru Yamasaki (1912-86), designer of the doomed Pruitt-Igoe. End-of-an-era symbolism was evident.

Similarly, in Britain, the municipal concrete Brutalism of post-war urban 'renewal' actually became the official architecture of the welfare state. It was a reaction against this which produced buildings dressed up to be what they are not, occupied by tenants pretending to be what they are not, designed by architects using a vocabulary they did not understand. More of this anon.

Transvestite architecture

Given the background, it is perhaps not surprising that Postmodernism owes most not to a great architect or patron, but to Charles Jencks, an ambitious American architectural propagandist living in London. Jencks, with independent means that allows a liberality of expression that would have been difficult in a conventional academic context, established the scripture of Postmodernism in his variously hyped and hyping books: *Meaning in Architecture* (1969), *Modern Movements in Architecture* (1973) and *The Language of Post-Modern Architecture* (1977). His tutor, the arch-Modernist Reyner Banham, once told me that the thing he regretted most was letting 'Charlie' have his PhD since this gave a spurious authority to the young man's sometimes eccentric proclamations.

Another architectural journalist, the conservative Gavin Stamp who used to affect a scrap of Pugin altar cloth as a necktie, perhaps thinking of these very books, called Postmodernism 'grotesquely vulgar, illiterate'. Its chief monument, its manifesto even, is Charles Jencks' own house in London's Notting Hill, a whimsically manic farrago of overwrought symbolism all executed in medium-density fibreboard which has not endured the passing of time any better than the flimsy ideas that supported it.

The movement's other great monument was the AT&T Building in New York (1984), which dates from the last years of the giant corporation before courts executing anti-trust legislation broke up the old US telecoms monopoly. A memorandum from Louis O'Leary, assistant vice president of public relations at AT&T, to the architect, Philip Johnson, is so extraordinarily revealing of taste in late twentieth-century architecture that it bears reproduction in full. Here, wholly evocative of how a craving for easy-to-read symbolism inflamed 1980s' sensibilities, is O'Leary describing the corporation's vision of itself, as expressed in the building:

If we had our portrait painted, it should be by Norman Rockwell.
If we were ancient builders we would have built the Roman aqueducts instead of the cathedral of Notre Dame.
If we were a baseball team, we would be the New York Yankees, not the LA Dodgers.
If we drove race cars, we would be Richard Petty, not AJ Foyt.
If we were a state, we would be Midwestern, probably Iowa. Twenty years ago we would have been Nebraska.
If we were a US general, we would be Omar Bradley, not George Patton.
If we were a tree, we would be a huge and utilitarian Douglas fir – not a sequoia, and certainly not a dogwood.
If we could choose an epitaph (never believing such a thing would be needed) we would choose 'Millions of customers, but it served them well and one at a time.'

A building designed along these lines would have been a colourful affair, but Philip Johnson (1906-2005) ignored the implied directive and instead preferred to satisfy Chairman John D deButts' playful, innocent whim to own

Right: Philip Johnson's AT&T Building in New York (1980-4), was intended to be the 'world's greatest skyscraper for the world's greatest corporation'.

'the world's greatest skyscraper'. It is a measure of deButts' sensitivity and humility that the skyscraper headquarters, unveiled on 30 March 1978, was part of a publicity programme initiated after an opinion poll in 1972 had revealed to his dismay that less than two per cent of the US population recognised his name. So much for architecture being frozen music. Architecture had become frozen public relations.

Johnson was already New York's most celebrated corporate architect. Hilton Kramer described his oeuvre as a demonstration of: 'publicity, showmanship and the exercise of power'. He had secured the support of a younger generation as keen to ape his social position and media profile, as he had been to imitate Mies van der Rohe's architecture. They included Robert AM Stern, Frank Gehry, Michael Graves and Robert Venturi. By exercising his considerable gift for patronage, without necessarily being patronising, Johnson recommended each camp follower for important commissions.

I'm a whore
William Shirer hinted at the darker side of Johnson's political motivation in *Berlin Diary* (1941). Rich, clever, vain, gay, patrician, and proud to be largely without principles or scruples – 'Remember, son, I'm a whore,' he once told me, and a lot of other people besides – Johnson had briefly practised a polished form of Modernism of the Bauhaus sort. His office on the thirty-seventh floor of the Seagram Building, which he designed with Mies van der Rohe (1886-1969), was full of Barcelona chairs and Frank Stella paintings, but it is probably true to say, as Johnson himself once did, that he liked Mies's architecture because it was easy to copy. He gave further evidence of the philosophy that informed his life and work in a BBC interview of 1965: 'What good does it do you to believe in good things? It's feudal and futile.'

Although he lived in the Rockefeller Guest House, in Manhattan, from 1971 to 1978, Johnson was moving away from pure Modernism. His departure from the Bauhaus aesthetic was emphasised by the evacuation of his office from the Seagram Building into his own 'Lipstick' building at 53rd Street and Third Avenue, which he described as 'an oval building in a square environment'. It is an architectural one-liner whose tiresomeness demonstrates the dominant superficiality of Postmodernism, which he did so much to champion.

In creating his monumental pastiche for AT&T, Johnson achieved the remarkable double of satisfying both the largest and most conservative American corporation ('The last thing in the world we want is to be trendy,' declared Edward M Block, AT&T vice president) and the tiny, self-styled claque of radical Postmodernists who, like Robert Venturi, were pleased to describe the profession that had once occupied Ictinus, Callicrates, Michelangelo, Bernini, Wren and Soufflot as 'decorating sheds'. Once the positivist ethic and aesthetic of Modernism had been reduced to no more than a temporary aberration, everything was available for copying.

Johnson's experience in Berlin in the 1930s may have stimulated his taste for the monumentalism of Albert Speer, Hitler's architect. The AT&T design was for a thirty-six-storey building 650 feet high (less monumentally, you could expect to get sixty floors into that height). The cladding was 13,000 tons of granite to cover up the fast-track steelwork, detailed to simulate structural masonry. Even the lifts were granite inside.

Inspired by the 1922 Chicago Tribune Tower competition (where Adolf Loos, of all people, submitted an entry in the form of a giant Doric column), Johnson wanted to advertise his break with Modernism by abandoning the canonical flat roof and putting something else in its place. Nearby, Hugh Stubbins (1912-2006) had done this brilliantly with his massive, single-pitched condenser roof for Citicorp, immediately raising the stakes for corporate statements in Manhattan skylines.

For AT&T, Johnson chose a broken pediment, somewhat like a Chippendale chair-back. (Later, in 1984, with even more spectacular kitsch vulgarity, he built the Pittsburgh Plate Glass tower with a profile like the Gothic of Pugin and Barry's Houses of Parliament.) That everybody in the vicinity of Citicorp had to reject a flat roof, even if they couldn't think of anything smarter, was demonstrated three years later with the completion of Helmut Jahn's thirty-six-storey Park Avenue Tower whose daft openwork pyramid has to light up at night in order to achieve an effect.

'We were classicising,' Johnson said in a subsequent interview, one of many about AT&T. Thus he called the orifice in the broken pediment an *orbiculum*. He pretentiously compared the AT&T lobby to Alberti's Basilica of Sant'Andrea in Mantua, and made his admirers gasp at his range of educated historical reference. More sensitive people cringed at what Ada Louise Huxtable called 'a monumental demonstration of quixotic aesthetic intelligence rather than art'.

The ultimate test of a building is the quality and validity of the idea that sustained it. Postmodernists talk of Alberti, but what they are really concerned with is public relations, gratifying philistine clients and winning cheap aesthetic thrills, while being certain to get into the international magazines. In a contemporary article in the *New York Times* Paul Byard, vice president for architecture at New York's Architectural League, explained that, except for some institutional work, virtually the entire province of new design has been left to corporations indulging their wealth in headquarters monuments of little perceivable social utility or to developers chasing wealth by meeting demands for products at the outer margins of the market. The result is profoundly debilitating for a profession that is ethical at its core.

Postmodernism is not about ethics, it is about effect. Robert AM Stern in his *New Directions in American Architecture* (1969) argued for historical allusion, context and ornament. Fair enough, but they demand educations that are not patchy, sensibilities that are as wide as they are deep, and qualities of imagination and inventiveness that are all too rare. Mies van der Rohe might have been easy to imitate, but Lutyens, who knew how to innovate with traditional elements, whatever sins are committed in his name, also said, 'You can't copy'.

The generation of architects who survived the garish, opportunistic errors of Postmodernism were faced with the challenge of moving on, as Le Corbusier did, from the Modernism of the 1930s, without denying its achievements, without taking refuge in a house in the country and without creating more transvestite architecture.

Meanwhile, the AT&T Building became the Sony Tower. And then Sony had a collapse all of its own.

MNMLSM

Since Socrates declared that a well-made dung bucket was better than a poorly made gold shield, a version of the Functionalist sensibility has been in European thought, if not always in European deed. From Plato to Saint Thomas Aquinas, philosophers contemplated the beauty of the absolute although architects took rather longer to appreciate the artistic opportunities of restraint.

Perhaps the very first reference to Functionalism, to which Minimalism is related in the many-branched tree of isms, appears in the eighteenth century when an obscure architect-priest called Carlo Lodoli (1690-1761) built the austere Pilgrim's Hospice at San Francesco della Vigna in Venice. Lodoli, influenced by the calculations of the mathematician Leibniz, disliked classical ornament and wrote '*Devonsi unire fabbrica e ragione e sia funziona la presentazione*' (We must unite building with reason and let function be the representation'). In the same century, the German poet Christoph Martin Wieland (1733-1813) wrote: '*Und minder ist oft mehr*',

Above: The interior of the Tetsuka House, Tokyo (2003-5) by John Pawson.

perhaps the very first expression of a trope that Mies van der Rohe and Dieter Rams later adopted. While, of all people, the Romantic poet Robert Browning was the actual source for the English form of words. In his lush poem *Andrea del Sarto* (1855), Browning writes: 'Well, less is more, Lucrezia'.

In retrospect, predictably, the fussy and flatulent bombast of Postmodernism was promptly replaced in the cycle of fashionable taste by the refined cool of Minimalism. Out went ham-fisted Egyptian details, inarticulate classical quotations and challenging colour schemes. In came polished concrete, the muted light of monasteries and finishes that spoke of philosophy and chastity, but whispered 'very expensive indeed'.

Design and food being so very closely related, the Minimalist sensibility also found expression in its near contemporary, nouvelle cuisine. Here you would find a large, plain white ceramic dish with naught but a pyramid of chopped chives, a colophon of oyster jus and a carpaccio of something transparent weighing no more than 15 grams, providing about 200 calories and tracing its origins back not to Mrs Beeton's kitchen, but to St Thomas Aquinas's monk's cell and his concept of *claritas pulchri* or the beauty of absolute clarity. Similarly, the French gastronome Curnonsky (1872-1956) said 'Good cooking is when things taste of what they are'. Minimalist designers apply this principle to interiors.

An enduring image of the period is of a thoughtful architect in Prada boots, black jeans and turtleneck contemplating the *claritas pulchri* of the immenseness of the nothingness he has just designed. Minimalism's apogee may have been 2008 when Cordula Rau, so tired of being asked the question herself, published an anthology of answers called *Why Do Architects Wear Black?* It was at about this same moment that ambitious estate agents began advertising properties as 'Minimalist-style', as once they had 'Georgian-style'.

Minimalism was not just easy to copy, as Philip Johnson averred of his master Mies, it was also very easy to parody. It was not something simple, limited, restricted and ascetic; rather it was subtle, wide-ranging, engaging and nuanced. Nor was it ever cheap. On the contrary, it costs a fortune to make things *look* simple. Simplicity is hard-won: *l'art difficile de faire simple* as the French say. Flock wallpaper, damask, scatter cushions, washed Chinese rugs, lion pelts, drapes, shag pile, statuettes, swags, stuffed zebras, bevel-glassed cocktail cabinets, sconces and escutcheons are convenient ways to disguise nasty constructional flaws or shoddy materials.

But if you want to live in serene emptiness, your waxed plaster white Venetian-style walls and black Macassar Ebony floors have to be expensively perfect in the first place (usually aligned by laser) and even more expensively maintained (by cleaners) in the long run. So living with very little became the ultimate pose of the very rich. 'There is no dirt in Heaven' according to Mother Ann Lee, founder of the Shakers, a nineteenth-century utopian sect whose strict furniture designs inspired some Minimalists. If there is dirt in a Minimalist house, it is always embarrassingly obvious.

And by about 2000, Minimalism had settled into the mainstream – with a repertoire of hidden lights, brushed gravel, flush surfaces and dry twigs – although acceptance was not universal. One London restaurant with a splendidly Minimalist men's room discovered, by unfortunate trial and error, that customers found it difficult to 'read' what was what and so, as an urgent retro-fit, had to label hitherto thrillingly discreet features with helpful instructions in declamatory mode: 'WC', 'Tap', 'Basin', 'Waste' and so on.

About the same time, one Minimalist architect took the roof off his house, hired a tower crane and shut down his street for a week or two so as to allow the installation of sheer, 80-foot planks of Douglas fir in the kitchen. It is said that the late Joseph Ettedgui, the brilliant clothes entrepreneur who popularised the Minimalist little black dress – Coco Chanel's *misérabilisme de luxe* – wrapped every book in his library in fine, art-quality white paper. They looked beautiful, but were impossible to identify. But convenience and logic were not chapters in The Minimalist Handbook.

So what exactly is a Minimalist interior? It is first necessary to achieve a bit of *claritas pulchri* in the vocabulary. The expression 'minimal art' cannot be found earlier than 1965 and it refers not to architecture and design, but to the dominant ism in painting that found expression in, for example, Frank Stella's geometrical stripes of the late 1950s or Ellsworth Kelly's colour fields of the next decade. These bold simplifications, following another cycle of taste, replaced the energetic – even neurotic – daubs of Jack the Dripper and the other paint-splattered exponents of Abstract Expressionism.

In this interior there would be appliances designed by Dieter Rams whose pursuit of stripped-back excellence reached its inevitable conclusion in machines that looked like white boxes or black boxes. The Rams food-mixer of 1957 was a near perfect exercise in Platonic form: formal, disciplined, tightly detailed, fuss-free. Its problem was that when you take perfect Platonic form into the kitchen, you get cake mixture and shredded carrot all over it. Another problem was what Braun engineers called the *Rams Ausschlag*: the designer's strict discipline was so expensive to manufacture that his signature cost an enormous surcharge.

143

Architectural Minimalism had its tribunes in the Portuguese architects Eduardo Souto de Moura and Álvaro Siza, the Japanese Yoshio Taniguchi and Tadao Ando, and the Swiss, Peter Zumthor. The latter's Bruder Klaus Kapelle (2007) has all the elements of absurd extremism and occult spirituality, which are Minimalism's characteristics: to memorialise a medieval mystic, Zumthor built a wooden structure, surrounded it with concrete and set fire to the core. Minimalism does not have to be without theatrical special effects.

Minimalism turned Functionalism into High Style. After all, art and artifice are only two syllables apart. But it had its absurdities: nothing matters quite a lot, and very little matters greatly. Or as Rem Koolhaas put it: 'If less is more, maybe nothing is everything'. Architecture is still struggling to escape from that conundrum of taste.

But now people say Minimalism has run its own fashionable course and has hit the buffers of history, collapsing into a muddle of chilly affectation. Some even speculate that we are through with isms of any description. History has exhausted itself. On his way back from the Basel Art Fair, Grayson Perry (wearing at the time a Bo-Peep dress, red patent shoes, white tights and gripping a pretty clutch-bag as though his media profile depended on it, said in mock dismay: 'Everything is now happening all at once'. He meant there is no ruling taste or style, as there once was. We are over schools and movements. It's the end of isms: there is today no common agreement on what is avant-garde and what is *retardataire*. Today, the happening thing is just what is … happening.

There is an equivalent hiatus in manners: today it is even difficult to be truly vulgar. No clothes can shock as a mini-skirt once did. Women smoke on the streets when once it would have been frowned upon. David Cameron's wife Samantha has a tattoo. Fat people are medicalised as 'obese'. Badly behaved children have psychiatric disorders. The trashy Kardashians get on the cover of US *Vogue*, territory once populated by Norman Parkinson and Richard Avedon.

What hope can there be for enthusiasts of kitsch when the *Mail Online* publishes the following as a matter of course: 'Fat Jew stands out from crowd by dressing up as Rob Kardashian and Blac Chyna's baby at Seriously Scary Halloween Ball'? The rules of taste have gone the way of Postmodernism.

The Starchitect
Just as there ceased to be any dominant ism in architecture, so new forces determined the public's perception of the building designer. This was the

Starchitect, a media construct force-fed by publicity, rather as a waddling Strasbourg goose stuffed by the cruel processes of gavage. After the decline of certainty in matters of architectural taste, after the battle of the styles had not so much been lost as effortfully drawn, the Starchitect emerged as a figure of influence. Chief among them are Rem Koolhaas, Frank Gehry, Norman Foster and the late Zaha Hadid.

The circumstances of this emergence were very specific. Starchitects are brands, not artistic movements. They work globally and show not much interest in locality, heritage, tradition or national characteristics. Their projects are mega-scaled and designed to photograph well. Starchitects do not concern themselves with, for example, low-budget housing. They show no resistance to working for despotic regimes in the Caucasus, Middle East or China. Indeed, among the monuments of these Starchitects are buildings conceived in the service of an authoritarian Kazakh ruler and China Central Television. Their culture is an art market where prices of modern masterpieces are edging towards the billion-dollar mark. Their clients have superyachts that cost $1 million a metre. They are all international celebrities. And celebrity is a mask that eats the face.

Zaha Hadid (1950-2016) became perhaps the most fully realised idea of what, today, it is to be a global architect. The expression 'global architect' may need explaining. This is not someone who merely designs beautiful and useful buildings that appear all over the world, patiently working to a client's brief, but someone who has celebrity allure and the cachet of a luxury brand. Global architects do not fix leaks or fret about drain schedules. Instead, they have high concepts. Or in Hadid's case a 'design vision'.

Often a global architect will move beyond mere architecture, pollinating other areas. Hadid designed a Liquid Glacial table that is not somewhere to rest drinks or pile books, but something that 'embeds surface complexity and refraction within a powerful fluid dynamic'. Global architects often have problems stating things clearly.

Zaha designed a superyacht for Blohm+Voss for a superlatively rich client. She told the builders of the *Bismarck* that her 'unique circle' concept avoided 'strict horizontal order' and instead offered 'intense connectivity'. She said nothing of hydrodynamics. You can get a humble engineer to do that. Hadid's superyacht looks like an acrylic cycling helmet, but no one knows why this is a good idea. With the art dealer Kenny Schachter, son-in-law of the late Marc Rich, the Clinton-era fugitive billionaire, she discussed designing a car, but was not herself much of a motorist.

For nearly fifteen years after establishing her studio in London in 1980, Hadid was absurdly famous for not actually having built anything. Instead, her reputation was boosted by a clique of fawning admirers, who saw in her uncompromising angles and later zoomorphic blobs, a fearless repudiation of stuffy tradition.

The competition entry for the Cardiff Bay Opera House was her celebrated cause. With this, with genius, she managed to alienate both the left and the right. The former thought it elitist, the latter outrageous. It was, after years of well-publicised struggle, abandoned in 1995. She thus became a martyr both to taste and sexism.

At about the same time, Hadid's first real building emerged above the ground. This was a tiny fire station in a Swiss-German furniture factory whose shrieking concrete angles and disruptive interiors photographed well and were dutifully recorded in the parish magazines of architecture, but were not much liked by the actual firemen. It was decommissioned and Vitra now uses it as an exhibition centre.

As if in revenge for years of neglect, Hadid now began a global strut in billowing drapery by Prada or Issey Miyake. She became the champion of an architecture that was more about personal vision than public utility. There was a Science Centre in Wolfsburg and a showroom at the BMW factory in Leipzig. Karl Lagerfeld had her design a pop-up exhibition for Chanel and, accordingly, she made it look like a quilted handbag.

Critics mumbled that she had no sense of context or locality, preferring to crash-land photogenic concepts whose function was not to serve her clients' needs, but to advertise her own status. Her fabulous, zoomorphic forms were always eye-catching, but often difficult to build. And almost always, so neglectful was she of tectonic practicalities that her buildings went deliriously over budget. Drowning in debt and impracticality, the Aquatics Centre for the London 2012 Olympics was described by an official as a 'joke'. For the same reason of doubling cost, a fatigued Shinzō Abe canned her design for the Tokyo 2020 Olympic Stadium.

But there were other reasons why Hadid's Tokyo stadium was a bad design. It too resembled a monstrous acrylic cycling helmet. But why? Two of the grand old men of Japanese architecture, Arata Isozaki and Fumihiko Maki, damned the project as monstrous and wasteful. And, more damagingly still, they said it was conceived with neither respect nor reference to its locality. That, of course, was almost certainly her intention.

In Qatar, Hadid's 2022 World Cup stadium with its almond-shaped opening and labial folds looks from the air bogglingly like a giant

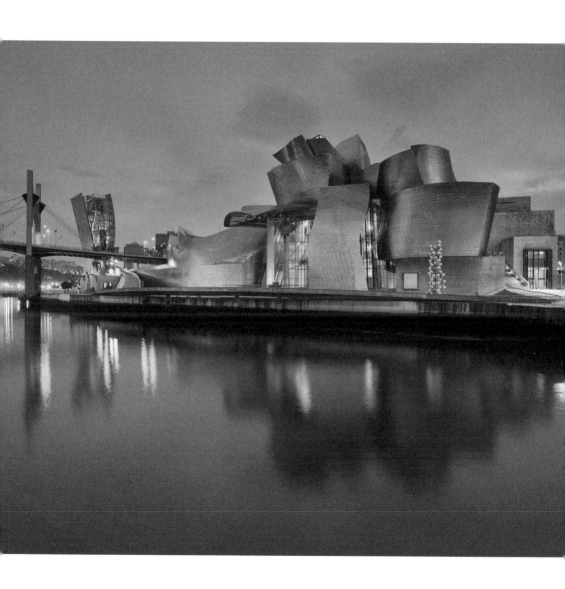

Above: The Guggenheim Museum Bilbao, Spain (1991-7), by Frank Gehry.

Above: Vitra Fire Station, Weil am Rhein, Germany (1990-3), by Zaha Hadid.

pudendum. Someone mentioned this and she said: 'If you think anything with a hole in it is a vagina, that's your problem'.

Brutal

The history of Brutalism is architecture's most revealing contribution to the absurd history of taste. Just as the term Brutalism had, thanks to Prince Charles, been accommodated into anathematising tabloid critiques of any sort of modern architecture, so a creeping movement of reappropriation began.

As early as 1966, Nikolaus Pevsner had detected a 'revived Expressionism', citing Le Corbusier's Ronchamp, Denys Lasdun's Royal College of Physicians and Stirling and Gowan's red-brick and faceted Engineering Building at Leicester University. All these bold statements rebelled against what was becoming the pallid orthodoxy of Modernism with its dismal piazzas, pools and reticent blocks animated only by tedious ribbon windows.

The term Brutalism was not originally a slur. It first seems to appear in 1949 when the Swedish architect Hans Asplund coined *nybrutalism* (or New Brutalism). In 1953, Peter and Alison Smithson defined the aesthetic in the *Architectural Review*: 'no finishes at all internally … bare brick, concrete and wood'. Later, their school at Hunstanton in Norfolk would demonstrate these qualities. Two years later, the *Architectural Review* became the scriptural source of the term when it published Reyner Banham's essay 'The New Brutalism'. Mad about planes and cars and gadgets while hip to the beat of rock and adept at hepcat demotic, it is hard to imagine anyone less in sympathy with Geoffrey Scott's *Architecture of Humanism* than Banham.

An architectural Angry Young Man, Banham (1922-88) greatly admired Le Corbusier's favourite *béton brut*, or raw concrete. Architecture, Le Corbusier was fond of saying, results when raw materials establish moving relationships with one another. Banham adored the clarity of buildings where 'water and electricity do not come out of unexplained holes in the wall, but are delivered to the point of use by visible pipes and manifest conduits'. Thus, the clear exposition of structure, the use of materials 'as found' and a strikingly memorable graphic image of the whole were what counted. Of course, these criteria of excellence were just as arbitrary and judgemental as any other fashionable preference.

In the cycle of taste, it's important to recognise that Banham's enthusiasm for Brutalism was not so much a reaction against the twee Arts and Crafts of heretofore but a red-blooded critique of the anaemic

Modernism of so much British public architecture, a style he derided as 'whitewash and patent glazing'. Thus, the design of Brutalist buildings emphasises texture, materials and construction. Often the windows are small, as in a bunker, while an emphatic ruggedness is underlined by externalised heating and ventilating equipment. The very qualities Banham admired – 'bloody-mindedness' he called it – were exactly what, after a twenty-year hegemony, brought Brutalism into disfavour. JG Ballard's *High-Rise* (1975), a grim dystopian masterpiece, is based on Ernö Goldfinger's thirty-one-storey Trellick Tower in west London, a building that magnificently satisfies Banham's requirement that a structure should have graphic stand-out.

The architecture of Ernö Goldfinger, Peter and Alison Smithson, Sir Basil Spence and Patrick Hodgkinson, designer of The Brunswick Centre, is now highly fashionable. At about the time that Boston's mayor planned to sell its Brutalist City Hall by architects Hellmuth Obata & Kassabaum, on the other side of the Atlantic fashionable Notting Hillbillies were moving into Trellick Tower. It had moved from eyesore to High Style within a decade.

Brutalism has been rehabilitated. So much so that there are now connoisseurs of concrete. Rightly so, as great architects go to special efforts to use it to extraordinary effect: at the National Theatre in London, Denys Lasdun said he took such care with the textured effects of the wooden shuttering that it would have been cheaper to clad the whole building in Carrara marble. At the Louvre in Paris, IM Pei's concrete is so fine it is indistinguishable from natural limestone. Maybe that is just how it should be, yet in *Raw Concrete: The Beauty of Brutalism* (2016), Barnabas Calder finds himself in praise of the *brut*: 'I love the way the buildings look: rough, raw concrete, streaked by rain and dirt, forming punchy, abstract shapes; soaring cliffs of tower blocks or entire cities within cities'. After the flimsy pastiche of Postmodernism, the angst of Deconstructivism in the 1980s and '90s and the ludicrous flimflam of Zaha Hadid's Parametricism, the Old Brutalism seems to offer us something refreshingly tough and honest.

The National Trust, for so long interested only in Georgian time warps and gift-shop novelty chutney, now speaks of Ernö Goldfinger as it once spoke of Robert Adam. A popular fan-base Tumblr blog is called 'Fuck Yeah Brutalism'. Trellick Tower, once regarded as a bloody-minded offence to

Right: Trellick Tower, London (1966-72), by Ernö Goldfinger.

Above: A House for Essex, Wrabness, England (2015), by Grayson Perry and FAT Architecture.

architectural intelligence, is now a listed building. It has not happened yet, but one day the Prince of Wales is almost certain to look upon it wistfully. Ultimate proof of re-acceptance is English Heritage publishing Elain Harwood's *Space, Hope and Brutalism: English Architecture 1945-1975* (2015). Appropriately, it weighs an impressive nine pounds.

The history of taste shows that such reversals are predictable and inevitable. People now mourn the destruction of Rodney Gordon and Owen Luder's spectacular Trinity Square Car Park, in Gateshead, and their imposing Tricorn Centre in Portsmouth, both products of the mid-1960s. In another entirely predictable development, the Twentieth Century Society has replaced the Victorian Society as Britain's policeman on the lookout for philistinism.

Notwithstanding the darkness of JG Ballard and his dystopian urban literature, Brutalism now seems a warm, nostalgic retro-passion: architecture for real people who lived in real buildings and performed real work, not abstract functions of the Internet era. Because whoever wrote the rule that bush-hammered concrete is inferior to Pietra Serena?

Why is rough texture less worthy than smooth? There really is no rational answer, and concrete itself is now finding a new acceptance of its own: a thermally efficient material, susceptible to many interesting treatments and finishes, it is also natural and can be readily recycled. You can even achieve a finish like Pietra Serena, if you so wish. Soon, someone will perhaps talk emotively about the Wabi-sabi of stained ferroconcrete and the haunting beauty of rusting rebar. The grim Thamesmead estate in south-east London (once thought so dystopian it was used as a location for Stanley Kubrick's 1971 film of Anthony Burgess's *A Clockwork Orange*) may soon move into imaginative space currently occupied by the gorgeous gardens of La Foce, Ninfa and Settignano. One thing is certain: our faith in the present moment is a very weak current.

Essex maniacs

As if to demonstrate a directionless plurality in contemporary architectural taste, Alain de Botton's Living Architecture programme of high-concept holiday lodging for aesthetes includes buildings of bold purity and, in the case of Grayson Perry's House for Essex at Wrabness, completed in 2015, frivolous kitsch. Perry, who has broadcast on taste, has noted that the problem with art today is that 'everything is going on at the same time' and that there is neither an avant- nor an arrière-garde, just an unmediated scrum vying for attention.

The House for Essex is a knowing assault on good manners, designed in collaboration with architects FAT (which stands for Fashion Architecture and Taste). 'Steal, copy, collage' might be Perry and FAT's motto. A person has been created to assume the *genius loci* of this house: Julie May Cope. Julie's house is a challenge to whatever orthodoxy you want to describe. Perry, who was born in Chelmsford, says it is: 'a homage to the single mums in Dagenham, hairdressers in Colchester and the landscape and history of Essex'. This fiction is now so popular that it has caused paralysing traffic problems on Wrabness's Black Boy Lane and Essex Highways has agreed to install new road signs and markings to discipline the admiring crowds of Mondeo Men who want to worship the Essex cult legitimised by the Turner Prize-winner Perry. It is not at all like Marie Antoinette's Dairy at Versailles.

So where are we today? There are few architects able or willing to produce new buildings that are absolute and true, even if anyone actually knew what 'absolute' and 'true' meant. There are few prepared to commit themselves to the realisation of contemporary possibilities, in anything other than a sardonic sense, as in Grayson Perry's case. Few find new clothes for new ideas. Construction technology has devalued art. Clients buy big-name architects rather than designs. Never before have taste and technology been so distinct, even as advanced construction gets ever closer to faithful reproduction of anything an architect-driven computer can deliver. Never has the public been so interested in architecture; never has it been so disenchanted with architects.

A digression on superyachts

The Superyacht Design Symposium takes place every year in Kitzbühel in the Austrian Tyrol, a nightmare environment of Nazi kitsch buildings, greasy food and the Streif, the planet's scariest ski run. It is rather as if the Caravan Club of Great Britain announced it was going to hold its AGM at Indianapolis Motor Speedway.

Enter the superyacht world and you meet a lot of strangely tanned people on the abyss of the ennui brought about by extreme wealth. They are the one per cent of the one per cent and operate in an environment where the merely rich feel as alienated as a shoeless beggar in a Rio favela might feel from an ordinary citizen.

Except probably more so. Advertisements in the house magazine of the global superyacht community often read: 'For charter: £500,000 per week'. In this world you learn wonderful things. Only fifteen of the world's largest superyachts have *two* helipads. Only seven have a heli garage.

Above: A concept for a 128-metre superyacht, designed by Zaha Hadid in collaboration
with Hamburg-based shipbuilders Blohm+Voss (2015).

The Eurocopter 145 superyachtsmen generally favour costs about $6.4 million, depending on paint job and trim. It is viewed as a mere accessory. President Trump probably has several.

But there are shocking new perspectives on taste and luxury available wherever people gather to discuss superyachts. At a time when the most significant innovation in luxury car design has been Mercedes-Benz's deliciously squidgy headrests and those nice soft sleeves they put over the seatbelts in the latest S-Class, the uninhibited creative bravura in the superyacht world amazes. True, it does not always produce vessels of reticent aesthetic good manners.

Lapo Elkann, the Fiat heir, a superyacht owner himself, says 'millions and millions of dollars do not equal taste'. The norm is an interior that is a deprived child's vision of glamour, humbling Trump Tower in terms of unblushing, crass, spectacular vulgarity. On superyachts, chandeliers are making a comeback. But in this ocean of aesthetic fatuity, there are currents of innovation that make the luxury car business look artistically impoverished and make architecture itself look flaccid and dull. And the interesting thing is this: once, the whims of the very rich directed the design of luxury cars. And there was a corresponding vitality in execution and quality of result. The Comtesse de la Saint Amour de Chanaz's 1936 Delahaye 135M with its glorious Figoni & Falaschi body would be an example. It speaks of sex, glamour, privilege and indulgence. The new BMW 7 Series, by way of contrast, looks like the damp wet dream of a modestly ambitious middle-ranking IT manager. And anyway, it's a contemporary German opinion that in the Fatherland, BMWs are now only ever bought by *immigrants*. The rich, you see, no longer drive quite so much.

The extremes of superyacht design are fascinating. A new design language, more fantastically architectural than traditionally nautical, is emerging. Indeed, Zaha Hadid, Frank Gehry, David Chipperfield and Norman Foster have all designed superyachts. Surely Grayson Perry will soon. You find yachts with a 23-metre beam with gardens, infinity pools and side-opening docks or garages. In some cases, the hull is treated not as a tool for hydrodynamic penetration, but as a platform to support a float-alone Modernist house.

And, dazed by a continuous diet of grande-marque champagne, cocaine and very brown girls in Minimalist swimwear, the very rich beguile themselves by competing with each other. Size matters and so too does shape. The competition is so intense that, like Detroit in the 1950s, there is the annual model change. Every year, there are more extremes of dramatic oviform, biomorphic, high-finish, drop-dead, look-at-me maritime bling. But there is also a trend towards military design. Obviously, but discreetly, many superyachts use propulsion, navigation and security systems known to the world's navies, but there is military *style* too. The strange, windowless faceted stealth profiles of modern destroyers are an aesthetic stimulus to superyacht designers who want to clean up the superstructure of their clients' yachts, if not clean up the infrastructure of their habits.

If you were a designer looking for a playground where excess was not merely tolerated, but actively encouraged, where new materials and processes appeared every year, and where your client has a boredom threshold that lowers itself automatically every twelve months, you would not look for work in the luxury car business. You'd go into superyachts. In their shameless tastelessness, refusal to be polite, extravagant commitment to phallic metaphors, unscrupulous veneration of tawdry status and sheer joy of excess, they make even extreme hypercars look dull. You will find more creativity at Blohm+Voss, builders of the *Bismarck*.

Interiors Vacuums of taste

Back on dry land and taking a holistic view of things, interior design is a travesty of the architectural process and a frightening condemnation of the credulity, helplessness and gullibility of the most formidable consumers – the rich. Yet it is a fascinating phenomenon in the history of taste, since a study of it reveals in the most explicit way much of the normally hidden structure of our value system.

Like all other episodes in consumerism, which put style in front of substance, interior design had its origins in the United States where it was and still is practised with the greatest professionalism, flair, energy and consequent vulgarity. Americans enjoy interior design for the same reasons they enjoy Coca-Cola: because, lost in a vast continent free of any but the most recent traditions, they crave symbols and symbolism. Coke gave the masses access to an inexpensive part of the American Dream. Interior designers gave the privileged access to what their forebears had left behind before Ellis Island … the European Dream.

In the 1980s, Conservative Arts Minister Grey Gowrie explained that when he was first invited to parties in New York the hostess would introduce him to an East Coast politician; ten years later he would be shown off to a fashionable academic or a Pulitzer Prize-winning novelist, but nowadays what he hears is, 'You *must* meet Norbert [*gnaw-bear*] Poubelle [*pooh-bell*]. *He* makes curtains!'

The story epitomises the rising status of the interior designer. Now that only sheikhs, Russians, South and Central Asian gas entrepreneurs, department stores and Japanese insurance companies can afford to buy paintings, and since there are few opportunities to build palaces, the interiors of private houses are empty canvases where fantasies can be created and lived out.

But interior design is required only in houses where the owners have no eye or capacity for discriminatory judgement of their own. Writing in *Industrial-Arts Magazine* in 1936, the Bloomsbury painter Duncan Grant condemned the nascent profession: 'The wealthy flat owner, distrusting his

own taste, engages the "experts" of a furniture shop to design, deliver and dispose about his rooms the elements which, as the expression of his own individuality, would have make it a home.'

There have long been firms of upholsterers and decorators who could create entire interiors. 'I have never met with a class of men who were so hopelessly confirmed in artistic error', Charles Eastlake wrote of them in his *Hints on Household Taste*. The interior designers' brief goes beyond providing furniture; they provide an image of self (both their own and their clients'). This is their age. And this is their history. Edmond de Goncourt (1822-96), writing in the late nineteenth century, after half a century of disruption in values relating to interior design, noted:

'I have often said that if I were not a man of letters, if I had not got money, my chosen profession would have been to invent interiors for rich people. I should have loved being allowed to have my own way by some banker who would have given me *carte blanche* to work out the décor and furniture of a palace with just four bare walls.'

After the Napoleonic Wars, the decline in influence of the Grand Tour and the explosion of mass consumption contributed to the deregulation of classical order and produced High Victorian styles which, now gloomy, now glorious, were a symbol of the end of Taste with a capital 'T', as it was understood by the eighteenth-century philosophers.

The requirement to have somebody else choose your domestic environment, either by default or by commission, originated in what Jane Ellen Panton called the 'evil days' of the nineteenth century, when the new middle classes in England and the United States made terrible mistakes on a budget. In her book *From Kitchen to Garret – Hints for Young Householders* (1890), Panton describes how mass consumption brought new and debased aesthetic standards. The graceful eighteenth-century furniture of Sheraton and Chippendale was discarded, put in the attic or sold at country auction to end up in a pub or the back room of a shop. 'And the heavy "handsome" furniture of mahogany and damask bore down upon us, and made us for a time the most depressed people, heavy with our ugly furnishings, and the mock of all nations that had better taste and lighter hearts than we were possessed of.'

Left: A Thonet No 14 chair. Thonet's furniture, like Palladio's architecture, transcended taste because its form and content were in perfect harmony and balance.

Panton's rhetoric is dolorously moral, befitting the conspiracy of 'good form' and propriety, which after the death of Prince Albert in 1861 became codified into what we now call Victorian values.

The age when parlours were stuffed with cherry-red Genoa velvet on cloth of gold, burnished brass, carved wood, gratings, swags of excess and a petrified forest of ormolu and damask, was the age of the decoration of deceit. Soon electric light would reveal the clutter and dusty drabness of the surroundings, and *horror vacui* would become *amor vacui*. The fact that the people who lived in these dens of brown nastiness were the very same who needed and bought etiquette books confirms the link between taste and morals in consumer society.

The Habits of Good Society (1859) advised 'gentlemen' not to spend more than a tenth of their income on their wardrobe, which should consist of: seven pairs of trousers, seven coats, four morning waistcoats and one evening one, as well as gloves, linen, hats, scarves, ties and boots. And all were dark. Like Venice in 1460, London around 1860 developed strict, if unspoken, sumptuary laws (whose ghosts are with us today). And the same deadly conformity applied to the middle-class interior.

Lenin's seat

Besides electric light, one other technical innovation prepared the ground for radicalising interior design: the mass production of furniture, and in this area the name of Michael Thonet is outstanding. Johannes Brahms used one of Michael Thonet's new bentwood chairs while composing at the piano. Lenin used them too, as did Le Corbusier. They appear now in smart New York restaurants, but not for the same reason.

Michael Thonet (1796-1871) was born at Boppard, near Koblenz in Germany. He trained as a cabinet-maker and experimented with the technique of lamination – gluing together thin strips of wood (or other material) proved stronger than using a single piece of wood. Lamination was also cheaper and more effective than hand cutting for making curved structures. Prince Metternich admired Thonet's first essays in laminated furniture on a visit to Koblenz in 1841, and he suggested that the market was more propitious in Vienna. Thonet settled there, receiving an imperial monopoly in 1842 and supplying the popular Café Daum in 1849.

Right: Bordello style adapted for middle-class American taste. In Europe, mass-produced furniture was decent and spare, like Thonet's. Its technical equivalent in America was the furniture of JH Belter, whose decoration is as much an offence to the mind and the eye as to the bottom.

Rising wages in Vienna forced Thonet to find a means of reducing the cost of making furniture using the labour-intensive lamination technique. His radical departure was to bend solid wood with steam. The parts of the chair were turned before they were steam-bent, and this innovation led to real mass-production furniture. A factory was established at Koritschan in Moravia to manufacture his No 14 chair – the Vierzehner – in enormous quantities: a hundred million had been made by the time the Thonet company switched to tubular steel in the mid-1920s.

The construction technique demanded simplification: the Vierzehner was made from six separate pieces of beech. The cross-section of each component varies continuously at any given point according to the demands of the structure. At the 1862 London exhibition, where William Morris was displaying his pseudo-medieval, pseudo-vernacular furniture, the jury, getting a sense that the evil days might be over, declared Thonet's design, 'An excellent application of a happy thought … they are not works of show, but practical furniture for daily use – they are simple, graceful, light and strong.'

While the technique certainly influenced the design, the style of Thonet's Vierzehner (as well as its less popular catalogue mates) is in fact a product of the taste for the Rococo that influenced Viennese craftsmen around 1840. In Thonet's case, clever and efficient development of technology subordinated this influence to the larger purpose of his furniture, whereas a similar influence acted as a deadening burden on his remarkable contemporary, Johann Heinrich Belter.

Belter (1804-63) was born in Hanover and trained as a cabinet-maker. In 1833 he emigrated to New York, where he set up in business in 1844. He may have been as ingenious as Thonet, but American taste compromised him. James Fenimore Cooper had written to Horatio Greenough that in America, 'You are in a country in which every man swaggers and talks; brains or no brains; taste or no taste. They are all ex-nato connoisseurs, politicians, religionists and every man's equal and all men's betters.'[8]

In such an environment, Belter could not simplify: he had to complicate. In 1847 he took out a patent for 'Machinery for Sawing Arabesque Chairs' and another in 1858 for the 'Improvement in the Method of Manufacturing Furniture'. This second patent related to the industrial application of

Left: William Morris was both good and original: what was good was not original, and what was original was not good. He did have a certain touch as a designer of flat pattern, but was otherwise a melancholy influence on British design.

lamination, but Belter did not make the technique explicit; he disguised it with grotesque and exaggerated carvings, sometimes politely known as rococo revival, but more nearly comparable to the louche decorations popular in New Orleans bordellos. The determination to suggest antiquity, even in so debased a form, calls to mind Henry James's remark about Nathaniel Hawthorne: 'It is only in a country where newness and change and brevity of tenure are the common substance of life, that the fact of one's ancestors having lived for a hundred and seventy years in a single spot would become an element of one's morality.'[9]

Belter's furniture and his 'parlour sets' were so popular that his name became a generic for any elaborately carved and upholstered furniture, however it was made. It dominated local taste until a remarkable woman called Elsie de Wolfe (1865-1950) had a better idea. Like Owen Jones, she believed that there were principles of taste, but while Jones perhaps overestimated the public's appetite for inspiration from history and nature, Mrs de Wolfe's great achievement was to establish her own aesthetic preferences as a saleable popular commodity, at least among a certain trashy, privileged class.

All the Looeys

While it would be a mistake to pursue the observation until it hardened into a theory, it is nevertheless irresistible to declare that, given historical perspective, interior design appears to be an almost exclusively homosexual activity (at least, from the supply side). In this respect, as in so many others, Elsie de Wolfe created the stereotype of the profession.

In a very curious way – and one that both parties would have repudiated – Mrs de Wolfe, an actress, predicted the tastes of the Modern Movement. The sensibility she confronted was created at least partially by the American influence of Eastlake's *Hints on Household Taste.* His popularity led to a style known laconically as 'Eastlake walnut'. In his splendid preface to the US edition of *Hints* (1872), Charles Perkins – one of Boston's own tastemakers – wrote: 'Nowhere is modern sterility in the invention of form so marked as in America ... We borrowed at second hand and do not pretend to have a national taste. We take our architectural forms from England, our fashions from Paris, the patterns of our manufacturers from all parts of the world, and make nothing really original.'

Perkins deplored the lack of expertise available to consumers. He argued that you have jurists to make judgments about law, theologians to settle theological disputes, but matters of taste left him waving his hands in

Above: The Tapestry Room of Kelmscott Manor, west Oxfordshire, the country home of William Morris from 1871 until his death in 1896.

exasperation in the void. The effect of desperation was made worse by the awfulness of interiors in the 1890s: according to an article in *The Decorator and Furnisher*, the ordinary customer would rather weigh a piece of furniture than consider it aesthetically. In her novel *The Custom of the Country* (1913), Edith Wharton describes a typical pre-de Wolfe interior:

'Mrs Spragg and her visitor were enthroned in two heavy gilt armchairs in one of the private drawing rooms of the Hotel Stentorian. The Spragg rooms were known as one of the Looey suites, and the drawing room walls, above their wainscoting of highly varnished mahogany, were hung with salmon-pink damask and adorned with oval portraits of Marie Antoinette and the Princess de Lamballe. In the centre of the florid carpet a gilt table with a top of Mexican onyx sustained a palm in a gilt basket tied with a pink bow. But for this ornament, and a copy of *The Hound of the Baskervilles,* which lay beside it, the room showed no traces of human use, and Mrs Spragg herself wore as complete an air of detachment as if she had been a wax figure in a shop window.'

Into this cluttered vacuum rushed Elsie de Wolfe, the very woman who introduced new American money to old French furniture. At one brief meeting in 1913 Henry Clay Frick bought a reputed $3million of French eighteenth-century furniture through Elsie de Wolfe, who was paid ten per cent commission as his adviser. A morning's work made her one of the richest independent women in New York and soon one of the most influential. Still today American collectors find it difficult to change the taste for French furniture implanted in the national psyche by de Wolfe's bravura shopping spree. Even the fabulously wealthy Getty Museum (which could afford to collect anything) steadily accumulates eighteenth-century French furniture on an industrial scale.

In the furniture columns of women's magazines in the late nineteenth century we can see the beginnings of popular neurosis, since methodically cultivated by the media. One contributor to the *Lady's Pictorial* answered letters privately for 7s 6d and would travel anywhere as a consultant on matters of taste for those suffering agonies of indecision for one guinea plus expenses. But Elsie de Wolfe brought it out of the closet. No longer anonymous, decoration became a branded commodity.

The chief, though never acknowledged, influence on Elsie de Wolfe was the book on interior design Edith Wharton wrote before her literary career really began. In 1897, at the age of thirty-five, Wharton published *The Decoration of Houses.* Her co-author was the architect Ogden Codman, also at the beginning of a career that in his case did not come to very much.

With the Knickerbocker hauteur of one who could count Rhinelanders and Schermerhorns among her immediate ancestors, Wharton encouraged her readers – goaded by aspirational photographs of chateaux and palazzi – to dispose of the parlour sets and the Eastlake walnut and start all over again.

The practical chintz lady

In *The Tastemakers: The Shaping of American Popular Taste* (1954), Russell Lynes described Elsie de Wolfe as:

'A woman of gusto, quick temper, good figure and striking but not pretty, appearance. She made a fetish of being unable to understand accounts and of always extracting from her business a whopping profit. She was sure of her tastes, all of which were expensive, and she was celebrated for standing on her head. She was an ardent devotee of calisthenics, raw vegetables and famous people, and if she was not the first woman decorator in America … she was certainly the first to turn her skill for the niceties of taste into a considerable fortune.'

The Colony Club at 120 Madison Avenue was her first major interior design commission, obtained through the intercession of the fashionable architect Stanford 'Stanny' White, junior partner of New York's McKim Mead & White, memorably described by Henry Adams in 1901 as the 'Moses, Aaron and Mahomet of the new rich'. De Wolfe's job of decorating White's 1905 design began with a voyage to England to buy Chippendale, mahogany candle-stands, chimneypieces and chintz, so that the ladies of the club could relax in an environment that was bright, but also suggestive of old European money.

The club's governing committee initially found it too plain and barren, but were eventually won over by the elegant practicality of the 'Chintz Lady', who made frills and heavy drapes and antimacassars a thing of the past. The Colony Club, and in particular its widely imitated trellis room, made Elsie de Wolfe famous and the club's far-flung membership took word of her triumphs back to Palm Beach, San Francisco and Chicago.

A popular concept of 'good taste' was necessary to her proselytising mission, which with skilful marriages, exercise and a cheerful sapphism became a lifetime's pastime. The term first appeared in her book *The House in Good Taste* (1915). (Ruskin and his contemporaries had discussed the opposite so much that 'bad taste' was a commonplace of popular journalism.) This book, together with her articles for the *Ladies' Home Journal* and other magazines, ushered into American homes a new form of dust-free brightness with the stirring motto, 'Plenty of optimism and white paint!'

Above: Fabric and wallpaper swatches for a 1920s 'withdrawing room' by Elsie de Wolfe, a cheerfully sapphic decorator and populariser of 'good taste'. Her aphorism: plenty of optimism and white paint!

The House in Good Taste was the climax of the attacks on 'bad taste', which was in fact the taste of the new middle classes for whom Thonet's elegant, inexpensive, mass-produced furniture promised so much. Mrs de Wolfe acquired a cultured persona on the flip side of ordinariness. She preferred the high places where she encouraged aesthetic defeatism, although her position relative to them was aspirational rather than occupational, as in Edith Wharton's case. She states her principles on page one:

'It is no longer possible, even to people of only faintly aesthetic tastes, to buy chairs merely to sit upon or a clock merely that it should tell the time. Home-makers are determined to have their houses, outside and in, correct according to the best standards.' And then, realising she has travelled too far too fast: 'But what are the best standards? Certainly not those of the useless, overcharged house of the average American millionaire.'

The de Wolfe theory, if such a practical doctrine may be so named, skilfully combined intelligent respect for the past ('our ancestors knew what they were doing'), with diluted proto-Modernism ('anything which works well, looks well'), and, most seductive of all to aspirational America, an anyone-can-do-it claim, perhaps intended as a slap in the face for the polite, but superior, Wharton caste: 'There never has been a house so bad that it couldn't be made over into something worthwhile.' This melded with a tempting introduction to creative self-expression: 'We must ... visualize our homes ... as individual expressions of ourselves.'

At her best, Elsie de Wolfe spoke and decorated with refreshing clarity. Listen first to what the *Lady* of 1894 expected to find on a table top: 'a Dresden china candelabra, an old Worcester pot-pourri bowl, one delicate figure, a pair of old paste shoe buckles in a faded velvet case and an antique miniature'. Now Mrs de Wolfe: 'When you have emptied the tables of rubbish so that you can put things on them at need ... your rooms will have meaning.'

Her terms of reference for the definition of taste were 'sham' or 'authenticity', bringing to light, yet again, the flirtation of taste with morals. But the authenticity she sought was not necessarily to be found in antiques alone; no woman of quality should trifle with fakes, but Elsie de Wolfe was, like Viollet-le-Duc, prepared to improve on the past if it was found wanting. She sounds very like the Modern Movement when she writes: 'We must learn to recognize suitability, simplicity and proportion, and apply our knowledge to our needs ... We can exert our common sense and decide whether a thing is suitable.'

The House in Good Taste was highly successful, going through numerous editions in the five years following publication. It was also influential; in 1926 John Wanamaker's store in Philadelphia even opened a department called 'Au Quatrième', where customers could have interior design counselling, and rival decorators set up in New York, including Ruby Ross Wood and Nancy McClelland, as well as abroad. In England, Syrie Maugham and the aristocratic Sibyl Colefax, driven into trade by the Crash of 1929, attracted particular attention, and for much the same reason: access to the press.

Elsie de Wolfe was one of the esoteric influences in the pages of American *Vogue* during the 1920s. She decorated the thirty-room apartment of its proprietor, Condé Nast, with crystal chandeliers, salmon pink moire curtains, Chien-Lung wallpaper and mirrored cornices in a style that was characterised as enthusiastic French. For his daughter Natica's bedroom, Elsie de Wolfe provided a design that was to be the first rebuff of her career and gave a sign of an imminent change in taste far more fundamental than the replacement of frills by *fauteuils*.

Natica Nast was a hard case. For her boudoir, de Wolfe proposed more mirrored cornices, eggshell taffeta curtains, fruitwood bergères, Aubusson carpet and a dressing table that had come from Versailles. Natica instead specified a modern dressing table which she had custom-made at a Third Avenue furniture store. An exchange, which included the deathless line, 'If it was good enough for Marie Antoinette it's good enough for you', did not prevent the rejection of the $10,000 piece.

Elsie de Wolfe did have a certain taste for simplicity and straightforwardness; in *Recipes for Successful Dining* (1934) she wrote, 'It is the humble dishes one comes back to with gusto and appreciation: the ragout, grilled sole, roast chicken, risotto dishes in which all the ingredients are of the first quality … where each dish tastes like what it is and is innocent of yellow sauces and pink and black stars, beloved of second-rate chefs.'

Her problem, if one can speak of so felicitous a life and career in such terms, was that she was unable to separate her theory of simplicity from her practice of laying on piles of glittering Looey with a trowel. Thus, dinner with Elsie might well be a humble grilled fish, but it was likely to be served by a butler on a gold lamé or *bourrette de soie* tablecloth, with bowls of white Mennecy filled with fruit and a centrepiece of salmon-coloured dahlias and zinnias with white Wedgwood china. You'd be lucky if you could even see the food.

Design as social insurance

Just days after the 1929 Wall Street Crash, the Museum of Modern Art (MoMA) opened in New York, offering a smarter European influence adapted for the Park Avenue palate. While Modernism in Europe was perceived as an intellectual and creative revolution handmade by Bolsheviks and whore-mongering, absinthe-soaked Bohemians, it was presented in Manhattan as a cleaned-up act, as if *Vogue* had styled the Bateau-Lavoir, or as if Lord & Taylor ran the Bauhaus. The rich social moths attracted by the bright flame of Modernism could scarcely be expected to identify with the political views of Picasso, even as they stashed away his canvases. They would not understand the social theory of Walter Gropius (despite his own dedication to Fordism), even though they gazed admiringly at Henry-Russell Hitchcock and Philip Johnson's seminal 1932 architecture exhibition at MoMA entitled *The International Style.*

When Gropius and his colleague Mies van der Rohe arrived from Germany, Tom Wolfe compared the scene to the stock movie reception of white gods arriving in the jungle in a crashed plane. Although by no means as radical as the name suggested – Abby Aldrich Rockefeller was one of the founders and the very rich are rarely subversive – MoMA changed American taste. Modernism became high fashion rather than revolution. Gropius, the social engineer, would have worried more about this change of purpose had he not become a Harvard professor with a house in Lincoln, Massachusetts, while Mies in Chicago became architectural adviser to corporate America.

Despite the sanitisation of Modernism, the elements of reform – so essential to its founders in Europe – remained inside the stylish carapace. MoMA's architecture and design department organised improving exhibitions, offering exemplary models of furniture to fill the vacuums of taste left when Elsie de Wolfe and all her Looeys were ousted.

In *The Personality of a House* (1930), Emily Post explains that Modernism is just another style: 'Its personality should express your personality, just as every gesture you make – or fail to make – expresses your gay ambition or your restraint, your old-fashioned conventions, your perplexing mystery, or your emancipated Modernism – whichever characteristics are typically yours.'

In 1937, one of the manufacturers in Grand Rapids, then the seat of the American furniture industry, introduced 'Swedish Modern' into his catalogue. The names Carl Malmsten or Bruno Mathsson were already known, but Swedish Modern was essentially vernacular and anonymous, rather than autograph. It was calm, gentle and unthreatening. Satirised as 'Moderna' by TH Robsjohn-Gibbings in his brilliant book *Homes of the Brave* (1954), Moderna was a 'benign and fruitful influence on the household arts of America'. Of course, 'Swedish' was a catch-all term that included Danish as well.

It is pleasant to think that this unobtrusive Modernism, which soon became integrated into what we understand as American, might have been esoterically influenced by a great oil painting. Vilhelm Hammershøi (1864-1916) specialised in quiet Danish interiors, so fine and sepulchral they make Vermeer or De Hooch look noisy. He painted *White Doors* in 1899. It is a perfect Scandinavian interior. The picture was soon acquired by Axel Otto Henriques and inherited by his daughter, Inge, in 1915. She became the wife of Sven Risom, an architect. Their son, Jens Risom (1916-2016), was the Danish-American designer whose Risom Chair of 1941 became a popular masterpiece of the Moderna sensibility. Risom kept and venerated the Hammershøi painting in his New Canaan, Connecticut, house until his death. With Eliot Noyes, Marcel Breuer and Philip Johnson all New Canaan residents, this quiet New England town became a taste incubator.

Another incubator, where Modernism in America was engineered to stimulate and satisfy the ambitions of the rich, was a modest building in the East 50s of Manhattan. Here, Philip Johnson created the Rockefeller Guest House (1950). It is in Midtown, in an area curiously known as Turtle Bay, but with artistic associations rather than aquatic ones. Peggy Guggenheim lived nearby in the 1960s, and Andy Warhol's Factory manufactured here.

The patron of this supremely austere brick, glass and steel jewel was Blanchette Ferry Hooker Rockefeller, wife of John D Rockefeller III. She served on MoMA boards and was an energetic proselytiser; the Guest House was an experimental lab where new art and new architecture were tested on patrons. It was a bubble of wealth and privilege where High Modernism – works by Giacometti, Robert Motherwell, Willem de Kooning and Clyfford Still, or chenille curtains by Anni Albers threaded with copper – could be shown to donors, Manhattan's gilded establishment and admiring visitors. It was where High Modernism could be demonstrated without any of the annoying impurities of everyday life.

Dishonest yellow
If in America, the acceptance of Modernism was a sort of approval insurance, in Britain, vestiges of social purpose clung to this sleek and

speeding bandwagon. While MoMA was a Narcissus pool for Knickerbocker social mountaineering using the art approach, Britain's Council of Industrial Design (COID) set about improving public taste.

In 1953, London's *Picture Post* ran a feature, the prototype of many to follow, showing two rooms decorated on the same budget, but to different effect. It reveals all the assumptions that the COID made about popular taste. They are like the beatitudes of popular Modernism:

> The furniture trade says people buy what they like; 'designers' say they should learn to like something else.
> One room is cream (called 'dishonest yellow'); the other is white.
> One choice of furniture is clumsy, dowdy (but admittedly comfortable); the other is richly coloured and takes up less space.
> One carpet is easy to clean (or easy to keep dirty) Autumn Leaves; the other has off-white Indian rugs and kilims.
> One has a crow-step sand-tiled fireplace; the other is a spare rectangle with matt-black tiles framed in mahogany.
> One has high-shine dark oak; the other a swivel-topped table in cherrywood and elm, with white-spotted tobacco-brown upholstery.
> One bookcase is walnut with semi-circular glass doors; the other has open adjustable shelves.
> One room has parchment shades on a central chandelier and a looming standard lamp; the other has articulated hanging lamps with Swedish red pleated shades and a plain metal desk lamp.

By such means were the ghosts of Italian, German and Swedish modern designs smuggled into a few English homes, but never into country houses. Here taste remained doggedly reactionary. In Evelyn Waugh's parody *A Handful of Dust* (1934), Mrs Beaver (clearly a version of the decorator Syrie Maugham) violates a Victorian morning room with chrome furniture and sheepskin mats.

That the Modern Movement never had much real influence on popular taste in America or Britain is clear from a cursory examination of Nancy Reagan's White House and the Duchess of York's wedding list.

Since 1961, when Jacqueline Kennedy set up the Fine Arts Committee at 1600 Pennsylvania Avenue, White House redecoration has provided interesting insights into the current American psyche. During President Reagan's first year in office in 1981, his wife Nancy spent nearly $1 million on interior design, which caused rather a stir at a time of federal budget cuts.

The work was done by Ted Graber (1920-2000), a decorator who revealed his nice sense of appropriateness in his preference for open-necked shirts in California and neckties when working on the East Coast. He was recommended to the Reagans by some of their show-business friends he had worked for in Beverly Hills.

The Graber style consisted of new Looey Says coffee tables, lots of colour coordination, framed family photographs and hotel palms; Chinese wallpaper, chintz and the general pastel ambience in Nancy's quarters of expensive nouvelle cuisine restaurants. Elsie de Wolfe might have been back from the dead and working in Washington.

Dorothy May 'Sister' Parish (1910-94), the Queen of American decorating, who decorated the White House private rooms during the Kennedy era, was commissioned to design the interiors of the Duke and Duchess of York's new house at Sunninghill. Following the ancient tradition adopted by the Kennedys and the Reagans, newly married or new incumbents have a strong and understandable desire to style their environment. The extraordinary thing here was that, while Sister Parish and her partner Albert Hadley had been recreating throughout the United States a pseudo-English style to please wealthy Connecticut matrons, this very style of over-stuffed, fussy, antiqued comfort had become so convincing an expression of Englishness that the Royal Family wanted to re-import it. Parish explained that: 'Our point of view is based very simply on the traditional values of quality, comfort, integrity of design and appropriate furniture.' Which is to say, olden days taste.

A designer called Kaki Hockersmith from Little Rock, Arkansas, worked for the Clintons during their White House years in 1993-2001. In the Oval Office you would have found a cast of Rodin's *The Thinker*. When she was First Lady, Hillary borrowed Kandinskys, de Koonings and Rothkos from national collections. And in The White House grounds beyond her private apartments, she saw to it that there were exhibitions by Isamu Noguchi, Alexander Calder and Georgia O'Keefe. In contrast, Barack Obama used to have a bowl of green apples.

Then again, the Clinton style was different to Trump's. In 1983, when he first occupied the triplex atop Trump Tower, Trump made his taste for Pharaonic interiors public. There is lots of gilt, marble, glass and chandeliers with a special emphasis on thrones and gold candy bowls, all of this

Right: The White House in the Kennedy era. Architect James Hoban designed the Yellow Oval Room as a private sitting room.

Above: The Linley Sambourne House in Kensington. It was in this cluttered glory hole, originally the home of the illustrator of *Punch*, that the influential Victorian Society was founded in 1958.

designed by Angelo Donghia who also worked on the SS *Norway* and for Grace Mirabella, then editor-in-chief of *Vogue*. Donghia was described by the *Detroit Times* as 'the Saint Laurent of sofas'. He died in 1985, but his website still shows that the surviving firm has a keen specialism in chandeliers. By contrast, the Clinton family home is an 1889 Dutch Colonial in Chappaqua.

The British Royal Family has a tradition of redistributing heirlooms as wedding presents. For their marriage in 1973, Princess Anne and Captain Mark Phillips received: a Chippendale desk from Prince Philip, a butler's table and a chest of drawers from the Duke of Gloucester, and a nest of tables from Prince Andrew. This hermetic, ritualised system tends to enforce a certain standard of taste by genetic drip. The context of all this real and imagined gentility, whether in the White House or in Kensington Palace, is the complete failure of Modernism to attract supporters other than fanatics. If you insist on heirlooms as status symbols, or seize on fake ones as caste marks, then it is inevitable that you will require 'period' decoration. Faced with a vacuum of taste, even presidents and princes of the blood have recourse only to hand-me-down interior design.

Buying your own furniture

Decorators everywhere turn to the eighteenth century. David Hicks (1929-98) was one of the first British interior designers to come to popular notice. He made a reputation in the 1950s for his daring use of colour, including the juxtaposition of orange and pink, skilfully reinterpreted eighteenth-century design with its strong colours and geometric patterns. At his own often-published house in Britwell Salome, Hicks achieved the desired 'mix'. You would have found modern light fittings in Palladian rooms, as well as the precious groupings of redundant objects that he called 'tablescapes'. In his book *David Hicks on Living – With Taste* (1968), Hicks explained: 'I have been accused of being dogmatic; I am. I would be useless to my clients if I were not.'

His estimation of his clients' opinions is clear and the remark is as revealing of them as it is of Hicks. Further on, he echoes Elsie de Wolfe: 'I have seen countless collections of incredibly valuable furniture, pictures and objets d'art where I longed to remove three quarters of the contents and inject something simple and fresh of today to give life and counterpoint to the individually beautiful pieces.'

David Hicks achieved a distinctive style that had some contemporary freshness, but not so much as to embarrass the historical buildings he usually worked in, to say nothing of the *arriviste* clients he tended to work for. But, compared with the dominant taste of the day, the Hicks style appeared almost revolutionary in its commitment to change.

The period since the Second World War, as most of the foregoing suggests, has been one of extraordinary nostalgia. Seeking value in a restless age, people look backwards as if the stability afforded by the dead and their buried reputations can provide certainty. Few looked further back than William Morris (1834-96) and, nowadays, he has crowds willing him back from the grave to send us all rushing headlong into a fake past. What Morris did not achieve in terms of turning the clock back himself, the guardians of his memory are doing in his name. To the decorator's repertoire gifted by Elsie de Wolfe to her followers, Morris's adherents added cultural inertia. The net result was inertia in interior design. Passing fads became permanent. The prospect of development promised by Thonet's mass production of furniture and so tentatively grasped by the Modernists was never realised.

The miserable tidemark of Morris's influence is smeared across every revival, every stick of reproduction tat, every conservationist, every 'antique' (even the eighteenth-century ones). That his significance has been exaggerated does not matter, even if the chief exaggerator was the pioneer Modernist historian, Nikolaus Pevsner (1902-83). The subtitle of Pevsner's *Pioneers of Modern Design* (1936) – *From William Morris to Walter Gropius* – suggests that the hairy stockbroker's son from Walthamstow was on the fast track to the twentieth century. Morris neither wanted nor deserved this role, but Pevsner misunderstood him because for a short while Morris's ideas about materials, techniques and morality seemed congruent with those of, say, Walter Gropius. To historians of Pevsner's bent the Whig interpretation of history was not to be questioned, and the mauve Victorian gloom of William Morris seemed necessarily to lead to a bright new century.

The English establishment did not take kindly to Morris being raised into the canon of Modernism. John Betjeman took revenge on the German-Jewish scholar (whom he saw as a coarse materialist) by calling him 'Plebsveneer'. Pevsner wanted to believe that Morris was a visionary with a workable social theory that only needed streamlining through the use of new materials for it to be transferred to the Weimar Republic (and Gropius spoke of his debt to Morris), whereas Betjeman and his cronies just shared his nostalgia for the olden days. Betjeman liked Modernism when it was exclusive, but not once it became the chosen style of creeping socialism.

Above: John Betjeman, poetaster, professional snob and voice of a divided nation. While modern architecture was an exclusive import he admired it; when it threatened social engineering he repudiated it. Betjeman's achievement was to turn English complacency and slovenliness into a minor art form.

This reaction is typically British. In certain quarters the view of Morris is still that he was a thinker of monumental stature, a guardian of values that remain relevant. The truth, of course, is somewhat different. Morris is easy to write about, even if his vast corpus of ponderous prose and thudding, limping verse is difficult to read. An inevitable product of his education at Marlborough, with its coarse mishmash of wistful antiquarianism, he inspired CP Snow's bitterly perceptive observation that the greater part of English 'traditions' have their origin in the second half of the nineteenth century.

Morris is admired by enthusiasts who share his reluctance, even his inability, to come to terms with modern life. His hatred of contemporary civilisation has been the most enduring part of his legacy. Although he was seventeen when the Great Exhibition opened in 1851 and therefore should have been old enough to understand Prince Albert's real purpose, he was not stimulated by industry, rather he recoiled from it. Unlike Albert, who saw the future as an indissoluble mixture of art and industry, Morris did not see the promise of technology, only the superficial dirt, only the divisions. Perhaps most importantly, he did not want to have his own life of wealth and privilege spoiled. He declared that 'we should do without coal' and revive the Middle Ages: an era in which his various repressed fantasies could take form.

Although revivalism has been a recurrent influence in Western civilisation, Morris's form of cultural regurgitation was different in that it was narrow, indulgent and sentimental. In his furniture he aped the vernacular. The books he published were not by modern authors, but by Chaucer. Not intended for an urban population hungry for education and delight, these were deluxe volumes for smug collectors, happy like Morris to be immersed in a selfish dream world.

Only in his paintings and graphic design did Morris achieve any originality. Morris's art was adolescent, but it had great power. With its gaudy eroticism, long-haired girls, constipated prose, bardic refrains, vegetarian colours, clumsy details and murky sensibilities, he provided his narrow public with an irresistible mixture of sex and nostalgia, made safe by historical reference.

In 1814, Friedrich Koenig's high-speed printing press was first used on the London *Times*; in 1866 Werner von Siemens demonstrated his first self-excited generator; in 1883 Daimler and Maybach produced the high-speed petrol engine and in 1893 Rudolf Diesel unveiled his 'rational heat engine'. Morris's contribution to the century of progress was to found the Society for the Protection of Ancient Buildings, an organisation that, as the prototype for all conservationist groups, was an important advance in the disease of nostalgia.

Sir Leslie Stephen (father of Virginia Woolf) once said, 'One thing is pretty certain; no one will ever want to revive the nineteenth century.' The influence of William Morris proved him wrong for, after the successful revival of the Georgians in the first half of the twentieth century, there was then enough historical space to revive the Victorians as well. In 1957, when the first effects of property speculation were being noticed in London, when new urban motorways were destroying their destinations, when JB Bunning's magnificent London Coal Exchange (opened by Prince Albert on 30 October 1849) had been made redundant by the post-war rationalisation of the industry, Anne Countess of Rosse, wife of the founder of the Georgian Group, gave a party in her home in Stafford Terrace (which once belonged to *Punch* illustrator Linley Sambourne) in order to launch a society dedicated to the preservation of nineteenth-century buildings. There were bloodlines all over the place. Among those present at the founding of the Victorian Society three months later were the decorator John Fowler and the poet John Betjeman (1906-84).

Although, according to Evelyn Waugh, Betjeman was a mere schoolboy doing brass rubbings while Sir Harold Acton was trying to revive the Victorian era during the 1920s, it was Betjeman's popularity as a public figure that helped make nostalgia so much a cult in contemporary Britain. While he poured scorn on most late-twentieth-century inventions, Betjeman was not prepared to disdain television in promulgating his aesthetic faith. Strange to say, in Betjeman we can trace the curious path of Modernism in British life and culture.

Queen Camilla's grandfather

Betjeman was attracted to Modernism because its first spokesman in Britain was an aesthete educated at Eton and King's College, Cambridge called Philip Morton Shand (1888-1960). Shand was a friend of Le Corbusier and Alvar Aalto and translator of Walter Gropius. Shand's granddaughter, Camilla, is now married to the Prince of Wales. From so sophisticated and cosmopolitan a source, Modernism seemed exciting and even elitist. Betjeman's *Ghastly Good Taste* (1933) in fact ends in praise of the Bauhaus, but this was an eclectic age when the *Architectural Review* published Georgian details alongside articles championing heliotherapy in International Style Swiss sanatoriums, Canadian grain silos and Soviet gymnasiums.

Above: The eighteenth-century Spencer House, in London, as restored by David Mlinaric. Mlinaric inherited John Fowler's reputation, and his fastidious and scholarly restorations have had a powerful influence on taste.

Indeed, for as long as Modernism was not a social threat, the English eclectic tradition encouraged it as an exotic creature. But as soon as it ceased to be a diversion for dilettantes, Betjeman and his followers dropped it like a proverbial hot potato. The Second World War was the turning point: just as Evelyn Waugh was moved to write his saccharine and sentimental novel *Brideshead Revisited* in response to the material and spiritual privations of 1939-45, so too James Richards, editor of the *Architectural Review* (for whom Betjeman was then working), was stimulated to write in 1946 a plausible, if rather sickly, panegyric about the suburbs. The title, *The Castles on the Ground*, alludes to what is usually said about the gentleman's home.

Shand also became disaffected with Modernism and instead took up the cultivation of endangered apple species. His last thoughts about modern architecture were expressed in a letter to Betjeman, which he wrote shortly before his death in 1960: 'I am haunted by a gnawing sense of guilt in having, in however minor and obscure degree, helped to bring about … a monster neither of us could have foreseen.'

To Betjeman and his circle, architecture was a pursuit comparable to birdwatching, having nothing to do with social purpose (except of a very conservative sort) and thus his artistic eclecticism and social snobbery soon got the upper hand in his febrile flirtation with the buildings of socialist realism. Betjeman was happiest when safe in a world of trains and buttered toast. He was always a conservationist, his dream-world doggerel was written to memorialise a genteel vision of a country that never really existed – except in the poet's imagination. He feared an 'England … all council houses and trunk roads and steel and glass factory blocks'.[10] And now with the Victorian Society there was a society to help him fantasise. It is true that Pevsner too had been in at the founding of the Victorian Society, but the great professor played a part because at first it seemed that any organisation dedicated to architecture must be admirable. What Pevsner really wanted was a *Forschungsinstitut*; what he got was a reactionary clique.

John Betjeman never wrote a serious book about architecture, but in his quirky television presentations he became its popular champion. He never wrote a decent poem, but became Poet Laureate. An apostate of Modernism, anti-intellectual, anti-serious, anti-Semitic and antiquarian, Betjeman was a quaint schoolmaster type who raised trivia to the status of a great national pursuit. He was the perfect topographer of the English soul. But the price of his persuasive, if rather smug, vision of all the nice things in the world – by which he meant brown garden walls, silvery frosty Sunday nights, a view of St Botolph's, a cup of tea, a sunny afternoon, a snooze, cigarettes and comfy chairs – was the loss of a positive view of the future which might be different to the cosy version of the past.

Betjeman defined and captured a certain middlebrow taste in Britain. His personal achievement at vicarage tea parties neatly complemented that of the National Trust at a national level. Only since 1945 has the National Trust been concerned with the preservation of houses. Originally, its founders – Octavia Hill, Robert Hunter and Canon Rawnsley – sought to preserve the countryside and coastline; its aim was to keep vile industry away and, more sensibly, in Octavia Hill's words, 'to provide open-air sitting rooms for the poor'.

The change in character of the National Trust from an amenity society to an antiquarian cult was, like so much else in modern Britain, made possible by the new tax structures imposed after the end of the First World War. The second National Trust Act of 1937, passed after years of lobbying by Lords Lothian and Zetland, allowed the owners of country houses to transfer their property and land to the National Trust, which, being a charity, did not have to pay taxes on them. The Trust would maintain historic buildings in perpetuity, while the owner's family continued to live in the property in exchange for agreeing to open it to the common people. Thus was the habit of visiting country houses born and a version of interior design based on an artificial reverence for the past was made public.

Under the administration of James Lees-Milne, the trust soon acquired a handsome portfolio of historic properties. Among the first were Blickling Hall, Cliveden, Polesden Lacey, Lacock Abbey, West Wycombe Park and Speke Hall. Many more were to follow and in this way a particular vision of Britain's heritage was imposed on popular taste.

The National Trust Country Houses Scheme set out to prove the assumption in Evelyn Waugh's comic novels that the past is always better. Each reveals a total disdain for theory, a distrust of the modern world. Waugh, who was born above a dairy in north London, even set himself up in his country house, Combe Florey, a case of life imitating art.

After the Second World War country house owners, who had mostly had their properties requisitioned between 1939 and 1945, had the opportunity to rethink the demands of the interior. They rethought and came to the same conclusions. John Fowler (1906-77) created the post-war country house interior very much according to principles of his own invention, and this became National Trust taste. His style of 'humble elegance' did not come cheap, particularly when his fastidious taste required sixteen different shades of white on one ceiling, or the lowering of an entire cornice by two inches to improve the proportions of a room.

Fowler's expensive shabby chic fixed a certain image of the 'quality' English interior. David Mlinaric replaced Fowler as the dominating influence on the National Trust and with this change historical accuracy replaced intuitive pastiche: a sign of the design professionalism that matched the ever-increasing status of the country house.

Yet some architects and designers who believe that the only responsible path is to explore contemporary possibilities have rebelled against this. As early as 1904 Richard Norman Shaw (1831-1912) would have none of it. In an essay in *The British Home of Today* he complained:

'The present day belief that good design consists of pattern – pattern repeated ad nauseam – is an outrage on good taste. A wallpaper should be a background pure and simple – that, and nothing else. The art teaching of today follows in the steps of William Morris, a great man who somehow delighted in glaring wallpapers. The kind of paper hanging that we need most of all is what I may describe … as the "tone" wallpaper.'

The aesthetic of a designer such as Dieter Rams – 'to me good design means as little design as possible' – derives from the declarations of humility taught by the Fathers of the Church. That less is more does not have to mean austere reductivism. In the modern world, with all its vulgar surplus and clutter, it represents a challenge that has as its objective not bland utilitarianism, but the thrill of refined, sensuous pleasure. It is far more difficult to make things easy than complicated. Mystification is simple; clarity is more demanding.

More is not only a bore, it runs against the strongest continuous element in European culture: a belief in progress validated by the fragile vision of perfectibility. The Thonet chair offered an idea of industrialised perfectibility, but in Britain and the United States the consumers with discretionary income preferred the heraldry of real or bogus pedigree.

Interior design is a business whose substance is a subterfuge; it derives its character from historical ignorance and its status from social fear. If the example of Thonet had been accepted, if there were more beautiful everyday things in the shops for fastidious people to buy, interior designers would be out of work. These pimps of taste flourish in the red-light district of culture.

Fashion Being and dressing

No one has ever taken very seriously the proposition that we are what we wear, but there is no doubt that we want it to appear to be so. At the height of the Depression, with shoeless waifs littering the streets of every major city, banking in chaos and manufacturing in decline, a Bohemian immigrant girl was reported saying 'After all, life is mostly what you wear', an apophthegm whose source, content and message nicely emphasise the richly charged language of clothes.[11]

When it comes to the meaning of things, there are no more powerful transmitters than clothes, those quasi-functional devices which, like an inverted fig leaf, put the heart of the matter in front of the skin. Ralph Lauren, whose business it has been to turn chain-store clothing into heraldry, said 'Clothing sets your taste; it's your outward expression, it's the first shot, it's what you say about yourself to the world.' But judging by appearances – a practice popularised but not originated by Oscar Wilde – exposes the contradiction that is central to fashion. Nothing is as crass and vulgar as instant classification according to hairstyle, clothing and footwear, yet it is an irresistible temptation and a cruelly accurate analytical form. In literature, from Laurence Sterne to Evelyn Waugh to Tom Wolfe, a sort of inheritor of an English satirical tradition, clothes are used to express character. In *The Bonfire of the Vanities* (1987), Wolfe assassinates all his characters with remorseless and sesquipedalian descriptions of what they are wearing: there is a professor in 'rotting tweeds' and all the black muggers wear Reebok trainers. Thus tweeds and trainers, to say nothing of their wearers, are categorised. That some critics have described Wolfe's laundry-list technique as malicious reveals its deadly accuracy in betraying taste and motivation.

Even in subsistence economies people rarely dress simply to avoid being naked. We think of our clothes as we think of our bodies: more so than other possessions, they are an extension of our self. We are grateful for any praise they excite and are dismayed if they cause disdain or indifference.

Clothes are a sort of theatre where the leading player – the self – is torn between function and decoration, protection and assertion, concealment

and display. This everyday drama reinforces the idea that clothes have a social and cultural function and as such are vital evidence in the study of aesthetic preference: what you wear is a matter of taste. And so, of course, is what you refuse to wear. Clothes have always been held to be the most explicit confessions of status, or distinction through decoration. That's why we know a Tom Wolfe hero is bound for a fall when we read he's wearing handmade shoes and a $1,800 suit. Equally, although perhaps less understandably, a man is morally suspect if his wife buys his trousers.

Clothes are so inflammatory that injunctions have existed since antiquity to moderate the power of dress to upset the status quo: there is a sort of politics to fashion. The purple border on a Roman senator's toga was wider than that of a Roman knight. Dress codes flourished towards the end of the Middle Ages as a means of buttressing the existing social estates at a time when the feudal nobility felt threatened by the emerging bourgeoisie, a class becoming increasingly able to articulate its position by visual means (and nowadays dedicated to the practice). Ostentatious dress was repeatedly cited as a characteristic of the worldly city life (think of the strictures of Savonarola) and met with disapproval from austere churchmen. Of course, the considerable increase in ordinances on the subject of immodest dress in the early modern period suggests a concomitant increase in their violation.

In Renaissance Italy, officials upbraided citizens for wearing ermine instead of sackcloth, buttons instead of studs. Such regulations in matters of taste were intended to enforce authority during periods of social change. The problem of sustaining rank was especially acute in England during the reign of Elizabeth I, who in 1597 passed a decree limiting silk embroidery and the general use of velvet to women who were married to knights, or above – the equivalent today of designer labels being restricted by statute to the wives of senior management. The vested interests of those most concerned to preserve the visible distinctions of class are described in Philip Stubbes' *The Anatomie of Abuses* (1583). On the one hand he cautions against 'the pride of apparel', which he felt was a cause of wickedness and sin, while on the other he argues for strict demarcations in dress so that one class might have its authority over another reinforced by visual means.

Left: Richard Sackville, third Earl of Dorset, by Isaac Oliver (1616). Dorset was a vainglorious spendthrift. Here the painter uses eye-wateringly expensive lapis lazuli for the earl's breeches, spangled with golden moons and suns.

Sumptuary laws expose the intimate bond between clothes and social competition, the conspicuously dressed *arriviste* always being a threat to the establishment. Imitation and emulation, the driving forces in fashion, compelled first the aristocracy and then the bourgeoisie to resort to increasingly elaborate devices to maintain the differentials upon which a comfortable and familiar social order depends. In those most conservative callings, the law, church and universities, ancient dress codes are frozen and the requirement still exists to exert authority by symbolic means.

There is now a free market in the consumption of clothes: an actress dresses as sumptuously as a princess and self-made businessmen can purchase a version of respectability at outfitters who once specialised in cladding gentlefolk. The messages are less clear, but not less significant. The first person to distance himself from this primal phenomenon in modern consumerism and report on it was Thorstein Veblen (1857-1929), whose celebrated dissection of the 'pecuniary canons of taste' neatly described how clothes operate as signals of wealth and lifestyle. His famous expression 'conspicuous consumption' explained the impulse to astonish and impress through costly ornaments. Inspired by sartorial devices such as slashing in order to reveal gorgeous undergarments, Veblen went on to explain that purchasing power is a crude but effective measure of sumptuousness and therefore of *intention.*

Teasing exhibitionism can be dramatic, but redundancy is a more subtle and effective means of communicating authority: clothes that inhibit physical exertion, such as high-heeled shoes, denote status because they suggest a privileged life of selective idleness. Similarly, clothes made from astonishingly impractical materials, such as linen, silk and cashmere, demonstrate powerfully an hauteur about maintenance and depreciation in the wardrobe. In cultures with different values, easy-care fabrics would quite properly be considered luxurious.

But the functionally redundant high-heeled shoe is more than a symbol of feminine inertia; it is, as Freud knew, a powerful sexual fetish. Discussing the merits of the high heel, the *Tatler* reported David Bailey as saying, 'It means girls can't run away from me.' This characteristic of high-heeled shoes has in itself made them victims of inertia in the fast-moving world of fashion. They are enduringly erotic. To find out why, you should perhaps think first of flat shoes. Summon up an image of an espadrille: salt-bleached, unravelling rope sole, rucked down at heel. The woman wearing it has a mid-calf denim skirt, a T-shirt and beads, a big, loose and toothy grin and straw-blonde hair, greying slightly. Swedish. Very nice in its way, but the style is domestic and maternal, fundamentally practical. It is the flagrant lack of practicality that makes high-heeled shoes so fascinating: in terms of static mechanics they induce a sort of insecurity, which some find titillating. If a woman wears a high-heeled shoe it changes the apparent musculature of the leg so that you get an effect of twanging sinew, of tension needing to be released. Her bottom sticks out like an offering. At the same time, the lofty perch is an expression of vulnerability, she is effectively hobbled and unable to escape. There is something arousing about this declaration that she is prepared to sacrifice function for form. A glossy finish enhances the effect: there is simply no knowing what a girl who offers herself in this way might do in pursuit of superficial pleasure.

Ultimately, it is the ironic tension between form and function and material that gives the high-heeled shoe its meaning. It is the same with a silk brassiere. The chosen material is so at odds with the task in hand: vacuum-bonded honeycomb composite would be a more effective way of containing the brave vibration of a bust. A silk bra shows you don't care and that you are a slave to appearances and to the senses: slavery, sense and appearance – the three sum up high-heeled shoes and, indeed, the erotic element in clothing.

Ever since a woman first wore a waist string (and little else), the protective function of clothing has been secondary to its ornamental purpose. A waist string holding up a kind of small apron front and rear draws yet more attention to the sexual parts, and hence is an extension rather than a diminution of the original erotic purpose. Even in cold climates, coloured body drawings, which have no thermal advantage against the weather, were evidently as highly regarded as clothes of more obviously functional character. Until relatively recently, Aboriginal Australians only wore decorative ornaments and went quite naked even in the coldest weather, preferring to clasp a glowing log for warmth. In Tasmania, the Aboriginals choose to relax by standing on one foot, further proof – if proof were needed – that contemporary European attitudes to comfort and to function are themselves mere matters of preference – of taste.

The very notion of 'modesty' in dress is culturally specific and when provoked reveals a deep ambivalence, rooted in its correlation with desire.

Overleaf: *Gabrielle d'Estrées et une de ses sœurs* (1594) is now one of the most popular pictures in the Louvre, but when it hung in the Paris Prefecture of Police it was covered by a curtain.

Above: The high heel is the most obvious expression of a sexual disdain for function in dress: a dedication to effect rather than use suggests a sensitive interest in pleasure, which is highly erotic.

The cosmetic tycoon Charles Revson had a beguiling little theory about the psychology of clothes and make-up: 'Women all hope they get laid', he said. Quoting this approvingly, fashion entrepreneur Les Wexner explained: 'Uptight women stockbrokers will put on a G-string when they get home.'

If the ostensible aim of modesty is to combat desire, the effect is often the opposite, as the frequency of nun imagery in pornography suggests. Concealment stimulates the imagination to a degree that exposure cannot hope to emulate. This game between prudery and style is a stimulus to fashion, and fashion is nothing more than clothing at work in the marketplace.

As the sexuality of the female body is more diffused than the male's, exposure of one part customarily concealed helps focus attention. Décolletage first appeared during the fifteenth century and since then the emphasis of fashion has shifted from one erogenous zone to another. Taking a synoptic look at fashion, men appear to be able to absorb only one zone at a time, rather as it is said to be impossible to feel pain in two places simultaneously. Thus fashion draws attention first to this and then to that, whether by exposing, concealing, emphasising, exaggerating or distorting.

The varying threshold of embarrassment and the movable limits of modesty characterise civilisation in its erratic progress. During the Middle Ages, indignation could be aroused by the wearing of pointed shoes, whose symbolism was made more explicit by the attachment of a phallus to one foot (perhaps an unconscious expression of the idea, untested by science and all the stronger for it, that the foot and the penis are related in terms of size, if not function). Similarly, when plunging necklines of the sixteenth century left breasts completely exposed, codpieces became less pronounced.

Like all forms of behaviour, manners in dress started as innovative fashions and through custom evolved to become a part of the social repertoire. Wherever codes govern dress, the partnership of taboo and desire lurks concealed. Modesty, we have seen, is simply a matter of taste. It is not natural and is meaningless outside a specific cultural context. Indian women were once shocked by Western women wearing hats, a practice felt to be a male prerogative.

In seventeenth-century Massachusetts, dress was part of a morality of taste inspired by a religion that abhorred ceremony, ritual and delight. It was, after all, said of the Puritans that they condemned bear-baiting not so much because it caused misery for the bear but more because it gave pleasure to the audience. Puritan clothes were designed to separate individuals from their own bodies, to say nothing of the bodies of others. Not for the first time these regulations had their origin in notions of modesty that benefited the ruling class or caste. While taboos restrict conscious behaviour, they stimulate desire in the unconscious. Today, fashion thrives on a similarly ambivalent relationship between convention and outrage.

The status of artists, beauty itself, female desirability and even posture and gait are aesthetic preferences, rather than absolutes. Even sickness and health are influenced by fashion, which, in turn, is influenced by fashionable disorders. The early Victorian enthusiasm for Romantic melancholy – think of Joachim's *Frei aber Einsam* – produced widespread and modish invalidism. Extraordinary numbers of young people went into decline and died before maturity, a particularly ironic case of life imitating art.

Tight lacing may or may not have been a predisposing cause, but women were certainly prepared to go to peculiar lengths to achieve a fashionable appearance of delicacy and fragility. Drinking vinegar and reading all night were known to achieve the desired pallor and the longed-for rings under eyes whose pupils were often dilated by belladonna. Gustave Flaubert's account of his sister's wake is shocking evidence of this taste for implied and real putrefaction.[12]

At about the same time, such fashionable ladies as there were in La Corrèze, in France, crowded into Tulle's courtroom to experience the stench from Lafarge's guts after his murder. For a moment in the nineteenth century, the world à la mode acted as if it had been briefly reprieved from the grave and was about to return to it.

The Romantic preference for yellow make-up and other manifestations of putridity was a reaction to the aristocratic Restoration taste for pink and white facial designs. Lady Wishfort in William Congreve's *The Way of the World* (1700) had 'cracks discernible in the white vernish'. This aesthetic was influenced by the rose and the lily, the flowers of chivalry, which had medieval origins. During the late Middle Ages, cosmetics began to appear in court circles and the quality of looking glasses improved. For the first time since Imperial Rome, portraiture was revived, although curiously, fashions in cosmetics soon drove the female – not long released from the veil – back into the anonymity of the stereotype.

It is a measure of the power of art over nature that we now perceive the invented formula of pink and white faces to be 'natural'. The first Queen

Right: Coco Chanel with Duke Laurino of Rome on the Venice Lido. Paul Poiret described Chanel's elegantly restrained style as 'misérabilisme de luxe'.

Elizabeth was addicted to ceruse, a compound of white lead and vinegar used to maintain virginal whiteness. Freckles were eradicated by sublimates of mercury. In pursuit of an ideal, her majesty's contemporaries might use Spanish hair pads, false hips, iron busks, panniers and high heels. In so manipulating human form, subjects were vulnerable to the charge of practising witchcraft.

After the eccentricities of later Romanticism, respectable women did not use cosmetics until the twentieth century. Pompadour's marmoreal complexion had already contributed to the middle-class notion that it was aristocratic to be white and the extraordinary cult of elegant cleanliness, described by Étienne Tourtelle in his *Elements d'hygiène* (1797) and the Comtesse de Bradi in her *Du savoir-vivre en France au XIXème siècle* (1838).

Public hygiene was the exercise in favour of the olfactory sense that lessons in taste, from Henry Cole and others, were to the visual. Just as persuading the workers to wash was believed to enhance their wisdom, so persuading them to prefer one sort of design was expected to do the same. Both are expressions of the values being forged for the middle classes in the various workshops of the world. The taste developed for cleansing the skin, rather than disguising it, and the pores were to be aired rather than clogged (but bathing itself was to be treated with caution).[13]

In the twentieth century, another form of facial coloration inspired by confused ideas of healthfulness, the suntan, became fashionable. Although related to the Victorian vogue for sea-bathing, the idea that tanned skin is attractive goes back no further than the 1920s, when pseudo-scientific theories of heliotherapy were developed by mad doctors in Swiss and German clinics. Heliotherapy went hand in hand with nudism, Modernist tea parties, the International Style in architecture and youth movements. Coco Chanel, frolicking with her beau the Duke of Westminster on the Côte d'Azur, made the suntan chic, which elevated it from a ragbag of crypto-fascist ideas to a high fashion statement. Evelyn Waugh's Gilbert Pinfold hated suntans as much as he despised Picasso, plastic and jazz.

Although the Côte d'Azur was christened by an obscure Burgundian poet, Stéphen Liégeard (after his birthplace, the Côte d'Or), the English made it a tourist destination. Lord Brougham was trapped in Cannes during the cholera outbreak of 1834 and acquired a liking for the area. Soon taken up by the fashionable, the Riviera's English patrimony is commemorated in the local names: Promenade des Anglais, Hôtel Carlton, and l'avenue du Capitaine Scott. The cult of the Mediterranean and its luscious brown skins burst over Britain with special force in the 1950s, at a time when DH Lawrence's books, with their frequent Mediterranean focus, were becoming popular.

BBB: bronzage de Brigitte Bardot

Intellectual monthlies such as *Encounter* often contained articles by latter-day Byrons, their skin the colour of a nicotine stain. Languishing in Ibiza or Capri, as they struggled to finish yet another fifteen-shilling novel, they mused wistfully about the beatniks on the ferry. The image was given extra force by Brigitte Bardot, whose first film, *Et Dieu créa la femme* (1956), vindicated not only her savage potency as a symbol of amoral sexuality, but also the attractiveness of suntans.

The questionable benefits to health of permanently tanned skin were successfully promoted and reinforced by films and advertisements, to say nothing of the perennial nut-brown President Kennedy. A tanned complexion is still read as an unmistakable sign of youth and vitality, and even the proletarianisation of Mediterranean travel has failed to diminish the allure of the tan. One hundred years ago it would have been considered impolite; two hundred years ago, repulsive. Edward Gibbon was fat, pale and proud of it. We are too conditioned in regarding prevailing conventions as necessarily desirable to recognise them as products of taste not of science.

Fashion is primitive in its insistence on exhibitionism, which withers in isolation. The catwalk fashion show with its incandescent hype is its apotheosis. A ritualised gathering of connoisseurs and the spoilt at a spot-lit parade of snazzy pulchritude, it is an industrialised version of the pagan festivals of renewal. At the end of each seasonal display, the fashion priesthood is enjoined to carry news of the omens to the masses.

In his book *Système de la mode* (1967), Roland Barthes showed how the rhetoric of fashion disguises the inherent contradiction of creating absolutes, only to discard them as *passé* after a predictable period of time has elapsed. The journalist or the copywriter blurs memories of the immediate past by discrediting the language that justified last season's style, while simultaneously embracing this year's models with enthusiasm.

Fashion is the most intense expression of the phenomenon of neomania, which has grown ever since the birth of capitalism. Neomania assumes that purchasing the new is the same as acquiring value. Adopting bogus algebraic formulae to dissect the tropes of the fashion writer's prose, Barthes describes the role of accelerators whose task it is to sustain

DANDY'S TOILETTE.

fashion by precipitating the renewal of clothing. If the purchase of a new garment coincides with the wearing out of an old one, then obviously there is no fashion. If a garment is worn beyond the moment of its natural replacement, there is pauperisation. Fashion flourishes on surplus, when someone buys more than he or she needs. In the motor industry this was known as planned obsolescence, or, more charitably, the dynamic economy. The more the rhythm of purchase dominates the rhythm of dilapidation, the stronger the submission to fashionable tastes.

Magazines suggest that fashion thrives on confusion and arbitrary change; their rhetoric is highly stylised, a selectively gushing narrative which defines its role in the marketplace. But if fashion is unpredictable and anarchic up close, it appears more regular from afar – distance lends order to the view. Women's fashions are subject to long-term cyclical variation, and by measuring certain parameters such as the width of the waist over a century it can be shown that major oscillations in fashion occur at a rate of about once a century, although perhaps with increasing frequency.

This observation was irresistibly attractive to determinists wanting to reconcile the great tides of history with the little eddies of fashion. Thus, it has been said that France, from just before the Revolution to the aftermath of the Napoleonic Wars, saw agitations in the wardrobe as complete and exciting as those on the national stage. Similarly, the peaceful and prosperous reign of Queen Victoria witnessed decades of subfusc tranquillity in dress.

The *bals publics* of the Directoire period offer tempting evidence that vast generic causes in history do in fact have minute specific effects. Emancipated Parisians celebrated their survival and their freedom at the Bal des Victoires in the Hôtel Richelieu. They dressed for the party by cutting their hair short at the nape of the neck as if in preparation for the guillotine and they wore a thin ribbon as if to indicate the cut of the blade. Friends were greeted with a sharp movement of the head, in imitation of the victim's spasm under the knife. Modelled on Aspasia, dancers with naked arms and breasts wore transparent draperies below which, it was said, would scarcely further offend prudes if they were removed in their entirety.

No doubt there was an element of relief in this licentious display, but it is ironic that the austere Neoclassical standards of the revolution only

Left: Dandies misunderstood (c.1800). The matter of success in being and dressing must be nicely judged. Lord Chesterfield wrote to his son, 'Never be the first or the last in fashion'.

achieved form when the ideals of Republican virtue had given way to a great deal of shameless hedonism. Attempts at imitating classical civilisation by aping classical dress were fascinating, but not contagious. The same spirit fired *les Barbus*, bearded classicising men contemporary with the beautiful, patrician paintings of Jacques-Louis David, but with less to offer history. The failure of these particular experiments in dress inspired leaders of fashion to seek democratic models that were nearer home in terms of both time and space.

English liberty and therefore English fashion were soon considered worthy of emulation. The early decline of the influence of the Court in English life had a profound effect on life and manners, particularly when compared with the French. While sun kings radiated and courtiers sunbathed, decentralised English society encouraged the cult of the independent amateur. The idle periwigs and indulgent rouge of the courtier contrasted with the stout boots and the coarse cloth of the country gentleman. Functional influences created new styles, which soon became stereotypes: the English country gentleman cut away the skirts at the front of his jacket to make it easier to mount and ride a horse. Crowns of hats rose to provide surer protection against falls. The button-down collar reflects the polo player's requirement that his collar does not flap in his face. No areas of human activity have shaped fashion so much as sport and 'politics'.

The end of the Terror in France allowed émigrés to return and they brought with them a taste for English modes and manners. As the final flourish of eighteenth-century artificiality died, a new cult of the dandy emerged. Dandyism was not a style, but an attitude, based on early attempts to codify the modern phenomenon of the 'gentleman'. Beau Brummell, despite his personal notoriety, emphasised that the essence of dandyism was not to be conspicuous. Lord Chesterfield wrote in 1745: 'Dress is a very foolish thing; and yet it is a very foolish thing for a man not to be well-dressed.'

Without heat and full of melancholy
Dandies developed this notion into a language of objects, regarding dress as an exquisite means of expressing an assumed superiority of character.

Right: Oscar Wilde (1854-1900), dressed down for the summer holidays, c.1893.

Thus the dandy played an important part in defining modern consciousness – we are all nowadays, to an extent, dandies. Charles Baudelaire noted in 1836:

'Dandyism appears especially in transitory periods when democracy is not yet all powerful, and when aristocracy is only partially unsettled and depreciated … Dandyism is a setting sun; like the star in its decline, it is superb, without heat and full of melancholy.'

Dandyism was an episode in the development of middle-class taste and while, as Baudelaire realised, in cult terms it was historically specific, it donated something to the emerging bourgeois personality that seems to be ineradicable. By the late-nineteenth century the dandy had developed into something extreme, characterised by more than just an attitude to clothes. Oscar Wilde epitomised it, and was described by George Macmillan as 'aesthetic to the last degree, passionately fond of secondary colours, low tones, Morris papers, and capable of talking a good deal of nonsense thereupon, but for all that a very sensible, well-informed and charming man.'[14]

Wilde's dandyism was, of course, a form of revenge on the bourgeoisie. Far from presaging a classless society, the decline of old aristocratic mores gave rise to yet more intricate codes of behaviour – this time restricted to and developed by the middle classes. Simplicity and appropriateness were the guiding principles of a doctrine that clothed the middle-class male in a variety of uniforms. In a conformist age, the only available distinction was the subtle one of the cut of a good tailor. The creation of the well-dressed English gentleman was a device to carry the burden of a nation translating itself from centuries of conquering into a future of trading and decline.[15]

The style of the gentleman spread, with the British Empire, across the world. Even in the tropics, black silk hats and frock coats were aped. In Vienna at the turn of the century a curious mix of Anglophilia and incipient Modernism produced an intense admiration for the English gentleman's wardrobe, as if John Buchan's Richard Hannay had read Freud. No aspect of daily life was too banal for Adolf Loos's system of aesthetics: to him, good manners in dress, as in architecture and design, depended on the absence of ornament and functional appropriateness. In *Das Andere* (1903), Loos attempted, among the aromatic vapours of Viennese decadence, a systematic analysis of everyday life. Loos execrated ornament with all the vigour that Freud had shown in excluding from his own vision of the soul every device that the nineteenth century had used to camouflage its primitive mechanisms.

Like the doyennes of American interior decoration, in the first edition Loos even undertook to answer readers' enquiries on the subject of dress.

'How should one dress? Fashionably. When is one fashionably dressed? When you draw least attention to yourself. I do not draw attention to myself. I travel to Timbuctoo or Kratzenkirchen. There everybody stares at me. Because there I draw attention to myself. A great deal. So I have to make a modification. You are fashionably dressed when you do not draw attention to yourself in the centre of Western culture on a particular occasion. It is afternoon and I am happy that I do not draw attention to myself in my grey striped trousers, my frock coat and my top hat. I stroll about Hyde Park. Stroll about and suddenly find myself in Whitechapel. And again I draw a great deal of attention to myself. I must make another modification. You are only fashionably dressed, when in the centre of a specific culture on a particular occasion in the best society, you do not draw attention to yourself.'

Loos's cult of the gentleman can be compared to Le Corbusier's passion for the *objet-type* in revealing a taste for conformism. The stagnation of the male wardrobe was influenced by the determined routines of the bank manager and the civil servant; any impulse for decoration and display was transferred to the dress of women, which, in the early years of the twentieth century, began to demonstrate an extraordinary variability in matters of taste.

The Victorian idea of the sombre conventional gentleman had its mirror image in the Victorian idea of femininity, which depended on what are nowadays regarded as dubious notions, such as helplessness, pliancy, weakness and dependency. A reduction in the volume of erotic signals served only to enhance the value of those actually emitted. The wardrobe enforced this, turning modesty into a subtle erotic language. Chastely attired during the day, a nocturnal décolletage demonstrated the rhythmic tension between prudery and prurience. Day or night, tight lacing and corsetry and huge skirts constrained movement and independence.

In this fashion system there was some room for change, but an innovation like the crinoline, which was momentarily liberating, was soon turned into another impediment. Designed to replace the layers of padded petticoats used to create an absurd version of the desired female shape, the crinoline was a bell-shaped metal construction (whose fabrication reflected other Victorian achievements in engineering) within which women's legs could move freely for the first time in centuries. But it soon grew to exaggerated and restrictive proportions. Heaving and swaying with

every bodily movement, it represented both the theory and the practice of the unapproachable, unavailable woman.

Function is a matter of taste

The popularity of crinolines is powerful evidence of the taste for images. At the same time, the cult of Byron and the French conquest of Algiers had made Zouave trousers familiar in countless engravings and popular paintings. In New York in the 1840s, Amelia Bloomer added a radical and functional element to this fashion with her emancipated baggy trousers, designed to combine practicality with an alternative image of femininity. Bloomers were only the first and most famous attempt to reform clothing.

Although many gestures in fashion have had a functional origin, a reappraisal of clothing on technical grounds had to wait upon the moral certainties and technical ingenuity (and not a little quackery) of the later nineteenth century. For reasons we have seen, dress is much more than mere function, and disposing of the weight of custom and practice in favour of technical norms required a revolution in values, which despite the zeal of the reformers was not – and is still not – forthcoming.

As early as 1834 Andrew Combe had published his *Principles of Physiology* in which, for the preservation of health, he argued for the development of physical education to promote clothing that was 'artistic, hygienic and rational'. There was obviously a latent demand, because fourteen editions appeared in less than twenty years. Combe was in the scientific vanguard of dress reform, being particularly exercised about the maintenance of body temperature and the condition of the skin. His anxieties focused on tight bodices:

'Not only is the insensible perspiration injudiciously and hurtfully confined, but that free play between the dress and the skin, which is so beneficial in gently stimulating the latter by friction at every movement of the body, is altogether prevented, so that the action of the cutaneous nerves and vessels, and consequently the heat generated are rendered less than what would result from the same dress worn more loosely.'

From the Goncourts to Flaubert, George Sand to Gaston Leroux, remembrance of smell has been used as a literary device. This is perhaps not unrelated to the popularity of perspiration as a technical subject during the same period. Reformers and sanitarians, dedicated to the proposition that wool was better close to the skin, were faced with the battle of convincing the public to abandon 'fashion' for the sake of their health. South Kensington's International Health Exhibition of 1884 was the epiphany of the movement. EW Godwin (1833-86), the progressive English architect-designer, gave a lecture on 'Dress and Its Relation to Health and Climate', claiming that:

'As Architecture is the art and science of building, so Dress is the art and science of clothing. To construct and decorate a covering for the human body that shall be beautiful and healthy is as important as to build a shelter for when so covered that shall be beautiful and healthy ... Beauty without health is incomplete. Health can never be perfect so long as your eye is troubled with ugliness.'

Perhaps the most remarkable exhibitor was Gustav Jaeger (1832-1917), a professor of zoology and physiology at Stuttgart University and an expert on confusing morality with taste. George Bernard Shaw, who was one of his followers, had remarked that 'good taste' was another expression for moral cowardice. His own point of view was, of course, in itself an expression of taste: to Shaw, the major challenge of the era was to establish a simple and rational way of life.

Shaw was a fringe member of the health and common-sense lobby. Like Mrs Bloomer, the lobby was driven by a taste for simplicity that was entirely original in Western culture and found expression in many different areas of life, clothing being only the most obvious. Into this reformist milieu came the astonishing Dr Jaeger with his book *Health Culture* (1884) arguing that animal fibre is healthier than vegetable material because it facilitated – he did not say how – the exhaust of noxious bodily vapours. His own best advertisement, Jaeger claimed that wearing wool (as opposed to, say, silk, which he stigmatised as the excreta of worms) had cured him of obesity, haemorrhoids and indigestion.

The demands made on his followers were substantial: the 'Woolleners' wore specially designed wool hats and digital socks. Dr Jaeger was discovered by Lewis Tomalin, a London accountant whose wife had taught him German. Tomalin became such an effective publicist of Jaeger's theories that in October 1884 the *Times* published a leader on 'Dr Jaeger's Sanitary

Right: Dr Jaeger's obsession with humours and with fresh air anticipated mid-twentieth-century fads for sunbathing and power walking.

MEN'S NORMAL NIGHT SHIRTS,

GRAY NATURAL WOOL, VERY SOFT.

Probably no garment of Dr. Jaeger's invention conduces more to health than this. As the plate indicates, they are double over the chest, and open only on the shoulder, thus affording *warmth to the vital organs in case of exposure at night*. They cover body and limbs with a soft, delicate texture of pure, undyed wool, than which nothing can be more healthy or agreeable.

Those who suffer from *neuralgic* or *rheumatic pains* in the knee joints or elsewhere, when subjected to contact with linen or cotton sheets, will find entire relief by using these garments.

☞ When ordering, give length of sleeve from middle of back to wrist.

Sizes (Chest)....Inches..36	38	40	42	44	46	48	50	52
Quality K............... 3 50	3 75	4 00	4 25	4 50	4 75	5 00	5 50	6 00
" B............... 3 75	4 00	4 25	4 50	4 75	5 00	5 25	5 75	6 25

See samples of material on page 15.

Above: Oregon lumberjacks wearing jeans in the 1880s. While fashion has traditionally been inspired by sport or politics, in the twentieth century leisure clothes were inspired by proletarian workwear.

Woollen System'. What started as a private hobby became a cult, and the cult soon became a business when Tomalin bought the machinery to manufacture Jaeger's patent knits as well as the licence to use the name commercially. Significantly, one of Tomalin's closest friends was the furniture-maker Sir Ambrose Heal, whose own designs were an expression in cabinetwork of the same simple, healthful ideas that inspired Jaeger and his followers.

Bicycling might never have had such an impact on the taste in women's clothes had it not been taken up by the same fashionable set who accepted the theories of Dr Jaeger. At first this most functional of devices was not treated functionally, but rather as an entertainment. Servants would cycle to parks where on arrival the carriage trade would dismount from their broughams and phaetons and take up the boneshakers for exhilarating, futile sport. The pantaloons necessary for safe and efficient operation of a bicycle were denounced as shameless, but the women who wore them demonstrated very neatly that taste and practicality could on occasions be united.

The paradox of restricting fashion by reason lies in the susceptibility of the latter to the former. The Victorian watchwords 'artistic, rational and hygienic' are not so much akin to the Vitruvian virtues of commodity, firmness and delight as to advertising's popular trinity: comfort, freedom and convenience. In the same way, the many religious prescriptions relating to washing, for example, show that ideas about cleanliness are also culturally conditioned, which is to say, they are matters of taste. Appeals to higher authorities in order to validate temporary aesthetic preferences, always fail to acknowledge that those very authorities are selected on the basis of local cultural preoccupations.

Bleu de travail

In nearly two centuries of mass-market consumerism there has been a curiously persistent taste for the affectation of working men's clothes. Once upon a time tough trousers with lots of utilitarian pockets made of *serge de Nîmes* were popular among Californian prospectors of the '49 gold rush, presumably for entirely rational reasons. Since then, these 'denims' have undergone a well-rehearsed – and latterly orchestrated – series of transformations from symbol of rebellion to symbol of status. No garment illustrates the fallacious nature of neutrality in dress so much as jeans: dressing down is as conspicuous a gesture as dressing up. Alan Hare, the English proprietor of Château Latour, the first growth claret, affected to wear French workmen's trousers with his very English ties.

From about 1936, when Levi Strauss & Co became self-conscious of its own image and inserted the distinctive red tab on the back pocket, jeans have been more than workaday. In *The Wild One* (1953) and in *Rebel Without a Cause* (1955), first Marlon Brando and then James Dean made jeans into symbols of alienation whose power was not diminished, but rather enhanced, by their familiarity and accessibility. Their adaptability made them perfect material for stylistic innovation both in and out of the commercial mainstream. While skinheads cropped and bleached, hippies attached bells and paisley patches. Jockey launched denim-look Y-fronts for 'executives' who wished to keep their rebellion discreet.

But the biggest pretence was the idea that wearing jeans was not really dressing at all, merely a value-free decision not to be naked. Of course, the very notion of sartorial egalitarianism is flawed. At this point, the fashion industry intervened and with 'designer' jeans avenged itself on hypocritical notions of normalcy, allowing the total victory of consumerism and exposing the fragility of functionalism as applied to fashion. Umberto Eco often pointed out that any garment that grips a man's testicles is bound to have a moderating influence on his behaviour and deportment – to say nothing of his appearance. Thus, the popularisation of jeans has forced men to realise something women have always known: that exterior appearance influences, even if it does not reflect, the interior life.

The relationship between exterior and interior is intimate and intense, but not straightforward. The degree of permissible affectation is hard to define, but like seeing through clothes, impossible to ignore: a man is under suspicion if he cares too much and if he cares too little about his appearance. As Baldassare Castiglione knew, an impression of effortlessness is attractive, but elusive, and requires a great deal of effort. 'You are what you wear' is, after all, an observation, not a creed. In an age when 'lifestyle' is more remorselessly marketed and more enthusiastically consumed than ever before, the collective neurosis of a generation that failed to make this distinction has become fascinatingly clear – at least in America's better shopping malls.

Ralph Lauren was conspicuously successful at marketing dressing up for the late-twentieth-century urban man and woman. His business is designing and marketing clothes that obsessively and cleverly articulate

Right: A fashion shoot for *Madame Figaro*, in Biarritz, April 2016. The model in the foreground wears a cardigan and skirt by Polo Ralph Lauren.

the ambitions of deracinated nouveaux riches, but he is in constant danger of reminding his customers of the vacuity of their desires. He packages appearances and sells an image of an image, based on romanticised myths about the Wild West and WASP society, sanitising new money with a pastiche of old clothes, somewhat like Elsie de Wolfe. But the tension that gives life to the venture depends on the idea that money is a necessary but not sufficient marker of status. The Lauren phenomenon shows that if you cannot buy class, you can at least buy classy things to wear. The irony is that this style is mostly inspired by those very people – sportsmen, English gentry, cowboys – for whom clothes are expressions of a culture and a response to function.

The Lauren story is astonishing, an odyssey involving a devotion to appearances and pseudo-events that would be merely eccentric were it not so successful. His shops suggest that if you acquire style, you acquire meaning as well. The capacity for simulation goes back through the generations: Lauren (born Lifshitz) is the Bronx son of a mural painter who specialised in *faux bois* and could match up more or less anything. He first wanted to be an athlete and only later, as he described it to *New York* magazine in 1985, did he want to be like Hopalong Cassidy. Later still he decided to be like Jay Gatsby.

He got close when he dressed Robert Redford in the screen adaptation. 'I wish I had gone to Harvard or Princeton or Yale, but I didn't', he sighed in the same interview. His declared ambition in the 1957 DeWitt Clinton High School Yearbook was to be a millionaire. Then he wanted to be a history professor – not so that he could study or teach the Pirenne Thesis or look at trade in South China during the sixteenth century, but so that he could dress in gum-soled shoes, tweed jackets and smoke a pipe.

It is no accident that Lauren's company markets its merchandise as 'Polo'. He liked the suggestion of European style and horsey society and the 'aristocratic demeanour' he thought he saw in Cary Grant and Fred Astaire. As *Forbes* noted in 1986, polo 'was not a well-known sport in the Bronx of Lauren's youth'. He chooses to advertise in large blocks, sometimes up to eighteen pages, because he is selling an image rather than a particular product. Indeed, it is the ads that create the Lauren image. The pictures by Bruce Weber are narrative rather than descriptive and show safaris, country houses and black-tie dinner parties.

Left: Rubber soul. Singer/songwriter Beyoncé Knowles attends the 'Manus x Machina: Fashion in an Age of Technology' Costume Institute Gala at the Metropolitan Museum of Art, New York, May 2016.

Lauren was after what Brooks Brothers once had, but packaged it more effectively so as to anticipate, appeal to and satisfy hitherto unrecognised longings among consumers. Interestingly, his critics (easily outnumbered by his happy customers) invoke arguments against him that echo the sumptuary laws of Renaissance Florence and England: 'How does a working-class Jew from Mosholu Parkway dare pass off the tribal costumes of the Ivy League as if he owned them?'

The epiphany of fashion as a billion-dollar language-of-objects industry was when Ralph Lauren moved into his new premises on Madison Avenue, thirty blocks north of Brooks Brothers, who, when they began using Dacron, started losing market. He didn't choose 50,000 square feet in a garish marbleised atrium. Instead he bought the historic Rhinelander Mansion (1898), accessorised it and created a Disneyland of status-related fashion that now takes its place with the Frick, the Met Breuer and the other museums as an inevitable cultural stopping place on the Upper East Side.

Perpetually suntanned, like his idol John Kennedy, Ralph Lauren became his own role model. Thus, his achievement in creating a role that is entirely separate from the merely functional needs of clothing is a paradigm of the fashion business: you can become what you wear — at a price. Still, Lauren, while slightly preposterous, has, in his dedicated pursuit of an elusive Brit gentility, something of the dignified aroma of scholarship.

Today, just as the gap between the quality of fine and mass-market wine is closing rapidly, while the price difference is enlarging absurdly (a 2009 Le Pin from Pomerol is about £4,000 a bottle, Errazuriz merlot £9), so fashion is experiencing a similar disorientating bifurcation.

In ever more desperate grasps at attention, catwalk shows are ever more distant from the marketplace. Meanwhile, a new generation disdains the notion of 'brand', which from Worth and Dior to Gucci and Versace has dominated the perception of fashion. Instead, the neo-disposable fast-fashion is preferred. And as for couture, it is no more relevant to the future of clothing than traditional coachbuilding is to the future of the automobile industry.

Kids find advertising toxic and shopping is for bores. *Vogue*, the fashion bible sustained by splashy ads, is in crisis as it struggles to come to terms with the atomised taste of a new world order. Although you might find little sense of crisis in New York at the annual Costume Institute Gala, now known as the Met Gala, a freak show that brings to the minds of the sensitive a suggestion of Pompeii the night before the lava flowed.

Once, the preening fashion business sought the approval of the august Metropolitan Museum of Art for its ghastly bash of air-kissing and pouting unrequited self-love, but now the mighty Met is itself in disarray, in debt and in question. If any illustration of fashion's present absurdity were required it would be guests arriving at the 2016 Met Gala. Kim Kardashian, with tattooed brute minders in attendance, wobbled on perilous heels along a Met Museum red carpet, wearing a silver Balmain outfit that matched her husband's. The *Mail Online* declared that Kardashian looked like a 'sexy droid', while really she looked like a tipsy Tsaghkadzor hooker on Armenian National Day. Yet more bizarrely, Beyoncé, the popular singer, wore a pearl-encrusted sheer latex Givenchy gown, apparently inspired by a condom. Someone on Twitter nicely described the lady's costume as 'a rough endoplasmic reticulum with ribosomes attached'.

If these be leaders of fashion, then fashion is no longer anything the sensate would wish to follow.

Food Acquired taste

Food is the acid test of taste. Dr Johnson said, 'I take it that he who does not mind his belly will mind little else', and Jean Anthelme Brillat-Savarin (1755-1826), the great French gastronome, has as the fourth of the ten aphorisms which introduce his *Physiologie du goût* (1826): 'Tell me what you eat: I will tell you what you are.'

People who would not think to discriminate about paintings, buildings or music, exercise exquisite taste in matters of food, but it is notoriously difficult to establish how and why. It is said that there is nothing on this earth that is not as much beloved by one nation as it is detested by another; our very preferences about what we eat are determined by social and cultural conditions as much as by nutrition.

While rotten eggs are prized as delicacies by the natives of Brunei and the English upper classes actually prefer their game putrefied, the Navahos find fresh fish disagreeable and the Old Bretons cannot abide hare.[16] Medieval Arab poets sang the praises of *kamakh, murri* and *bunn*, condiments made of rotten barley dough now known to contain aflatoxins, among the most lethal of carcinogens. In his book *Travelling Sketches in Egypt and Syria* (1836), Alexandre Dumas tells a story of being required by social convention to eat a dish made of camel-milk cheese, oil and chopped onions pounded into a 'filthy mixture'. This may seem odd, but Eskimo taste is especially curious by modern Western standards: according to LR Wolberg's *Psychology of Eating* (1936), 'there is no sight in the world more revolting than to see a young and gracefully formed native girl stepping out of the carcass of a putrid whale', whence she comes with a select rotting morsel of subsequent delectation.

Anthropologists have not yet discovered a group that eats everything available to it. It has been said that the world has perhaps ten to the power of six recipes, yet the potential is ten to the power of fifteen. Even non-agricultural nomads are picky. The Mbuti pygmies of Angola do not eat leopard because a leopard might, earlier, have eaten one of them. Kalahari Bushmen eat only fourteen per cent of the edible plants available to them.

However, the rules of nutrition appear to be universal. The distinguished English gastronome, Alan Davidson, was surprised to react with conventional disgust at a feast in Turkey when fellow guests picked eyeballs and tongues from roast lambs. That he recorded his feelings in an elegant short essay[17] and confessed to his exploratory intellect being at odds with his cultured feelings shows just how vexatious taste can be, even to someone who makes it his business.

Apparently Keats dusted his tongue with pepper the better to savour the taste of iced claret, but his contemporaries in France were already serving Bordeaux with a warm napkin around the neck of the bottle to bring out the flavour of the wine. Clearly, taste is influenced by forces beyond the understanding of science. Of the five senses, taste is the most complicated because it involves the intellect as well as physiology. In an epic sentence in his paper 'Science and the Experience of Eating', delivered at the Oxford Symposium in 1987, EG Richards defined gustatory taste:

'The experiences encountered whilst eating and drinking are mediated by nerve endings in our mouths and noses and modulated by our knowledge, our beliefs, our predilections and what the morsel looked and felt like before we popped it in our maw.'

For this very reason, perhaps, social and cultural factors influence taste more than they do touch or sound. Traditionally, there are only four basic taste sensations that occur in the mouth: sweet, sour, salt and bitter – a gustatory map of the tongue's receptors. The complex taste sensations take place not in the mouth, but in the brain. The only one understood scientifically is sourness, which can be defined as the taste of a solution with a pH value of less than seven.

Umami burger

Since 1908, we have had umami. This is a neologism meaning 'delicious taste' coined by a Tokyo academic chemist called Kikunae Ikeda (1864-1936). He was in pursuit of what made kelp, rich in glutamate, so especially good to eat. In 1909 he commercialised his researches and began manufacturing monosodium glutamate (MSG), a taste-enhancer as well as a taste in its own right. The old Roman garum was also rich in glutamates.

Food scientists call MSG the most abundant excitatory neurotransmitter. It was also the inspiration in 1968 of 'Chinese Restaurant Syndrome', the title of a paper published in *The New England Journal of Medicine* by Dr Robert Ho Man Kwok who had noticed headaches and dizziness after his chow mein. It is also sometimes known as the 'won ton soup headache'.

Above: Vauxhall Pleasure Gardens. At this pre-industrial mass entertainment visitors allegedly drank gin made from sulphuric acid and oil of turpentine.

Above: Nightclub owner Sam Nazarian's UMAMIcatessen in Los Angeles (2012).

Far from being a source of malaise, umami has recently advanced to high fashion food. An ambitious Los Angeles restaurateur called Adam Fleischman has a chain of establishments called Umami Burger. Here those in search of the fifth taste can order their beef patty with shiitake mushrooms, caramelised onions, roasted tomato, a parmesan crisp and 'umami ketchup'.

Smell is perhaps even more fugitive. Again, associations help. Oz Clarke says wines made from Chenin Blanc smell of nuts and vomit. One sniffing wine buyer was heard to say in the cellars of Haut-Brion 'I think I am getting a little Brazilian woman'.

These sensations are considered in the olfactory bulb, neighbour of the temporal lobe, the home of our memories. This propinquity explains the power of smell to excite memory. Richard Llewellyn, author of *How Green was My Valley* (1939), claimed he could smell hens' feathers every time he ate roast chicken. In fact, the meaning of what we eat and drink is determined more by sensation in the nose than sensation on the tongue. Gastronomists and oenologists use the word taste to cover both flavour and aroma.

Rough definitions may be useful: aroma is smell, flavour is gustation, and taste – at least as far as the gastronomists and oenologists are concerned – is the combination of the two.

While sweetness, bitterness, acidity and saltiness can be scientifically measured, their meanings and our reactions to them are altogether less determinate. Brillat-Savarin suspected that 'smell and taste are in fact but a single composite sense, whose laboratory is the mouth and its chimney the nose'. But the laboratory is built on shifting sands. One simple example of changing taste is the fluctuating demand for dry and sweet. Vauxhall Pleasure Gardens in London, which flourished from 1661 to 1859, provides an example. It was a haunt of Samuel Pepys, whose idea of fun was to go there for a stroll, a lobster and a syllabub. Later it was opened up to people of all ranks as well as diarists. Whereas in 1802 champagne was available for eight shillings a bottle, most visitors preferred 'Vauxhall Nectar', containing rum, syrup and Benjamin flowers, as their summer tipple. Hock and Rhenish were offered with or without added sugar; claret was available at five shillings a bottle; 'Frontiniac' – presumably, Muscat de Frontignan, a heavy, sweet, undistinguished wine from the plains of Languedoc – was priced at six.[18]

If the taste for dry and sweet changes, so too does the dimension of the appetite. George Musgrave, author of *A Ramble through Normandy* (1855), watched a honeymooning couple at lunch on a steamer near Rouen. They consumed soup, fried mackerel, beefsteak, French beans, fried potatoes, omelette *fine herbes,* a *fricandeau* of veal with sorrel, a roast chicken garnished with mushrooms, a hock of pork served on spinach, an apricot tart, three custards, an endive salad, a small roast leg of lamb with chopped onion and nutmeg, coffee, absinthe, *eau doré*, a Mignon cheese, pears, plums, grapes, cakes and three bottles of Burgundy (two red, one white).

Similarly, ideas about fatness and thinness are not absolute. In peasant societies a thin wife brings disgrace to the husband, and for long periods of European history overeating was a familiar symbol of wealth. Even as late as the turn of the twentieth century, at least as described by Vita Sackville-West in *The Edwardians* (1930), overeating was a ritual. Yet in civilisations where starvation exists as a possibility, anorexia is unknown.

Because cooking involves the conception and execution of an idea, the assembling of functional components into a pleasing whole, it has both a practical and an aesthetic character. This makes it similar to design, a subject which in the past has lent itself to as much moralising as food (although the real sense of 'good' design is as fugitive as that of 'good' food). When Marcella Hazan said defiantly to her students, 'I don't measure, I cook', it was not a confession of carelessness, but an affirmation of high artistic purpose and personal conviction.

Impulsive caviar
Patterns in cooking are as cyclical as patterns in art and, viewed historically, betray similar characteristics, a period of excess being followed by a period of austerity, and so forth. Elizabeth David's *faites simple* was as much a moral and aesthetic instruction as a culinary one, if the two may be separated, and, as we shall see, an aesthetic instruction peculiarly located in culture. Her conviction that a bad meal is always expensive is similarly moral and democratic (although not to be confused with GK Chesterton's happy remark that there is more simplicity in a man who eats caviar on impulse than one who eats grape-nuts on principle). The fear of simplicity, which Mrs David said undermined Britain, is itself a subtle and fascinating matter of taste whose background this chapter will try to explore.

James Bond perhaps represented the conventional English taste that Elizabeth David wanted to undermine with garlic and oil. In *Moonraker* (1955) Bond is having dinner with his controller, M; Bond says: 'The best English cooking is the best in the world – particularly at this time of year.' It is May.

While any general discussion of taste follows a wandering path between prescription and philosophy, it is perfectly possible to talk about the historical development of taste in French culture. Here, more than anywhere else, very self-conscious and very influential styles of eating first emerged. Luxury is anything in excess of what is merely necessary for survival. In his book *Economy and Society* (1922), Max Weber provided a definition: '"Luxury" in the sense of a rejection of the purposive-rational orientation of consumption is, to the feudal ruling-class, not something "superfluous" but one of the means of its social self-assertion.'

French cuisine may be a luxury, but it is perhaps in French cooking that the very idea of 'good taste' first appears. Significantly, its first connotations were social and directed against proletarian or peasant values and in support of bourgeois ones. This sort of improved taste was definitively that of the improving grandee: in Molière's *L'Avare* (1682), the despised meanness of the lower orders provides the setting. Three successive titles offer evidence of this trend: La Chapelle's *Le Cuisinier moderne* (1733), Menon's *La Cuisinière bourgeoise* (1746) and Mme Mérigot's *La Cuisinière républicaine* (1790s). Clearly, a process of social orientation is at work in the titling of cookery books.

The fact that cooking and eating were becoming another aspect of social competition is demonstrated by the tendency, which accelerated after the Revolution but was present before it, to name dishes after the chefs or their patrons. It began when the Marquis d'Uxelles gave his name to the dish of quails in a mushroom sauce, which is still known as *cailles à la Duxelles.* Louis XV prepared his own omelettes and *les filets de volaille à la Bellevue* was named by its creator, Madame de Pompadour, after one of her favourite houses. Thus were social distinctions conferred on certain dishes and architectural taste and food interestingly mixed. This process of distinguishing 'designs', now applied to everything not just food, is known as the valorisation of surplus.

Three great chefs exemplify the development of French cuisine up to the beginning of our own age: La Varenne (1618-78), once employed by the Marquis d'Uxelles; Carême (1784-1833), once employed by the Rothschilds in Paris and at Ferrières; and Escoffier (1846-1935), chef at London's Savoy Hotel and elsewhere. French cuisine was initially influenced

by Italian cooking (brought to France by Catherine de' Medici, consort of Henri II). In La Varenne's *Le Cuisinier françois* (1651) a distinctive national French cuisine emerges from a common European medieval inheritance. La Varenne was the first of those cooks responsible for turning the artisan craft of cooking into the art of gastronomy, and in the course of doing this laid patterns of behaviour, ideas about manners and assumptions about the cultural role of food that have not yet been seriously challenged.

La Varenne was originally a *marmiton*, or saucepan boy, in the kitchens of the Duchesse de Bar, Henri IV's sister. It was Henri IV who said that in his reign the poor should be able to have a chicken every Sunday (the famous *poule au pot*). *Le Cuisinier françois* was the first systematic cookbook, an influential refinement of traditional practice. The subtitle reveals something of the burden of the author: '*Enseignant la manière de bien apprêter et assaisonner toutes sortes de viandes grasses et maigres, légumes, pâtisseries et autres mets qui se servent tant sur les tables des Grands que des particuliers.*' (A primer on how to properly dress and season all kinds of lean and fat meats, vegetables, pastries and other dishes for the tables of the Great and the private individual.)

To his critics La Varenne was vulgar and rustic. There is much in his book that carries the medieval sense of awe and wonder, to say nothing of sorcery. He used spices more sparingly than his medieval predecessors, but still savoured contrasts that are to us odd. He insisted, for instance, on adding sugar to meat dishes. This is his recipe for capon pie:

'Take the white meat of a capon and chop it fine. Mix with it two egg yolks, fresh butter, salt, pistachios, and a lot of sugar. If it is too dry, dampen it with a little bouillon. After that, make a very fine, sweet, puff pastry. Line a pie dish with some of it. Put your stuffing into the dish and add some dried currants.'

His critics said that what they were looking for in their cuisine was refinement, delicacy and 'good taste', and these attacks were perfect little models of the avant-garde's opposition to the establishment, recreated a thousand times since, but here applied uniquely and importantly to the kitchen. La Varenne's was essentially a medieval technique subject to modern systematisation. In a turkey recipe he suggested slinging on some raspberries 'if you have them'. The transformation that was about to overwhelm cooking and social behaviour around the table was one from 'superposition' (i.e. sugar and capon, raspberries on top of turkeys) to a cuisine of 'imprégnation et des essences'[19] – a good metaphor for the manners of the emerging middle classes.

The fine art of cake

Marie-Antoine Carême was abandoned by his parents and taken up by a humble cookshop. His astonishing career demonstrates how social progress could be made both by cooking food as well as by eating it. Beginning as a fifteen-year-old kitchen help he moved to Baily, the *pâtissier* in rue Vivienne, whose most famous client was Talleyrand. The *pâtissier* taught him culinary sculpture and Carême's most extraordinary creations were set pieces with dishes got up to look like buildings cribbed from designs he had seen in the Bibliothèque Nationale. Anatole France quoted him as saying, 'The fine arts are five in number, to wit: painting, sculpture, poetry, music, and architecture – whose main branch is confectionery.'[20] Here we may see the beginning of an impulse, since frequently repeated, to accommodate rogue and trivial subjects into the canon of art.

Carême achieved far greater sophistication than La Varenne. The minor cookery writers of the eighteenth century had, in respectful response to the spirit of the age, included an element of encyclopedism in their books. Carême built on this basis, but added something original: he had clients. As an apprentice he had cooked for Napoleon and was eventually employed by Talleyrand, whose dinners became famous. He then came to England to work for the Prince Regent, he cooked at the Russian and Austrian courts, but he met his destiny in the employ of the Rothschilds.

The founder of *la grande cuisine*, he made some claims to universality, but his attitude to his chosen career was specific to his time and culture; the sort of sophistication that made him a celebrity was only possible in an advanced economy. Indeed the social transformation that allowed Beethoven to be an independent genius while fifty years earlier Haydn had been a servant, also affected the role of the chef. Carême was an arbiter, an artist, a creator and a tastemaker. Dinner was a painting with chiaroscuro, iridescence and limpidity. He used spun sugar and moulded lard to make his *pièces montées* with palm trees, military trophies, lyres, perfume pans and ornamental plinths straining under the weight of red-legged partridges afloat in his beloved and epically complicated Espagnole sauce.

He explained in *L'Art de la cuisine française au XIXème siècle* (1833) that it is 'an error for those of lesser station to try to pattern their tables after the rich, crowding them with badly prepared food, badly served because of inexperienced help. Better … a simple meal, well-prepared; and not to try to cover the bourgeois table with an imitation of the rich'.

The Italian composer Rossini was a frequent houseguest of the Rothschilds and for him Carême created the vile *Tournedos Rossini*: filet steak, foie gras and truffles. Another visitor to the Rothschild household, Sydney, Lady Morgan, said in her *France in 1829-30* (1831) that a Rothschild dinner was a 'specimen of the intellectual perfection of an art, the standard and gauge of modern civilisation'. In their employ Carême wrote *Le Cuisinier parisien* (1828): 'In this wealthy household, I could spend as much as was necessary in order to prepare things as I wished. This is the only way in which a creative cook can fully profit from his talents, for what good is talent if one doesn't have the money to buy the best provisions?'

This is an apt summary of the vicious constraints of consumerism and strangely reminiscent of Racine's remark that '*Sans argent l'honneur n'est qu'une maladie*'. But in his cooking Carême achieved a high degree of creative freedom. Completely abandoning medieval contrasts he worked on complementary (which is not to say subtle) flavours. He always strove to extract in an interesting way the essential character of the food he was preparing. Although Baron de Rothschild invited him to retire to Ferrières, Carême refused. It was the rebuff of one nouveau riche to another: '*Je lui dis encore que mes livres m'avaient créé un revenu qui allait bien au-delà de mes besoins.*' (I also told him that my books had created revenue that went far beyond my needs.)

Carême was the first truly modern cook and, perhaps more significantly, regarded himself as such. His interest in purity was a gastronomic expression of a broader urge in culture as a whole. He refused to garnish meat with fish (a noxious practice which not all of his less skilled descendants have abandoned). His *fonds de cuisine* with the three expensive and intricate sauces provided the basis for 'classic' French cuisine and for a gastronomic culture whose development both Rossini and Dumas (who believed that his own *Grand dictionnaire de cuisine* (1873) was a far superior work to *The Three Musketeers* or *The Count of Monte Cristo*) encouraged in their different ways. But perhaps the key figure in this development was not a musician or writer but another cook, Escoffier.

Auguste Escoffier made French cuisine into an international standard. It was he who canonised restaurant French by the popularity of his *Livre des menus* (1912). In 1893, following the tradition of Pompadour and Colbert, he created for Nellie Melba the pudding that bears her name.

In 1890, in company with César Ritz (of the Grand Hôtel, Monte Carlo) and Louis Echenard (of the Hôtel du Louvre, Marseille), Escoffier created the Savoy and thus perpetuated for generations of Englishmen certain assumptions about haute cuisine. Part of his achievement was to reject the architectural fantasies of Carême and instil the Savoy kitchens with

Above: A selection of cakes by Marie-Antoine (Antonin) Carême (1784-1833) an early exponent of the elaborate style of cooking known as *grande cuisine*.

Above: Tastes change. In the 1890s fashionable young Frenchwomen would visit abattoirs to drink a glass of fresh blood. Mrs Beeton's *Everyday Cookery* presented many choices for carnivores but few for herbivores.

a new spirit so that heavily decorated food did not arrive stone cold and inedible at the guest's table.

But his revolution at the Savoy had more than thermal advantages for hungry, jaded diners. He restructured the operation of the kitchen so that there was a division of labour: thus, with nice symmetry, the new rich of the joint stock enterprises could benefit at table from the process which helped them acquire their wealth. The clientele, newly aware of the concept of efficiency, relished the innovation. In Escoffier's kitchen, different divisions carried out different operations, rather than distinct dishes. The structure he established is still in use today:

Garde-manger: supplies the kitchen and prepares cold dishes
Entremétier: prepares soups and desserts
Rôtisseur: prepares meats
Pâtissier: prepares bread and pastry
Saucier: makes the sauces

The Escoffier period at the Savoy and later at the Ritz was the time when all the grand hotels – Claridge's, the Piccadilly, the Hyde Park and the Berkeley – were becoming established, and the first cookery competitions took place. That Escoffier put peasant dishes (such as Provençal potato and artichoke) on the menu at the Savoy and turned them into expensive haute cuisine reveals the curious relationship between English class and French cooking.

Carême and Escoffier were not the first French cooks to work in England. Against a background of notorious philistinism (one Elizabethan writer attacked the 'affected gestures' of France and even the knife and fork of Italy), there was always a minority who took an expert interest in cuisine. Queen Anne's physician published a commentary on Apicius's *De re coquinaria* (*On the Subject of Cooking*). The curious and erudite *Closet of the Eminently Learned Sir Kenelme Digby Kt. Opened* (commonly known as *The Closet Opened*) was published in 1669. But historians and anthropologists have long laboured to understand why cooking in France and England is so different. While in France it did not take long for the sophisticated *cuisine d'imprégnation* to replace coarse medieval contrasts, in England the battle still has to be won. The familiar explanation is that the continued existence of court life in France, at least until the Revolution, encouraged sophistication, while in England with its decentralised social life, country (which is not to say peasant) values were more acceptable. Simple food was preferred to ostentatious refinement. The English lived on the land and preferred rural models; the aristocracy and gentry in England paid tax, but their French equivalents lived at a rarefied level of isolated privilege.

It is extraordinary that the most famous, although not the first, modern cookery book in England was written by a woman. As author of *Beeton's Book of Household Management* (1861), Isabella Beeton (1836-65) made her husband's name a generic in much the same way as Lux and Hoover. She was twenty-five when the book first appeared and twenty-nine when she died, just before the dictionary edition appeared. If cookery writing of the eighteenth century had been encyclopedic, then the most influential cookery books of the nineteenth were concerned with something especially appropriate to the age: scientific management. Beeton's preference was for what Elizabeth David described as sound, solid, sensible, middle-class mid-Victorian food. Much was derived from her predecessor Eliza Acton, whose *Modern Cookery for Private Families* (1845) was the first English cookery book to systematise ingredients, quantities and timings. Her contemporary, Alexis Soyer, the erratic French chef of the Reform Club, was also a source. Like her other contemporary, the Queen's cook Charles Elmé Francatelli, author of *A Plain Cookery Book for the Working Classes* (1852), Beeton had an admirable interest in economy. But the synthesis she created from disparate sources had the originality of genius. *Household Management* is at least as capable of capturing the spirit of its age as a conventional work of art.

Food historians are much exercised by the problem of why certain cultures prefer certain foodstuffs and Mrs Beeton is a determining influence in England – Mrs Beeton the publishing phenomenon, that is, rather than Isabella Beeton, the spirited and independent Victorian original. Successive editions of *Household Management* lost the original clarity and purity of Isabella Beeton's concept and added the editors' own conceits. It is not too fanciful to suggest that the aversion to foreign food endemic in Britain until very recent times – curry, according to the Welsh author and mystic Arthur Machen, is 'the most nauseous of all the massacres which go to form English Cookery of our doleful day' – can be traced to horrible recipes infiltrated into *Household Management* by unscrupulous editors at work for the opportunistic publishers. With copies of *Household Management* in virtually every home in the land, it took two world wars and a social revolution to rid the British of a phobic disregard for exotic food. Fish Klosh, Roast Wallaby and Parrot Pie from the 1906 edition are perhaps to blame.

Above: A well-laden supper table with places set for sixteen people, from *Mrs Beeton's Book of Household Management* (c.1860).

Above: Restaurateur Marcel Boulestin, the first television chef, filming in the BBC studios. Beginning on 21 January 1937, Boulestin presented a weekly fifteen-minute programme called *Cooks Night Out*. The onset of war brought the series to an end.

National tastes tease scientific analysis because they defy reason. The stories are legion about the curious foreign visitor to England finding that English food is the way it is because of a clearly defined national preference, not because of lack of opportunity. In an article in the *Evening Standard* in 1935, Osbert Sitwell attacked the Wine and Food Society as pretentious. In a 1983 television interview the patrician Harold Macmillan exclaimed that, at least in his household, it was considered bad form even to talk about food.

The splendid Edwardian Lieutenant Colonel Newnham-Davis, gastronomic correspondent of the *Pall Mall Gazette* and author, with Algernon Bastard, of *The Gourmet's Guide to Europe* (1903), was one of the first Englishmen to take gastronomy seriously (although it was characteristically English that he did so as an amateur). He cites Brillat-Savarin as an epigraph: 'The pleasures of the table are common to all ages and ranks, to all countries and times; they not only harmonise with all the other pleasures, but remain to console us for their loss.'

Anything so long as it's hot

This was the beginning of a European perspective in English cultural life. Enforced by the world wars, it led to the slow awareness that food was a pleasure and that preparing, serving and eating it were pleasing rituals that carried great meaning. Yet in 1921 it was possible for a gentleman to write: 'An Englishman will eat anything if it is served hot, there is plenty of it, and he is sure he knows what it is. The fear that a designing foreigner may one day make him eat cat is still present in one form or another in most British minds.'[21]

The process could be said to culminate with the quixotic restaurateur Marcel Boulestin (1878-1943) doing cookery demonstrations on television, the first of their kind. He describes the experience in the second part of his autobiography, *Ease and Endurance* (1948). But before the 1950s there was very little change in English attitudes to food. The prevailing philistinism is described frequently by Boulestin:

'I remember dinner at an MP friend's house – lovely house, superb silver, expensive fruit; no male servants, but several parlour maids in lace aprons. The white wine was so incredibly bad that, pretending to be interested in it, I asked its name. My hostess did not know it, nor did the parlour maid, who went to the pantry to look at the bottle.'

Of English waiters he writes: 'Some ... such as the old provincial waiters are not educable. I saw two superb examples. One of them, who served an abominably corked Lafite, confided the secret to me: "What can you expect, sir, when the cellarman keeps the bottles lying down so that the wine touches the corks?" Another time I saw to my great surprise an Yquem 1921 on the wine list, and I told the waiter to serve it properly cold. "Oh, you need not be afraid here, sir," he said proudly. "Our white wines are always in a refrigerator."'

Since the 1960s, England has become the sixth largest wine consumer on earth. That the English can now claim to have a better general knowledge of wine than any other nation, French and Italians included, is much to do with the influence of Elizabeth David and some of her contemporaries. In an article written for the *Spectator* in 1963, she describes the conditions in Britain just after the Second World War:

'It was not feasible, in 1947, to go out and buy food as nowadays I would. When you stayed more than a night or two in a hotel you gave them your ration book, retaining only coupons for things like chocolate and sweets … Hardly knowing what I was doing … I sat down and … started to work out an agonised craving for the sun and a furious revolt against that terrible, cheerless, heartless food by writing down descriptions of Mediterranean and Middle Eastern cooking. Even to write words like apricot, olives and butter, rice and lemons, oil and almonds, produced assuagement. Later I came to realise that in the England of 1947, those were dirty words that I was putting down.'

What was required now was not encyclopedic cookery books, nor those about scientific management, but cookery books full of social criticism and cultural modelling. Aspirational, some might say. The key word in Mrs David's account is, of course, 'description'.

In the age of the motor car, Curnonsky and Rouff, in their influential series *La France gastronomique* (1921 onwards) were genially adding tourism to the list of delights at table, thus creating for Michelin, Bottin, Gault & Millau, Kléber and Claude Lebey a genuinely popular movable feast. Meanwhile Elizabeth David was patiently turning English taste into continental taste. Mrs David, Raymond Postgate, Primrose Boyd and Patience Gray wrought a revolution in English values. The two last named published *Plats du jour* in 1957. Gray had been associated with the *Architectural Review* during its great period and her treatment of exotic food in this book had at least as much to do with radical social criticism as with what to put in your skillet or bain marie. Just as during the 1950s the Council of Industrial Design urged the salvation of English taste by importing and imitating Scandinavian furniture, glass and hollowware, David, Gray, Boyd and others sought to do the same with Mediterranean food. Their attack on beige food opened a path that led to chromatic experimentation and variety in all areas of English life, not just in the kitchen and the restaurant. Raymond Postgate's *Good Food Guide* (1951 onwards), André Simon's Wine and Food Society and Elizabeth David's *Mediterranean Food* (1950) are landmarks in the history of national taste as a whole. Each led to more choice and more discrimination.

Mediterranean Food, the magnificent result of the jottings mentioned above, was published by the avant-garde John Lehmann and 'decorated', in a style owing something to Eric Ravilious, by John Minton, whose familiar and easy pictures seem to anticipate a lot of what was to happen later in interior design. Mrs David had lived in Greece and Egypt; in her attitude to the Mediterranean we can see something of that ineradicable English longing for the south which goes back at least as far as Keats, but is perhaps at its very strongest in DH Lawrence and Norman Douglas.

Other influential books soon followed: *French Country Cooking* (1951), *Italian Food* (1954), *Summer Cooking* (1955), *French Provincial Cooking* (1960), *Spices, Salt and Aromatics in the English Kitchen* (1970) and *English Bread and Yeast Cookery* (1977). The titles read like the subtext of the changes in the British psyche during those years. Elizabeth David presided over the late-twentieth-century rebirth of British consumer awareness. She was interested in equipment as well as in the preparation of food; when a shop bearing her name opened in Chelsea it was national news. That you can today buy a demi-lune in a department store in Lincoln is due to Elizabeth David's influence on English life.

She declared that the kitchen should be 'the most comforting and comfortable room in the house', whereas most architects in the 1950s, still struggling under the continuing and baleful influence of *Existenzminimum*, wanted to do to the kitchen what even the most radical architect had failed to do in the 1930s: make it into a tiny functional annexe. Now the mandolin grater and the marmite moved in to alleviate the Formica as surely as ratatouille replaced the gristle rissoles. Of course, it was a small conceptual jump from familiarity with salade niçoise to the wholesome acceptance of a Provençal kitchen. And that meant: Habitat.

Terence Conran's Habitat grew out of these influences and was enhanced by personal experience of France.[22] He did not actually invent France, but artfully sold an Englishman's interpretation of it. It was a short step from selling a better salad bowl in Habitat to serving *frisée aux lardons* in one of his restaurants.

'Taste' is a concept that unites design and cooking. 'Le Goût Conran' is a designer's version of Escoffier's command: *'faites simple!'* On his Berkshire vegetable patch Conran aped a peasant in his bin-man's *bleu de travail* (while a witheringly expensive and aristocratic bottle of Corton-Charlemagne was chilling in the refrigerator). Conran detested the term 'lifestyle'. Instead, he called it '*l'art de vivre*'.

A certain class of Englishman has always been exposed to France for education. In the eighteenth century, privileged youth were sent on the Grand Tour. They bought fancy clothes in Paris, did a spot of whoring, and then moved on to Lyon, Grenoble and southwards. Conran's introduction to France was as a passenger in the Lagonda of Michael Wickham, an old-school bohemian, who mentored him.

Conran grew up with French ideas *dans le vent*, and *Plats du Jour* by Patience Gray and Primrose Boyd was a reference point. They write: 'We know perfectly well that many people live in far from modern homes' and their remedy, in so far as kitchens were concerned, was to visit Madame Cadec in Soho's Greek Street and buy a *turbotière* and a chinois plus lots of lovely white porcelain. This is exactly what Terence Conran did.

In 1964 the result was Habitat: a glorious mixture of the vernacular and the modern. Habitat recognised among the English a lot of frustrated yearnings for exoticism in food and design. While a Danish open sandwich has its exact conceptual equivalent in a Hans Wegner chair, so perfect roast chicken requires that famous (and useful) terracotta brick.

There were sources in *la France profonde*. Anthony Denney's photograph of a lunch at Hôtel du Midi in Lamastre was used on the jacket of Elizabeth David's *French Provincial Cooking*. It accurately predicts a Habitat or, indeed, a *Sunday Times* photoshoot from the later 1960s: crusty bread, windowpane cotton tablecloth, a bottle of southern red, big glasses and a hunk of *galantine de foie de volaille*.

To describe a generalised Francophilia among the insular English is not to diminish Conran's stylishly packaged version of it. His achievement was to have been a brilliant editor and publisher of ideas. Because 'Le Goût Conran' would be totally mystifying in a gritty Parisian *banlieue* full of cross *racaille* is only to describe its enduring magical quality.

In France Terence Conran found a nice combination of sensualism and earthy practicality: he would sniff the cleft in a peach and mutter about a woman's bottom. In the same way, his favourite shop in Paris was Deyrolle, on Rue du Bac, whose speciality is taxidermy, which combines a delight in display with a certain refined cruelty. Conran's favourite dish? *Poulet en demi-deuil*, a telling mixture of the simple and the sophisticated: a good Bresse chicken with slices of black truffle inserted beneath the skin as if in half-mourning.

Above: *Le carrefour des rue Bailleul et Jean Tison*, by Thomas Shotter Boys (1831); Boulanger, depicted here, was the world's first restaurant.

Conran's France is the place we all want to be. It is the France of long, convivial lunches in the sunshine, of nights in river-washed, air-dried bed linen and bowling down a tree-lined D road to search for breakfast in a classic Citroën Traction Avant. Thank God for fantasies. So persuasive was this vision that, like Ralph Lauren selling England back to the English, Conran even sold his version of France to the French. However, Andrée Putman, the Simone de Beauvoir of design, witheringly described the Paris Conran Shop as merely a '*succès de curiosité*'. It was, indeed, inundated by later tide of taste.

Michel Guérard published *La Grande Cuisine minceur* in 1976. It was the most extreme version of the self-styled nouvelle cuisine, although by now it should be clear that 'new cooking' is not very novel; it is rather a consistent feature in the history of gastronomy and taste. Periods of deliberate complexity and grossness are followed by periods of simplification and lightening – artifice versus authenticity to nature. After all, Rousseau condemned elaborate cooking in his *Confessions* (1782), and Jean-François Revel, in *Un festin en paroles* (1979), wittily and exasperatedly demanded of an eighteenth-century recipe cited by Massialot: '*Fait-il considérer … le canard aux huîtres comme une survivance médiévale ou une anticipation moderne … on ne sait.*' ('Does he consider … the *canard aux huîtres* a medieval survivor or a modern anticipation … we do not know.')

Nouvelle cuisine was a supreme artifice. It offered *le monde à l'envers*. The weekly review *Paris Match* noted in 1978 that the new cooking entailed a curious inversion of standard restaurant French: starters had to be given the names of puddings, *sorbet de fromage de tête*, for instance; the main course deliberately confused traditional appellations of fish and meat, *rumsteak de sole*; similarly vegetables – *gâteau aux carottes*; and puddings were given the names of entrées: *soupe de figues*. It is perhaps not surprising that, at least in England and the United States, many restaurants purporting to offer nouvelle cuisine also had their own interior designed to look Postmodern.

Most people learn the fundamentals of interior design from their experience of restaurants. Again, the concept of 'anticipatory socialisation' introduced by Robert Merton in his book *Social Theory and Social Structure* (1949) is a useful analytical tool. It would be naïve to believe that what one was paying for in every restaurant was the food: the aspiration and the ambience cost money too. Anticipatory socialisation is perhaps best explained in terms of drink: most people drink not so much because of alcohol dependence, but because of the often bitterly misplaced association of intoxicating liquor with good humour and good company.

The modern meal with its carefully structured progress – which has been analysed by Mary Douglas, the anthropologist, in 'Deciphering a Meal', *Daedalus* (1972) – is historically something of a novelty. The debased contemporary formula of starter, entrée, cheese, pudding is known in pretentious hotels and bad restaurants everywhere. The result of a progressive contraction of the bourgeois appetite, it is a simplified version of the food symphonies established in the early nineteenth century. A supper described in Émile Zola's *Nana* (1880) provides examples of the dishes that were served for each course:

Soup: the purpose of soup, Carême says, is to 'moisten and stimulate the digestive tube' (*purée of asparagus comtesse, consommé à la Deslignac, crépinettes of young rabbit with truffles, gnocchi and parmesan*).

The remove: the first solid food (*Rhine carp à la Chambord, saddle of venison à l'anglaise*).

Entrée: meat, offal, poultry, game (*chicken à la Maréchale, fillets of sole with ravigote sauce, escalopes de foie gras*).

Entremet: either a pudding or a fish; a chance to prepare for what is still to follow (*mandarin sorbet*).

The roast: imposing meat dishes (*hot fillet of beef with truffles, cold galantine of guinea fowl*).

Second entremet: vegetables and fruit (*cèpes à l'italienne, croustades of pineapple*).

Dessert: defined by Jean-Paul Aron in *Le Mangeur du XIXème siècle* (1973) as 'the counterpart to the soup. It was the task of the latter to create the right atmosphere; it is for the dessert to soften the blow of departure, that plunge into the void which engulfs the eaters until their next indulgence'.

Until about 1860 this bewildering array was presented not sequentially, as it would be today, but virtually simultaneously, or at least in three broad sequences: soup, removes and entrées; roasts and entremets; dessert. This, a survival of the medieval fashion of serving fish, flesh and sweet pell-mell, is known as *service à la française*.

This was superseded by *service à la russe*, which has some very important distinctions peculiar to modern, democratic societies: carving is done in the kitchen, or at a *guéridon*, or, at home, on a sideboard; waiters serve the diners who are expected to eat something of every dish.

The free-for-all of *service à la française* is replaced by the more uniform, but more manageable linear process of succession, which has proved more durable.

The service and presentation of the food communicate the abstract ideas underlying the menu to the consumer. Grimod de la Reynière (1758-1838) established the norms. He declared for the benefit of the bourgeoisie that napkins should be genteelly placed on laps, not stuffed manfully into collars; that the fork should be on the left and the knife and spoon on the right; that there should be a variety of glasses for different wines and water. It was expected throughout the nineteenth century that cutlery and crockery should be replaced for each course. This failed to happen in only the humblest homes. In the grandest, a virtue was made of profligacy: the French Rothschilds owned a dinner service and a vermeil dessert service consisting of 112 pieces.

Movable feasts

It is usually assumed that the French eat out more than the English, but this is in fact difficult to corroborate.[23] According to Brillat-Savarin, even in Paris in the days before the Revolution, 'the stranger within the gates … found few resources in the way of good cheer'. But the Revolution put a lot of the aristocrats' cooks on the labour market. It also changed meal times. Because the National Assembly sat at 10.00am, breakfast was served as early as 9.00am. Dinner, which Louis XIV enjoyed alone in his bedchamber, moved from 2.30pm to after 5.00pm. The new restaurants catered for this fashion. So in France as well as in England the restaurant, which soon became a cauldron of aspirations and assumptions about taste, is a relatively recent cultural institution, a product of industrial urban society.

Brillat-Savarin makes it clear that the restaurant was created for the middle classes who, with fewer resources, wanted to eat like Colbert or Pompadour or Louis XIV. It was only from the rise of the middle classes after the Revolution that the dining-room furniture came into existence. Since then, of course, the dining room and what goes in it has been a consistent preoccupation of the bourgeoisie, as the most cursory examination of home-furnishings magazines reveals. A well-equipped dining room confers prestige by suggesting worldliness.

Left: From the Middle Ages to the nineteenth century, all the dishes in any meal were placed simultaneously on the table.

Restaurants were public dining rooms. In Brillat-Savarin's account of their evolution, gustatory relish vies with economic expediency. It is clear that the restaurant was something special and new – a custom-made arena for the very first consumers:

'Having once come to a reckoning with his purse, the consumer may indulge at will in a light or solid, sweet or savoury repast, wash it down with the best French or foreign wines, make aromatic with coffee, and perfume it with the liqueurs of both worlds, and all with no limit but the vigour or the capacity of his stomach. The restaurant is the gourmand's Eden.'

It is clear from Lieutenant Colonel Newnham-Davis's account in *Dinners and Diners* (1899) that the new hotel restaurants were providing for an itinerant and free-spending middle class a great deal of the heraldry previously sported and enjoyed by the aristocracy. He writes of Claridge's:

'The windows are draped with deep red curtains and purple *portières*; the carpet carries on the scheme of quiet reds, and the chairs have morocco backs of vermilion, with the arms of the hotel stamped on them in gold. The white plaster ceiling is supported by great arches, the bases of which and the walls of which are panelled with darkish oak, in which patterns of olive wood are set. The quiet-footed waiters in evening clothes, with the arms of the hotel as a badge on the lapels of their coats, are in keeping with the room.'

The new restaurants also introduced competitive culinary inventiveness. So much the stock-in-trade of today's media treatment of food and cooking, it takes an effort of imagination to realise that the demand for new dishes is, like the restaurant itself, a product of modern bourgeois culture.

Before the French Revolution, the word *restaurant* had the same meaning as *fortifiant*. It did not refer to establishments or institutions, but rather to a liquid concoction – a sort of tonic soup – usually given to invalids. In 1765, in defiance of the tradition that gave *traiteurs* (caterers) sole rights to sell prepared food, a man called Boulanger opened a shop in rue des Poulies selling 'restaurants'. A sign was hung outside his establishment saying '*Boulanger débite des restaurants divins*' (which Larousse translates as 'magical restoratives').

As in many other episodes in the history of competitive consumption, the story of Boulanger's *restaurant* involved a certain amount of imaginative entrepreneurialism. Boulanger wanted to expand beyond mere soup and, although barred from selling ragoûts (a privilege jealously guarded by the litigious *traiteurs*), he devised a dish of sheep's feet in white-wine sauce. The *traiteurs* sued and lost, bringing Boulanger enhanced fame. By 1786,

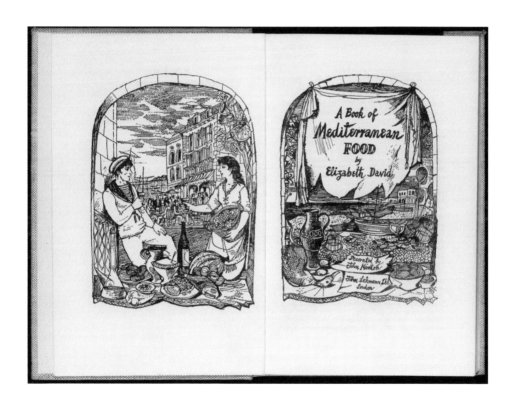

Above: There is a mournful, elegiac quality to John Minton's illustrations for Elizabeth David. To his publisher, John Lehmann, he wrote about 'art needing above all now a relationship to a meaning in our human lives'. He killed himself at thirty-nine.

in large part due to the *succès fou* of the vinous *pieds de mouton*, the word *restaurant* was appearing in legal documents in the sense we understand it today: it was not a soup, but had become an establishment, and restaurateurs were those tradesmen who made a living from welcoming strangers on to their premises and offering them prepared meals.

A commonplace today, it should be emphasised that this practice was a novelty at the time of its introduction. The very concept of the *table d'hôte* speaks volumes about the social, cultural, practical and economic assumptions of early bourgeois civilisation: after all, eating with a host whom you do not know is a surprising thing to do. No wonder that the restaurant soon established all manner of comforting and familiar rituals.

The things distinguishing the restaurant from the *auberge* or the tavern were cleanliness, luxury and the quality of the food. Brillat-Savarin describes the clientele, a nice cross-section of an emergent consuming class: there are solitary diners; out-of-towners; a conversation-less couple; lovers; regular patrons who know the names of the waiters; 'a type only met with in Paris, which has neither property, income, nor employment, but yet contrives to spend freely'; and lastly, the tourists who 'cram themselves with double portions, insist on all the most expensive dishes, drink the strongest wines, and do not always leave without assistance'.

Boulanger's prototype was followed by an establishment created, in 1783, by Antoine Beauvilliers (1754-1817). According to Brillat-Savarin, Beauvilliers could recognise the faces and recall the names of his clients even after twenty years. The very essence of the perfect host, he gave an impression that his restaurant was being opened especially for you. Indeed the establishment of the 'cover' is evidence of the emerging sense of the individual – eating in restaurants is a romantic experience in more senses than one.

Beauvilliers employed great chefs and was at the service of the new liberal society, at just the same time as he was out to benefit from it. Supply and demand, universal suffrage and freedom of the press were the muses in this progressive game. For instance, in his *L'Art du cuisinier* (1814) he lists thirty-six soups; but by 1856, when Urbain Dubois's *La Cuisine classique* appears, that number has risen to more than one hundred.

The restaurants that followed Boulanger and Beauvilliers each specialised in one dish – salt cod and garlic at Les Frères Provençaux, entrées with truffles at Véry, oysters at Balaine – but the repertoire was growing: before Balaine's Rocher de Cancale closed in 1860, it was offering more than two hundred dishes. The increasing sophistication of the menu suggests that restaurants cannot be understood outside the world of competitive bourgeois consumption.

Parallel with the creation of restaurants is the emergence of the gastronomes, the grammarians of taste, often majestically named: Jean Anthelme Brillat-Savarin, who was said to carry a dead woodcock and sometimes other small game birds in his pocket to savour the aroma, and his great contemporary Alexandre Balthazar Laurent Grimod de la Reynière (1758-1837). The gastronomes were not necessarily cooks themselves, but were certainly consumers. Most of all and most typical of liberal bourgeois society, they were commentators and critics. As Curnonsky said, gastronomes reconciled cooking with manners. In his *Considérations sur la cuisine* (1931), Pierre de Pressac explained the role of the gastronome: 'There is such a thing as bad taste ... and persons of refinement know this instinctively. For those who do not, rules are needed.'

Brillat-Savarin has been quoted to exhaustion, a fine testament to the rich menu of ideas he proposed. Grimod is less well plagiarised, but nonetheless significant. He established the Jury des Dégustateurs, who met regularly at the pioneer restaurant Rocher de Cancale. They produced the prototype of all subsequent guides: the *Almanach des gourmands*, published irregularly between 1803 and 1812.

Pan-fried ego

The guide, like the restaurant, depends on consumers. Curnonsky and Rouff, and later Samuel Chamberlain, established a relationship between food and travel. This has helped broaden expectations of restaurants and their environments, leading to regional dishes which Brillat-Savarin might have disdained being assumed into the culinary canon. But still there remains the phenomenon of the three-star Michelin restaurant, or the Gault & Millau twenty points (twenty in fact being virtually unattainable). Although Gault & Millau was established as a champion of nouvelle cuisine to challenge the *ancien régime* of cream and butter favoured by Michelin, it is interesting to note that year in and year out their judgements about quality tend to coincide.

The 'best' French restaurants all tend to look the same and that look is without exception vulgar. The furniture is imitation Looey something, with ormolu and gilt. The proprietor's portrait may be acid-etched on the drinking glasses. The celebrated restaurants inevitably belong to ideal couples, the woman with a certain hairdo, the man with a fixed smile. Why should sophisticated dishes such as *gigot d'agneau farci en croûte*, which demand extraordinary patience and skill in preparation, be served in restaurant environments of such hideous vulgarity?

The commercial preparation of food by third parties for sale to strangers in establishments called restaurants was, as we have seen, the first experiment in the full-blown consumer service. Since the 1780s the process has been one of continuous proletarianisation.

One of the changes that occurred when *service à la française* was replaced by *service à la russe* was that some discipline was imposed on the consumption of wine: there was no compromise with its quality, but now everyone drank the same vintage. This indulged form of egalitarianism was perfectly suited to a new age where the entire population above the poverty line had the economic resources to choose the services or commodities offered them.

Boeuf stroganoff, named after a Russian prince, is now frozen, freeze-dried and available in restaurants where they print (but do not speak) restaurant French; it has become a proletarian dish. Donald Trump once offered guests *noisettes* of Texas Roebuck Deer with heart of artichoke, chestnut purée and pumpkin polenta, thus completing the circle between peasant and vulgarian.

This process applies to personalities as much as to dishes. Imagine a provincial French restaurant, where the young cook struggles to achieve his first star. Yet more stirring endeavours still are required to achieve two. By the time the Parnassus of three rosettes is achieved and the first articles appear in American gourmet and travel magazines, the standards that got him there have been abandoned as surely as he has been abandoned to the media. At Le Moulin de Mougins, near Nice, as in some other three-star French restaurants – the late Bernard Loiseau's at Saulieu, for example – you have to walk through a shop selling the chef-patron's branded tea towels and oven gloves before you are shown to your expensive table. The experience is, perhaps, only an obvious extension of the consumerist one. In *Myself, My Two Countries* (1936), Marcel Boulestin recalled his youth in Périgord and in so doing captured the associational element which is inseparable from the perception of quality in food:

'There were the baskets of fruit, perfect small melons, late plums, under-ripe medlars waiting to soften, peaches, pears hollowed out by a bird or a wasp, figs that had fallen of their own accord, all the fruits of

September naturally ripe and sometimes still warm from the sun. Everything in profusion. It is no doubt the remembrance of these early days which makes me despise and dislike all *primeurs*, the fruit artificially grown, gathered too early and expensively sent, wrapped in cotton wool, to "smart" restaurants.'

There is more choice and meaning in the selection, preparation and consumption of food than in any other activity. Brillat-Savarin was correct: tell me what you eat and I will tell you what you are. Tell me *where* you eat and the conclusion will be the same.

Eating your art out

Whatever its stiff absurdities, haute cuisine offered a reliable standard of excellence when certain techniques and ingredients were universally admired. A classical canon of recipes helped reinforce this, but the decline of French prestige in politics, cinema, literature and art was soon followed by a decline in French prestige in matters of the kitchen. No one wants to fold a napkin in the shape of a swan and no one wants to cook, or eat, *blanquette de veau*. Except perhaps in French military hospitals. At the same time, the idea of a restaurant with rising cloches and a servile hierarchy of wait-people is now redundant. No one is going to open another restaurant soon: instead, we will have bars, grills, bodegas, taquerias and churrascarrias.

Sixty years ago, Elizabeth David caused a revolution when she published her *Italian Food*: in 1954 it was most unusual to find any cookbook not slavishly devoted to France and its high culinary arts. Since then, a profligate expansion of the cookbook genre hints at widening gustatory possibilities, approaching parody. An arbitrary selection of recent titles confirms the decline of haute cuisine: *Cooking in the Nude*; *Manifold Destiny: The One! The Only! Guide to Cooking on Your Car Engine*; *A Man, a Can, a Plan*; *The Secret Lives of Baked Goods*; *Fifty Shades of Chicken*; and *The Road Kill Cookbook*.

But then came the clean-eating cults that cut across the established genres of national kitchens or recipe types. Instead, the clean-eating cults suggested a fanaticism that separated food from pleasure, elevating, or demoting, it to the level of a moral cause. In 1972, the nutritionist Dr Robert Atkins created his low carbohydrate diet. As a response, in extreme cases, some US restaurants actually removed bread from their offer lest wheat-flour dough cultured with yeast pollute the customers.

Above: The Pool Room at the Four Seasons restaurant in New York (1959), designed by Philip Johnson.

Above: Whitebait on a board – rustic *chic* has overwhelmed *haute cuisine*.

The life and death of health food

The idea of 'health food' was popularised in 1961 when Cranks opened on Carnaby Street, five years before *Time* magazine declared London to be swinging from the Carnaby fulcrum. At the time, the espresso bongo era that preceded Pop, London's burger culture was represented by Mr Wimpy's Hamburger Parlor on Coventry Street, the subject of a 1955 *Washington Post* satire by Art Buchwald called 'Europe's Culture Falls to the Hot Dog'. Here you could enjoy a Whippsy shake and admire the 'atomic age efficiency' of service. There was a no-cutlery lore and condiments were offered in convenient sachets. Thus, Cranks offered a different set of values – a 'Health Food' environment had to be sympathetically designed: vegetables met their decorative equivalent with oak trestle tables, wheaten quarry tiles and blotchy, textured craft pottery.

And the vegetarian movement had a true dynamic, forcing more refinements and distinctions on true believers: mere vegetable lovers became more extremist vegans. These vegans avoid consuming anything which once had a face, or lactic products thereof, preferring to eat artisan nut cheese, coconut-based bacon substitutes and Paleo-scavenged granola. The Paleo Diet is the ultimate statement in debasement, which in some iterations features mammoth flavoured crisps, but whose adherents reckon their appetites on unproven assumptions about the caveman's menu of nuts and berries. Paleo faddists prefer unprocessed foods, going back to the early history of self-conscious eating c.10,000BC when style leaders wore fur leggings.

And then vegans begat freegans who, pushing the taste question, reject packaging and enjoy eating waste. This is tribal. This is identifying with a common cause. This is very little to do with the pleasure of eating or the science of nutrition.

For a while, the competitive arena of food was not concerned with the style of what and where you ate, more so its moral character. In 1977 Dr Dean Ornish started the low-fat and low-cholesterol campaign whose influence is only now being diminished after long technical scrutiny of its claims. Canola oil, which smells of urine and straw and tastes disagreeable, was mandated to succeed more delicious, but deadly, fats.

Gluten-free diets followed, again putting bread under threat although, evidence of the sinusoidal nature of the history of taste, artisanal bakeries have been enjoying a revival for the past twenty years. In the UK, Waitrose now stocks more than thirty types of bread, where once steam-baked white sliced reigned uncontested. A related fad for omega-3 oils led to popular absurdities such as fish tacos. Interestingly, only about twenty per cent of gluten-free tribalists actually suffer from coeliac disease. Anathematising gluten was a matter of taste, of preference, of identity, not of medical necessity.

French nouvelle cuisine partly addressed these fashionable dietary concerns, but not always consistently. It was a *rappel à l'ordre* of the type that has recurred in French culture over the centuries. The scriptural home of nouvelle cuisine is Michel Guérard's Les Prés d'Eugénie, in Gascony. Guérard redefined nouvelle cuisine. Fat, butter, cream and brandy would be reduced or avoided. Additionally, it would be *cuisine minceur*: a cooking that would help slimming. Perhaps in the same way that French pharmacies believe that you can get slim by rubbing in potions.

Les Prés d'Eugénie is an establishment of refined haute luxe, offering a poached oyster and difficult claret for a fat Belgian millionaire and his skinny *poulet* wobbling on her heels half a step behind. But alternative catering is on offer: around the back of the austere, Neoclassical temple of disciplined cooking and eating you find a more artisanal La Ferme aux Grives. Here are groaning trestle tables of terrines, meats and cheeses and breads and foaming carafes of *garagiste ordinaire* for hungry people who like to eat. A schism in taste made its demonstration here.

One of the great beneficiaries of the cook book cult and the rise of the television chef has been Nigella Lawson, a member of the Joe Lyons catering family that introduced Chicago's Wimpy hamburgers into London. At some level, very probably a highly self-conscious one, Nigella realised that erotic suggestion was a good career move. If you don't want to eat her plumptious chicken in its own hot juices, you might want to consume Nigella instead. In her very many television appearances she is wont to look unblinking at the camera and lick a wooden spoon in a way that brings to mind, even in the imaginations of the innocent, a really quite unambiguous notion of fellatio. Nigella might even have said that fellatio is a rude Neapolitan pasta dish, possibly related to puttanesca, the whore's pasta. And finger-licking Nigella says she is 'disgusted' by the idea of clean eating. Adding, 'you'll never hear me talking about healthy food'. In Q3 2016, sales of Nigella's hitherto popular books collapsed like a soufflé in a draught. Her dish of ham cooked in Coca-Cola has disappeared from the national consciousness.

In New York, changing tastes in food are illustrated by the fates of the great restaurants. The epochal Four Seasons has closed, awaiting relocation; Le Cirque has filed for bankruptcy. The food-cart and the pop-up have replaced restaurants with fine napery, bucket chairs and deep-pile carpet.

The robust peasant and the principled food explorer now have more prestige than the classically trained chef and his unctuous maître d'. The validation of peasant food found no higher point than the fad for *grano arso*. This is pasta made from the floor-scrapings of burnt husks, once a staple of only the meanest and dirt-poor Pugliese peasant. Now you buy it in Dean & DeLuca.

Globalisation has made novelty in dishes competitive. One recent list provided by *Harper's Magazine* included: risotto in a mug, tapas in a teacup, peas in a latte glass, bread in a handbag, vegetable tempura in a shoe, gin in a Converse sneaker, squid in a clog, soup in a stiletto, soup in a coffee percolator, coleslaw in a shopping cart, pickles in a Russian doll, toast in a tin bath, chicken fingers in a skull, breakfast on a surgical tray, cheese on a skateboard, raspberries on a rock, sponge cake on a tree, cotton candy on a horse's head, fish and chips on a Ferris wheel, sausage rolls on a bathroom tile and fish in a stick in a rock on a mirror …

In that bizarre list are represented ingenuity and folly, in equal measure.

Ghosts in a Hades of futility

It is now smart to eat a sardine on a rough-hewn plank. Michelin has become as farcical as the Turner Prize; haute cuisine, nouvelle cuisine, neo-bistro have given ground to *cucina di Nonna*, a sort of Arte Povera.

Spain, once notorious as the source of salmonella paella in Torremolinos, is now the source of all excellence in food. Santander and San Sebastián have disproportionate numbers of celebrated restaurants and chefs. A Basque name is, at least for the moment, as reliable a sign of kitchen ambition as a French one once was: Monsieur Jules has ceded to Jauna Azinak. If Michelin ever creates a new symbology, the traditional chef's toque might be replaced by a pair of pelotas.

A stream-of-consciousness account of food fads from a young London restaurateur went like this: 'natural', regional, endless variations of naturalness, natural yeasts, endless yeasts, natural sweetness, natural cloud, blackboards still, re-purposed curry, sharing plates, restaurants called Rabbit, ironic re-uptake, beetroot is never ending, shipping containers, Tube tile walls, serving food in shoes, craft craft craft craft, craft beers, pine, a lot of pine, sweet potato chips which are revolting, salted caramel (although this feels 1980s), smears on plates are still used, weirdly menus with lots of commas, gravy underneath the meat.

Of course, the natural food movement can trace its intellectual origins to a sophisticated taste for primitivism that has been a recurrent feature in European culture. 'Locavore' is the key term, the *Oxford American Dictionary*'s 2007 word of the year. A locavore is someone who forages in his own backyard, even if that is defined as within the M25 or the island of Manhattan. 'Eat in your zip code' is the locavore's New York motto as he protests against Big Food.

At some point in the last decade, subsistence foraging entered high culture. Processed food, once considered a sophisticated treat, especially if served with atomic age efficiency, is now demonised. It is morally toxic, if not medically so. Bioregionalism has replaced Francophonic internationalism as a global standard. Nor does anyone want food that has been air freighted: the stigma of out-of-season Peruvian strawberries is now almost unbearable! Farm-to-fork, and nose-to-tail are expressions of the same sensibility. Then there is the spectre of 'Foodscaping'. Restaurants now design their recipes for publication on Instagram rather than the delight of the customer. How far is that from Boulanger?

In wine tasting, the rise of popular criticism enabled by blogging has challenged the authority of established critics, or 'noses' as they say in the trade, because wine tasting is as much olfactory as gustatory. There is an irreverent opinion that an untutored autonomous response is as valid as the consensus of a snobbish elite. The academic philosopher Barry Smith has robustly defended educated expertise. In *Questions of Taste: The Philosophy of Wine* (2007) he writes that any champion of an autonomous response 'neglects the possibility that there really are features to discern a great Bordeaux or Burgundy and that it takes experience and practice to get oneself into a position to come to recognise and understand them'.

Perhaps the food micro-culture's best demonstration of taste's slippery sine wave of adoption and refusal is the fad for 'natural' wines, which became current in the middle of the second decade of the twenty-first century. Up to this point, wines that were, in fact, highly adulterated, even as they were delicious, had satisfied global taste. The consistency, clarity, familiar flavour and depth of colour in Chardonnay or Merlot are achieved only with the addition of sugar, potassium sorbate, Ovo-Pure desiccated egg white 'Mega Purple' for colouring, fish bladder extract and Bentonite powder for clarifying. Oak chips in stainless-steel barrels provide the flavour once created by a wooden barrique. Never mind, there is tradition here: the Romans doctored their wines with pig's blood, lead and marble dust. So much for terroir contributing to a classic wine's enjoyable qualities.

A great deal of it is lab work. If you crush and ferment Sauvignon Blanc grapes, you do not end up with a nice bright Sancerre unless you get assistance from chemical secret agents.

Unfiltered, unmolested 'natural' wines offer a purer alternative, even if that purity means the wines are often cloudy, variable in quality, usually sour and smell of an insanitary chicken-shed. None of that counts against the urgent need that opinion-formers have for authenticity. And authenticity is given greater value than deliciousness and reliability.

The wine debate is a miniature of a much larger debate about natural versus artificial. And another large debate about top down or bottom up.

At a big commercial wine-maker in California, there will be taste engineers who calibrate their palates so as to get consistent readings on what is, for instance, oaky or jammy. Wine can be made delicious for a focus group, but experts will call this good result bad. Meanwhile, expert-approved fine wine is good, but most people will find it not delicious, therefore bad. Good is bad and bad is good, as Bianca Bosker explains in *Cork Dork* (2017). That's what the mouth tells us. The brain, however, says something else. Should the taste of wine be created backwards from the consumer, using data-driven focus groups gathered in a Space-Age Napa winery? Why is this an inferior method to relying on the taste of a solitary throwback knuckle-dragging Burgundian farmer with his mimsy little parcel of five hectares in Puligny?

The larger picture is this: the classic wines with familiar and predictable tastes are well suited to the structured formality of great French cooking. But no one wants any great French cooking any more. People who eat out may now want sweet potato chips served in a clog, cronuts, Rwandan tacos and Momofuku's compost cookies, macerated strawberries with celeriac grenache, Noma's pork skin sandwich, a dirty burger or Magnus Nilsson's locavore Neanderthal rotted carrots dredged with guano and preserved by Arctic permafrost. In the context of this baffling, deracinated, globalised but local eclecticism, the most appropriate wines to drink are wildly various and unpredictable 'natural' wines, even if they look like pond water and taste like an error.

But taste and deliciousness are not to be confused: the natural wine fad is just the latest expression of a recurrent taste for primitive authenticity whose first and most famous expression was Rousseau's Noble Savage. Of course, it will not last.

Consumption The sport of things

People whose most active form of exercise is jumping to conclusions
are too exhausted to come to terms with taste. The idea that we have
proclivities formed by our upbringing or our education and that these
proclivities distinguish us – for good or for bad – from our fellows is
rendered no less harrowing by the fact that it is central to the life of the
modern consumer. New communications techniques, mass markets, and
new technologies have made all things available to all men – at a price.
Global advertising by ever-bigger networks in the service of ever-fewer
multinational corporations has turned the world into a shop, but what to
choose? When anything goes it is perhaps not surprising that so often
very little does. Never before has there been such a democracy of choice;
and never before has there been such inhibition and confusion.

Does taste have any meaning today? Investigate the newspapers
and you see that there is a feeling, to put it no higher, that such a thing
as national taste does exist and that the influence of certain events and
personalities can either advance or retard it as if it were a current. There is
considerable evidence that occasionally individuals – such as Coco Chanel,
Elsie de Wolfe, Elizabeth David, Kenneth Clark or Ralph Lauren – with
a sense of style or purpose in fashion, interior design, cooking or art
appreciation, influence their own and subsequent generations. On the
basis of their proclivities, public expectations are formed. In this sense
there are indeed tastemakers, but the assumption underlying most
journalistic comment is that good or bad taste exists independently,
and that the art, literature, architecture, design, food or manners of any
particular moment can be judged against some ill-defined or unarticulated
standard established at some unspecified point in the past. This feeling
presupposes the existence of an idealised notion of excellence – even if it
sounds absurd to say something so highfalutin in so irredeemably low-
falutin an area as blogging.

The influence of impressive individuals in imposing, or at least offering,
their own taste to the rest of us has to be judged against the sempiternal

observation that there are no fixed standards in art or behaviour. For instance, in his *A Manual of Diet in Health and Disease* (1875), Thomas King Chambers had this to say about the dangers of garlic:

'Another article that offends the bowels of unused Britons is garlic. Not uncommonly in southern climes an egg with the shell on is the only procurable animal food without garlic in it. Flatulence and looseness are the frequent results. *Bouilli*, with its accompaniment of mustard sauce and watermelon, is the safest resource, and not an unpleasant one, after a little education.'

Nowadays we are more inclined to agree with the views of Elizabeth David. Seminal is an abused term, but Mrs David's *Mediterranean Food* (1950) was a genuinely seminal book, containing in its brief 191 pages a *vade mecum* for an entire generation avid to exploit the exotic. In her Introduction she quotes Marcel Boulestin: 'It is not really an exaggeration to say that peace and happiness begin, geographically, where garlic is used in cooking.'

Again, today the last word in the absurdly sophisticated culinary refinements of Californian cuisine are baby pizzas with gossamer goats' cheese, made of foetal fish, demineralised mineral water, Perrier and soda. Yet when President Benjamin F Harrison had lunch at Sutro Heights on 12 April 1891, he ate the following: oysters and beef tea with California Riesling, Rüdesheimer and Sauternes; cold turkey, goose, ham, tongue, goose liver, sardines, sardelles, caviar, asparagus and artichokes with Zinfandel; sweetbreads with mushrooms (an intermediate course) with Château La Rose; roast chicken and duck with Château Lafite; followed by sponge cake, wine jelly, ice-cream, macaroons and strawberries with Sauternes, champagne, cognac and Chartreuse.

As we have seen, the history of wine also shows that taste in the gustatory sense is not constant. Patterns of wine growing, no less than patterns of wine consumption, have changed dramatically in the past and will, no doubt, continue to change dramatically in the future. What we now regard as 'traditional' wine-growing areas are in fact the result of a radical redrawing of the French agricultural map after the introduction of industrial standards of farming in the nineteenth century. Before then the grape had been well established in such northerly territories as Picardy, Normandy and the Île-de-France, which, during the Middle Ages, were producing some of the most respected wines, but in the nineteenth century it retreated south to the Loire and east to Chablis. Never mind that Dom Pérignon's historic discovery of sparkling wine at the Abbaye d'Hautvilliers

U . BON MARCHÉ, rue de Sèvres, PARIS

Above: The first modern department stores appeared in Paris. Described by Zola as 'cathedrals of business', they began a century of mixed metaphors and literals in the history of consumption.

has a specific date; medieval scholars make no mention of *any* wines of Champagne.

Human behaviour is no less variable. It is presently fashionable, as well as highly desirable by contemporary standards, to revile child pornography, except when it is written by effete intellectuals. Jean Cocteau's *Le Livre blanc* (1927) contains passages such as this:

'This boy, who for me represented good luck, bore on his chest the words PAS DE CHANCE tattooed in blue capital letters ... Was it possible! With that mouth, those teeth, those eyes, that belly, those shoulders, those iron muscles ... with that fabulous little underwater plant, lying dead and crumpled on the moss, which unfolded, grew bigger, reared up and threw its seed far away as soon as it found the element of love.'

This is hardly distinguishable from the sort of filth you can find on the highest shelves of the bookstore at Copenhagen airport in shrink-wrapped packets or three clicks away on the Internet. Walther Killy made a similar point in *Deutscher Kitsch* (1962), where he produced a fascinating pastiche by mixing purple pulp fiction with a little bit of Rainer Maria Rilke. In the context, the lines of Rilke were undetectable. Umberto Eco did exactly the same in his *Opera aperta* (1962); sentences taken at random from DH Lawrence appear grotesque.

It is not only the value of specific works of art that changes; it is also the significance of any given genre. Gore Vidal wrote:

'As a source of interest for the serious, film has replaced the novel as the novel replaced the poem in the last century ... The half-serious reader of yesteryear is now the film-buff. The "educated" – that is, functionally literate – public looks at television a great deal and reads many magazines and newspapers. They read few novels ... If a new novel is highly praised it might be consumed by five thousand readers. Edna St. Vincent Millay's verse used to be read in greater quantities.'[24]

Of course, film has now been replaced by streaming. All these examples should teach us to be cautious about assuming that the current status quo has anything more than temporary significance, but the examples concerning literature also teach us something else: that in making judgements today we are constantly having to come to terms with the mass market.

Right: The interior of Le Bon Marché, at 24 rue de Sèvres, Paris, designed by architect Louis-Charles Boileau with engineer Gustave Eiffel.

ESCALIER CENTRAL : VUE INTÉRIEURE

ALICK. P. F. Ritchie.

Vincent Brooks Day & Son Ltd lith

The fact that mass markets tend to homogenise our preferences, while people with style may prefer to break away from them, makes taste both a totem and a taboo. There is a residual feeling that 'good' taste is necessarily exclusive: dim bulbs who still believe in it find the idea of the mass market repulsive. The couturier Balenciaga would reputedly, without regard to function, performance or starving millions, spend thirty-six hours without food, drink or sleep, the better to fashion an armhole. He lived long enough to witness the arrival of *prêt-à-porter*, which should, at least in theory, have made his prodigious technical skills available to a larger audience, thereby enhancing the gross volume of appreciation upon which creative vampires nourish themselves. His reaction to the opportunity of creating fine clothes at moderate prices was not to welcome the democratisation of luxury, but to condemn the proletarianisation of culture. '*Je ne me prostitue pas*', he said. Kitsch may be a type of art which lacks any value except popularity, but that is not to say that everything that is popular needs to be kitsch.

Instagrammar
In *Ways of Seeing* (1972), John Berger noted that the creation of new reproduction technologies, not just *prêt-à-porter*, suddenly made art of any type 'ephemeral, ubiquitous, insubstantial, valueless, free'. That was the whole point of the Modernist adventure, which from today's perspective we now regard as a touching, even tragic failure. The story of contemporary taste is marbled with the history of Modernism, itself a sort of high-minded form of consumerism. Its purpose was to democratise luxury by the application of technology and social engineering to fundamental human needs, as well as to art. Either in the breach or the observance, the Modernist aesthetic was the one fixed point in a story of art and manners, which otherwise leaps and swerves confusingly. The abstract painters, severe prophets of a new objectivity, believed they had discovered an absolute. Piet Mondrian, for instance, thought that all human expression could be contained in a rectilinear grid of primary colours.

The idea that history is a linear process, a Hegelian march, which necessarily ends with Modernism, is now considered quaint. We may have been brought up to despise suburban villas, but we can see more clearly that they met a real need. James Richards remarked on it first in *Castles on the Ground* (1946). The Modernists overstated a case in order to be heard; now that we are more liberal, not to say promiscuous, the history of art has become a supermarket of effects. Styles that once belonged to a certain historical period, dishes that were once the privilege of kings and courtiers, paintings that were the property of popes, are the common currency of an extraordinary age when, with everything accessible, there is unprecedented uncertainty about what things mean.

It is an age of material prosperity and poverty of faith. It is the best of times and it is the worst of times. Everything is for sale. Not for nothing did the Victorians use the word 'spend' to suggest sexual excess as well as profligacy in consumption. Shopping is one of the chief cultural experiences of our age. The Duchess of Windsor once said she would prefer to shop than eat, a preference memorialised at her funeral service, where the flowers surrounding her emaciated corpse came predominantly not from mourning individuals but from the boutiques of Dior, Van Cleef, Alexandre de Paris, and other jewellers and couturiers. 'So much,' said novelist Dominick Dunne 'for style.'

Online click culture has changed almost every assumption about consumerism. Yet a global freedom of choice and next-day delivery have not created conditions of universal ease in matters of consumption, but rather the opposite: inhibition, apparently, remains a stronger force than extravagance when consumption betrays the character of the soul. Taste retains some of the characteristics of religion. This religion once had rites, which were celebrated in department stores and museums, two institutions whose origins lie in exactly that historical period which witnessed the explosion of popular consumption.

The department store rose with the middle-class consumer and each helped to define the other. The range of merchandise and the hierarchies into which the department store was organised helped create a notion of middle-class normality, which even today is difficult to escape. To many people brought up near Harrods, stationery has an ineradicable connection with perfumery in the landscape of their imaginations. Pets are related to hi-fi for the same reasons. Here, for the first time, there was the opportunity to inspect without commitment, one of the great and unique experiences of the twentieth century. In *Au bonheur des dames* (1883), Zola describes the luscious window displays of his imaginary store, but does not comment that window-shopping provided the very first opportunity for *speculative consumption*, a phenomenon which today also takes the form of television advertising and magazine journalism.

While Restoration Paris had several large *magasins de nouveautés,* such as Au Masque du Fer, La Fille Mal-Gardée, Le Diable Boîteux, Les Deux Magots and the Coin de Rue, the department store as we know it is a creation of the later nineteenth century. In 1852, Aristide Boucicaut (1810-77), who worked in the rue du Bac, decided to expand and in 1869 he commissioned a *grand magasin* to be built at the corner of the rue de Sèvres and rue Velpeau from the architect MA Laplanche. Extended by Louis-Charles Boileau and Gustave Eiffel, by 1906 Le Bon Marché occupied an entire block and had a staff of 7,000.

In Le Bon Marché, Les Grands Magasins du Louvre, La Samaritaine and Le Bazar de l'Hôtel de Ville, lower prices fostered mass consumption and broadened the customer base. Zola was inspired by Le Bon Marché; he describes the store in *Au Bonheur des dames* as a 'cathedral of business'. In the old shops, where haggling was commonplace, the presence of respectable women would have been unthinkable, whereas Zola saw Bon Marché as a 'temple to woman'.

Although the department stores helped create the middle classes, it is interesting to note that the owner-entrepreneurs who created them, like Boucicaut, were usually themselves of peasant extraction. Samaritaine's Ernest Cognacq was an orphan and Félix Potin a smallholder.

Aristide Boucicaut deliberately made Le Bon Marché similar to an exhibition, and, appropriately for a cultural institution, it organised tours, had a reading room and held concerts. In London, the greatest attractions of the new department stores were the elegant but inexpensive restaurants. When Harry Gordon Selfridge opened his huge store in Oxford Street in 1909 he said he wanted it to be 'not so much a shop as a social centre', where customers could not only have tea, they could watch a fashion show and listen to Strauss, Lehár or Gilbert and Sullivan. He used the impressive Free-style Classicism of his Oxford Street store as advertising, using architecture to sell knickers. While some declare the end of bricks-and-mortar retail, Selfridge's remains packed with global consumers gathered to celebrate certain rites.

Just as department stores were cathedrals of commerce, museums became emporiums of style. The architect Philip Johnson, no less, exclaimed that museums are taking the place of temples and palaces in cultures that have abandoned God but still require higher values to defer to; especially, one might add, those represented by money. The philosopher Benedetto Croce once explained that everyone knew what art *was*, but no one knew how to define it. Hence, the connoisseur was brought into the drama of human behaviour, a specialist of refined knowledge who could determine art from non-art.

In 1925 Le Corbusier predicted in *L'Art décoratif d'aujourd'hui* that the museum would cease to be a marble hall with a knackered Apollo and a limbless Aphrodite; the quotidian would be raised to the monumental:

'A plain jacket, a bowler hat, a well-made shoe. An electric light bulb with bayonet fixing; a radiator, a tablecloth of fine white linen; our everyday drinking glasses, and bottles of various shapes … A number of bentwood chairs … we will install in the museum a bathroom with its enamelled bath, its china bidet, its wash basin, and its glittering taps … clearly, this museum does not yet exist. Such a museum would be truly dependable and honest; its value would lie in the choice that it offered, whether to approve or reject; it would allow one to understand the reasons why things were as they were and would be a stimulant to improve on them.'

There is a sort of consensus about what constitutes quality in design, what features make a manufactured artefact useful and desirable. You could gather together a collection of department-store buyers, museum curators, Sorbonne intellectuals, web entrepreneurs and consumers, and there might be little serious dissension about what constitutes excellence. At a time when doubt and utopianism replaced the moral certainties of the nineteenth century, the polemical Adolf Loos, the high-minded Walter Gropius and the maverick Le Corbusier were searching for some sort of order to replace the academic principles that had been thrown out with the *beaux-arts.*

Do the definitions of 'good' design pioneered by the Modernists have a relevance that transcends time and remains relevant in the digital era?

There may well be some rules that are fashion-defiant. Respect the nature of materials. Never force unnatural forms or contrived patterns. Whenever possible, choose the simplest and most direct alternative. Ornament is usually reprehensible, but especially so if applied by machine. Avoid the bogus. Pay attention to the intended function, which will usually provide a key to the form. Look to nature and to science for inspiration. Respect tradition, but do not ape it. Express your intentions honestly and clearly. Ensure that the details harmonise with the whole.

There is an underlying substance to the Modernist doctrines of 'functionalism' and 'truth', which lend quality to artefacts and buildings as certainly and as surely as classical laws of detail and proportion. John Ruskin believed that inanimate things have a sense of spirit and, in a surprisingly similar way, so did the Modernists. Perhaps we should still believe that today. The spirit of something pleasingly functional, such as a revolver or a milk bottle, can best be described in metaphorical terms: honesty, integrity, guts and good manners – exactly the same qualities we admire in attractive people.

If quality in design may be defined objectively, 'good' taste cannot. To attempt to do so would be to reduce all the subtleties of human proclivity to a technical formula, rather as if the chemical character and composition of a fine wine, expressed in terms of pH value and unions of hydrogen, carbon and oxygen molecules, can in any way account for its flavour and aroma (which, it seems, can be conveyed only by the most poetic allusion). A Richebourg '64 is more than the sum of its molecules. Our minds are more than an electro-chemical dance.

Yet there are times when people recognise 'bad' taste so irrefutably that it is tempting to regard the reaction as instinctive. There are social gaffes, combinations of colours, incongruous juxtapositions, jarring contrasts, impositions of effect, strident appeals to emotion, that most people find discomforting. Equally, there are examples of exquisite 'good' taste that are similarly upsetting – Highgate or Atlanta McMansions or Scottsdale ranch-burgers, for instance. Here the proportions may be fine, the colours and materials judiciously chosen, but the effect is unsettling to the aesthetically fastidious.

The answer to the conundrum is where and how an artefact is used. There are few things so discomforting as an exquisite exercise in good taste. You can imagine all sorts of different 'tasteful' interiors in almost any part of the globe. The same pseudo-sophistication will be on show in London, New York, Paris or Milan: holly green walls with eighteenth-century console tables, a Turkey carpet; a bathroom with red granite basins; glorious Fortuny stuff hanging from a William IV four-poster; piles of glossy books on fenders and footstools; eighteenth-century prints of Africa glued to Cosmati work panels; Ralph Lauren linen stacked on a bed; more plumped-up cushions than it would ever be possible to use; table pieces; anything with bows, swags or drapes; a Barcelona or Eames chair; tin toys.

These items may or may not pass the old Modernists' test for excellence, but the judgement of taste in art, architecture, manners, food or fashion depends on the *context* rather than the object itself. It is not necessarily the chair, the swag, the tin toy, the pile of magazines or whatever, which is in 'good' or 'bad' taste, but its relations in time and space. It is the intention behind its use. Any attempt to excite respect or any other response by the quickest possible means is in questionable taste. Hence our revulsion at the bogus gentility of Ionic columns used on contemporary architecture, or at Savile Row tailors faking country-house atmosphere in their lobbies the better to calm the excited nerves of rich dentists from Tennessee or zip manufacturers from Nagoya.

Taste is overwhelmingly a matter of personal preference, a person's ability to interpret style or add meaning to gestures, flavours or objects. There are individuals who use their taste to impressively good effect, but when someone else's taste is copied in dress or interior design, the effect is at best derivative and at worst witless. Take Coco Chanel: her artful use of a sailor's handkerchief created a style that Paul Poiret memorably described as '*misérabilisme de luxe*'. But the creation of such a style has nothing to do with good or bad taste. As the architect Richard Rogers said:

'Taste is the enemy of aesthetics … It is abstract, at best elegant and fashionable, it is always ephemeral, for it is not rooted in philosophy or even in craftsmanship, being purely a product of the senses. As such it can always be challenged and is always being superseded, for how can one judge whose taste is best … Good design on the other hand speaks to us from across the ages.'[25]

Rogers, of course, is now himself consigned to architectural history as a one-speed technophiliac.

In an age when commerce and culture have elided, it is instructive and amusing to watch the brief, tinsely passage of colourful trash through the spreads of the lifestyle magazines, through the racks and shelves of modish boutiques, while demand for the enduring quality of classics has never been stronger. After decades of uncertainty in matters of taste, simple truths, even simple half-truths, are very alluring.

Taste is not a particular set of values, but the ability to discriminate between things in order to enhance enjoyment of them. Thus, taste depends on knowledge and the exercise of it presupposes an appetite for aesthetic pleasure. In 1273 St Thomas Aquinas wrote:

'Beauty … has to do with knowledge, and we call a thing beautiful when it pleases the eye of the beholder. This is why beauty is a matter of right proportion, for the senses delight in rightly proportioned things as similar to themselves, the sense-faculty being a sort of proportion itself like all other knowing faculties. Now since knowing proceeds by imagining,

Right: Ralph Lauren's flagship women's store in New York occupies the Renaissance Revival chateau that heiress Gertrude Rhinelander Waldo built for herself in 1898, on Madison Avenue.

and images have to do with form, beauty properly involves the notion of form.'

And, of course, form carries semantic value. Edith Wharton said in *French Ways and Their Meaning* (1919): 'The essence of taste is suitability. Divest the word of its prim and priggish implications, and see how it expresses the mysterious demand of the eye and mind for symmetry, harmony and order.'

Properly speaking, design has little to do with taste. Or, at least, needs to be understood as something apart. Performance, durability, economy and functional efficiency can be measured in a way that approximates to scientific accuracy, but when most people speak of good design what they are really referring to is their own taste. The character of an object is a matter of design; the meaning of an object in use is a matter of taste.

The whole world is a cabinet of curios. Potentially, everything is for inspection and consumption. In the 1947 movie *Magic Town,* James Stewart played an opinion pollster who discovered a town, inhabited by Jane Wyman, which was a perfect microcosm of American taste, full of typical consumers. Now, American market researchers (such as Chicago's Information Resources Incorporated, Time-Life's Selling Areas Marketing Incorporated and AC Nielsen) use computers, cable television and supermarket barcode readers to monitor consumer reaction to new advertisements. The consumers (who are on a sort of electronic leash) can immediately signal their preferences to manufacturers, while advertisers can find out exactly what programmes their customers prefer to watch. As an American public-TV producer explained in a 1985 interview in *New York* magazine: 'You used to have an idea, or burn to do a certain series. You'd shop it around for funders. Now you find out what the funders' ideas are and craft their series for them.' Today, crowdfunding has further complicated old distinctions between supply and demand, author and consumer.

The world is becoming more complicated and never before has simplicity been so elusive. The story of taste is a history of abstraction, from a passive human sense, via capitalisation of the initial letter and via industrial capitalism, to a generalised attribute of certain designers or a grail for every active consumer. In an age of popular mass consumption and global markets, while there are types of behaviour and aesthetic preferences that the fastidious find dismaying, there cannot be the 'rules of taste', which Addison and Reynolds once described.

Taste is not nowadays the same as reason, but as the expression of choice it does have something to do with meaning. Economists are wrong:

the law of diminishing marginal utility of goods states that when survival needs are satisfied, the appetite for consumption declines. It is demonstrably a false law. The appetite may change shape and direction, but it remains.

In an age robbed of religious symbols, going to the shops replaced going to church. In our own time, conventional bricks and mortar retail is undermined by online commerce. Instead of a noun meaning premises, 'shop' has become a verb. And a testament: I shop therefore I am. True, we have the un-brand, a disdain for tribalism and fast-fashion is diminishing the prestige of labels. Advertising is disintegrating as a cultural form. Display ads in newspapers will soon be a thing of the past while television audiences are either disappearing or meaninglessly fragmented. The thirty-second television slot aimed at a homogeneous audience is now as culturally irrelevant as late Imperial consular diptychs. But still we must make choices and still those choices tell stories about us.

By our patterns of consumption our tastes are betrayed. It is a beguiling and disturbing drama of ideas. We have a free choice, but at a price. We can win experience, but never achieve innocence. Marx knew that the epic activities of the modern world involve not lance and sword but dry goods.

Notes

Scenario

1   On the relation of taboos to manners and to taste, see Archibald Lyall, *The Future of Taboo in these Islands*, 1936

2   So too did the German Expressionist painter Franz Marc, who compared El Greco to Cézanne in *Der Blaue Reiter Almanac* (1912). Describing them as 'spiritual brothers', Marc wrote, 'Despite the centuries that separate them … today the works of both mark the beginning of a new epoch in painting.'

3   Perhaps the most remarkable was Erik Satie, the pianist. A Rosicrucian who had founded the Metropolitan Church of the Art of Jesus the Conductor, he saw in El Greco's *duende* a prototype of the anarchic mysticism he was rather hoping would undermine society.

4   Keats was, in fact, joining a poetic discourse on the relationship of beauty and truth which goes back at least as far as George Herbert; in his poem *Jordan*, Herbert wrote, 'Who says that fictions and false hair/Become a verse? Is there no truth in beauty?'

5   Claude Lee Finney, *The Evolution of Keats's Poetry*, 1936

6   See, for instance, ER Curtius, *European Literature and the Latin Middle Ages*, 1953

7   Some of the sense of taste being related to manners (and of manners being related to restraint), is preserved in the French saying '*Le secret d'ennuyer est celui de tout dire*', a maxim that should be observed by all those reckless enough to tackle so formidable a subject.

8   There is more of this in JE Spingarn, *Critical Essays of the Seventeenth Century*, 1908. Spingarn explains that, to the virtuosi, taste was a 'guide-post to what they sought and a touchstone of their success in finding it'.

9   The document was suppressed by his executors in 1714 and only added to *The Characteristics of Men, Manners, Opinions, Times* in the 1733 edition.

10 There is an amusing passage in Harold Nicolson's *Small Talk* (1937): 'There are many men who would prefer it to be said that they had acted cruelly, selfishly, perhaps even unfaithfully, than that they were guilty of lack of taste. "Your action", so runs the accusation, "appears to me, and I may say to others with whom I have discussed the matter, to have been in singularly bad taste." One squirms at receiving such a letter.'

11 In a pamphlet by 'Mrs Sidney Webb', *The Discovery of the Consumer*, 1928

12 See Umberto Eco, *Art and Beauty in the Middle Ages*, 1959; English translation, 1986

13 PN Furbank, *Unholy Pleasure*, 1985

14 For instance, Hugh of St Victor, *De institutione novitiorum;* Petrus Alphonsi, *Disciplina clericalis*; and Johannes von Garland, *Morale scolarium.*

15 In his *Civilitas* (1560), Erasmus remarks: 'The Germans eat with their mouths open and think it unseemly to do otherwise. The French, on the contrary, half open their mouths and find the German practice rather disgusting. The Italians eat delicately, the French more vigorously so that they find the Italian practice too refined and precious.'

16 The *Independent*, 14 January 1987

17 Lasinio, *Pitture a fresco del Campo Santo di Pisa*, 1828

18 See the Preface to *Lyrical Ballads*, 1800

19 Dr Albert C Barnes is typical. The fabulously wealthy inventor of Argyrol, an optician's liniment, he was soon on the trail of modern

art and ambitiously created a 'philosophy' to support his taste. The Barnes Foundation at Merion, Pennsylvania, became the centre of an education programme based on principles so transparent and scientifically compelling that no one, according to Dr Barnes, could deny them allegiance. These principles included a complete lack of labelling, so as to encourage an innocent response to the art from the visitor.

20 *Ins Leere Gesprochen*, 1897-1900; English translation, *Spoken into the Void*, 1982

21 For example, Gabriel-Désiré Laverdant, *De la mission de l'art et du rôle des artistes*, 1845

22 Clement Greenberg, 'The Avant-Garde and Kitsch', *Partisan Review*, 1939

Imbroglio

1   In a speech at the Mansion House in the City of London, 1987

2   *The Architects' Journal*, 16 and 23 December, 1987

3   Guy de Rothschild, *The Whims of Fortune*, 1985

4   Rothschild, ibid.

5   Adolf Loos, *Ornament und Verbrechen*, 1908

6   Later, Rodker turned towards sexology and psychoanalysis, eventually bringing the Imago Publishing Company from Vienna to London and completing the publication of all Freud's works.

7   Ada Louise Huxtable, 'The Troubled State of Modern Architecture', *New York Review of Books*, 1 May 1980

8   Russell Lynes, *The Tastemakers*, 1954

9   Lynes, ibid.

10 John Betjeman, *Summoned by Bells*, 1960

11 Elizabeth Hurlock, *The Psychology of Dress*, 1929

12 Recorded in *Selected Letters*, ed. F Steegmuller, 1980-2

13 According to the Comtesse de Bradi, 'There is an indefinable element of idleness and flaccidity that ill becomes a girl in the taste for settling down on the bottom of a bathtub.'

14 Rupert Hart-Davis, *More Letters of Oscar Wilde*, 1985

15 See Robin Gilmour, *The Idea of the Gentleman in the Victorian Novel*, 1981

16 According to H Henning, *Der Geruch*, 1924

17 In *The Three Course Newsletter*, No 3, 1987

18 Warwick Wroth, *The London Pleasure Gardens of the Eighteenth Century*, 1896

19 Jean-François Revel, *Un festin en paroles*, 1979

20 Stephen Mennell, *All Manners of Food*, 1985

21 Lord Edward Cecil, *The Leisure of an Egyptian Official*, 1921

22 Ironically, another famous Englishman with an interest in France and French food, Sir Jack Drummond, author with Anne Wilbraham of *The Englishman's Food* (1929), was murdered there, as Roland Barthes noted in *Mythologies*, 1957.

23 See Stephen Mennell, *All Manners of Food*, 1985

24 *Times Literary Supplement*, 22-8 June 1990

25 Bryan Appleyard, *Richard Rogers*, 1986

Select bibliography

Since the idea of taste includes all human endeavour where choices are made, its bibliography is potentially vast, uselessly so. The following includes items that amplify points only hinted at, or perhaps even ignored, in this book. No attempt has been made to include periodical articles or the hundreds of eighteenth- and nineteenth-century works, of no particular originality, which use the word 'taste' in their titles. The editions cited are not necessarily the first, but the most convenient. The place of publication is London, unless stated otherwise.

Addison, Joseph, *Essays on Taste, and the Pleasures of the Imagination*, 1834

Alison, Archibald, *Essays on the Nature and Principles of Taste*, Edinburgh, 1817

Allen, B Sprague, *Tides in English Taste*, Cambridge, MA, 1937

Ames, Winslow, *Prince Albert and Victorian Taste*, 1967

Aron, Jean-Paul, *Le Mangeur du XIXe siècle*, Paris, 1973

Barrère, Jean Bertrand, *L'Idée de goût de Pascal à Valéry*, Paris, 1972

Bate, Walter Jackson, *From Classic to Romantic: Premises of Taste in Eighteenth-Century England*, Boston, 1945

Bayley, Stephen, *Ugly: The Aesthetics of Everything*, 2012

Baudrillard, Jean, *Le système des objets*, Paris, 1968

Beanland, Christopher, *Concrete Concept: Brutalist Buildings Around the World, 2016*

Betjeman, John, *Ghastly Good Taste; Or, a Depressing Story of the Rise and Fall of English Architecture*, 1933

Bourdieu, Pierre, *La Distinction: Critique Sociale du Jugement*, Paris, 1979

Boyd, Robin, *The Australian Ugliness,* 1960

Burke, Edmund, *A Philosophical Enquiry into the Origin of Our Ideas of the Sublime and the Beautiful*, 1757

Clark, Sir Kenneth, *What Is Good Taste?*, 1958

Cooper, Nicholas, *The Opulent Eye: Late Victorian and Edwardian Taste in Interior Design*, 1976

Curnonsky (Maurice-Edmond Sailland), *Souvenirs littéraires et gastronomiques*, Paris, 1958

de Zurko, ER, *Origins of Functionalist Theory*, 1957

Dorfles, Gillo, *Kitsch: An Anthology of Bad Taste*, 1969

Driver, Christopher, *The British at Table, 1940-1980*, 1983

Eco, Umberto, 'Reading Things', 1976, reprinted in *Faith in Fakes*, 1976

Elias, Norbert, *The Civilizing Process*: Vol 1, *The History of Manners*, Oxford, 1939

Gloag, John, *Victorian Taste: Some Social Aspects of Architecture and Industrial Design, from 1820-1900*, 1962

Haskell, Francis, *Rediscoveries in Art: Some Aspects of Taste, Fashion and Collecting in England and France*, 1976

Haskell, Francis & Penny, Nicholas, *Taste and the Antique: The Lure of Classical Sculpture, 1500-1900*, 1981

Hogarth, William, *The Analysis of Beauty: Written with a View to Fixing the Fluctuating Ideas of Taste*, 1753

Irwin, David, *The Visual Arts: Taste and Criticism*, 1969

Krestovsky, L, *La Laideur dans l'art*, Paris, 1947

Laver, James, *Taste and Fashion*, 1945

Lynes, Russell, *The Tastemakers*, 1954

Mennell, Stephen, *All Manners of Food: Eating and Taste in England and France from the Middle Ages to the Present*, Oxford, 1985

Moles, Abraham, *Théorie de l'information et perception esthétique*, Paris, 1958

Pazaurek, Gustav, *Geschmacksverirrungen, im Kunstgewerbe*, Stuttgart, 1909

Silber, John, *Architecture of the Absurd: How Genius Disfigured a Practical Art*, 2007

Smith, Barry, 'The Taste of Wine', *The World of Fine Wine*, No 40, 2013

Vanderbilt, Tom, *You May Also Like*, 2016

Zeldin, Theodore, *France 1848-1945*: Vol 2, *Taste and Corruption*, Oxford, 1977

Index

Photo credits